INTRODUCTION

You made it! You've managed to achieve the grades you wanted and been accepted by your chosen university, or perhaps you've found a place through the clearing system. Either way, you're going to be starting a college course, probably at the end of the summer. Fame, fortune and debauchery await. OK, so I lied about the money bit. It's going to be a rollercoaster ride of good times and hard work, and hopefully you'll come out of it at the end with a top-class degree and excellent career prospects. Or at least a pass and a job that's slightly more interesting than flipping endless burgers in the nearest take-away joint.

Gaining a degree can make a world of difference to your career prospects, but going to university is about much more than academic qualifications. Strong friendships are forged and your social life and love life will probably take off like a rocket. Most new students throw themselves into the student societies and the bar and club scene with enthusiasm, and many get to satisfy their taste for travel. This all costs, of course, and the money-handling skills that you develop over the duration of your course will hopefully last a lifetime. The majority of undergraduates need to take out loans to cover the rising costs of education, such as their day-to-day subsistence and tuition fees, and the ability to budget well is now absolutely essential. Being able to sweet-talk the parents and the bank manager doesn't hurt either.

After taking on all of this enormous financial outlay, you might just want to get a decent degree out of it. Stranger things have happened, you know. This calls for good time management and new ways of learning and analysing information that are completely different from the traditional school environment. There's no 'spoon feeding' and you're totally responsible for your own workload, in spite of all those wonderful distractions that are constantly going on around you. Putting some effort in right from the beginning pays dividends later and it's useful to know how to stay motivated, or where to go for extra help and information at times when you get a bit stuck.

Throughout your course you'll have to contend with living in halls and moving in with friends, and may have to cope with the perils of budget accommodation (free mice and damp, anyone?) or wrangle with the occasional dodgy landlord. If you can get through all of this and have your deposit returned intact then that's an achievement in itself. Student life can sometimes be stressful, so along with your living situation, your overdraft and that overdue essay, it's good to know that there's a big support network of university advisors, health staff and representatives from the National

Union of Students to back you up when something goes wrong. There's also a careers service who can help you to decide whether you want to go straight into a job, sign up for further study or take off for a gap year after you've graduated.

It's all there waiting for you. Enjoy!

THE VIRGIN UNIVERSITY SURVIVAL GUIDE

Also published by Virgin Books:

The Virgin Alternative Guide to British Universities
The Student Cookbook
The Virgin Guide to Courses for Careers
The Virgin Travellers' Handbook
The Virgin Guide to Volunteering
The Virgin Travel Health Handbook
The Virgin Guide to Working Abroad

THE VIRGIN UNIVERSITY SURVIVAL GUIDE

KARLA FITZHUGH

First published in Great Britain in 2004 by
Virgin Books Ltd
Thames Wharf Studios
Rainville Road
London
W6 9HA

Copyright © Karla Fitzhugh 2004

The right of Karla Fitzhugh to be identified as the Author of this Work has been asserted by her in accordance
with the Copyright, Designs and Patents Act, 1988.

This book is sold subject to the condition that it shall not, by way of trade or otherwise, be lent, resold, hired out
or otherwise circulated without the publisher's prior written consent in any form of binding or cover other than
that in which it is published and without a similar condition including this condition being imposed on the
subsequent purchaser.

A catalogue record for this book is available from the British Library.

ISBN 0 7535 0818 4

Typeset by Phoenix Photosetting, Chatham, Kent
Printed and bound in Great Britain by Mackays of Chatham, Chatham, Kent

CONTENTS

Introduction   vii

Chapter 1: Getting Ready   1

Chapter 2: Freshers' Week   13

Chapter 3: Your Course   25

Chapter 4: Hedonism   59

Chapter 5: Housing   91

Chapter 6: Money   111

Chapter 7: Work and Careers   131

Chapter 8: Health and Stress   151

Chapter 9: Crime and Safety   171

Chapter 10: Graduation and Beyond   183

Appendix 1: The Basics   199

Appendix 2: Contacts   219

Thanks   223

Index   225

1. GETTING READY

Heading off to campus tends to be the first time that students have lived away from home for any long period and there can be a steep learning curve if you've never had to pay the household bills or do your own cooking, cleaning and laundry before. Then there's the awkward first few days to contend with, when you don't know your way around town and you're thrown in at the deep end meeting hundreds of new people. In the meantime you have a few weeks or months to get yourself ready to go to university and being prepared for what lies ahead makes things much easier.

- **Think hard about what you want to take with you, and remember that you need to strike a balance between travelling light and having your favourite things around. Leave the giant collection of stuffed toys at home (nobody's going to fall for the 'but they're all my mascots' story).**

- **Keep all paperwork, such as acceptance letters and offers of accommodation, together in a safe place, and preferably inside something waterproof like a reusable ziplock bag. Then it will always be on hand when you need it in a hurry, and it won't get ruined by rain showers or coffee spills.**

- **If you don't have them already, there are a few life skills that you need to pick up that will help you to be more independent. They include the ability to cook, do your own laundry and handle your finances.**

- **Most students get excited or stressed about all the new people they're going to meet when they arrive, but it's also good to pay some thought to the people you are leaving behind. It can be a very emotional time for them as well as you. Aww.**

- **There are also several arrangements that you probably want to make before you leave home, such as getting insurance for your belongings, applying for university accommodation and opening a student bank account.**

STUDYING NEAR TO HOME

While there is an increasing trend for students to apply for degree courses near to their families and friends, the majority of them prefer to study in a different town. If you do stay in the family home while you're at university, you'll have cheaper accommodation costs and many more of your creature comforts will probably be provided. You won't have the upheaval of packing up and moving out, or have to cram yourself into tiny hall rooms or eat hall food. On the other hand, it may feel more difficult to meet new people if you live off campus, or you may find it annoying if you still have to live by your parents' rules. Even though you're not moving away, you'll still need to get your documentation together, arrange your finances by opening a student-friendly bank account and maybe put together a small cash fund.

SOMEWHERE TO LAY YOUR HEAD

Once you've been accepted onto your course you can start arranging your accommodation. Most universities send out a brochure to potential undergraduates that outlines the facilities available at various halls of residence and flats, and shows how close each building is to campus. They will also probably have lots of lovely pictures of smiling gorgeous students in clean and spacious rooms. Do bear in mind that they will always take those pictures in the newest and most deluxe rooms, and certainly will not illustrate broken heating, bad-tempered door staff or corridors that smell of overcooked broccoli and bleach. And the cute boys and girls might be models that they've shipped in to make an impression. If possible, talk to someone who attended the university recently and either lived in or visited lots of friends in the hall you're most interested in. You can also chat to current students on the message boards of websites such as www.virginstudent.com. Just remember that wherever you plump for, it isn't quite going to be the Ritz and you may not even get your first choice.

If your priorities are convenience and making lots of friends, then go for a big hall as close to campus as possible, perhaps one with its own bar or social rooms. For people who like to eat what they want, when they want it, self-catering accommodation or at least a catered hall with small kitchenettes might be ideal. There has been a big move in the last few years for universities to build student villages or halls based around small self-catering flats, with kitchens and communal areas that are each shared by around four to eight students. If you want somewhere much quieter, or are a mature or postgraduate student, find out whether you can get a place in a university-owned house slightly away from the main campus, preferably with people nearer to your own age.

Fill the forms in as soon as you can with your first, second and third choices, then stick them straight in the post and keep your fingers crossed. You may even be asked a few questions on the application form about your interests, what time you like to get up or go to sleep, whether you smoke or not, if you are a vegetarian and so on. Do not be fooled into thinking that it will ever be used to match you up with your ideal flatmates because most university accommodation services are way too frantic, understaffed and under-resourced to spend time doing this. You get what you're given most of the time, unless you have special religious or cultural requirements. Also bear in mind that if your family live within a certain radius of your college, you may not qualify for university accommodation, or will be given much less priority.

It's the norm for a university to have more students arriving each year than they can actually house. There may be a mad scramble at the start of term, with a few unlucky students unexpectedly finding themselves in temporary accommodation such as bed and breakfasts, living miles out of town with an unfamiliar family, or even sleeping on camp beds on the floor of the gym. If it happens to you, do your best to grin and bear it, because things will get sorted out eventually and people much prefer to help you out if you're managing to stay polite and friendly. Other students might drop out or change courses or accommodation, so a hall place could well come up soon if that's what you really want.

You may prefer to rent privately. Unless you're prepared to lodge with your landlord or landlady, or take a tiny bedsit somewhere, you'll probably end up taking a room in a shared house because it's the cheapest option. Speak to the accommodation office to see whether they have a list of recommended housing agencies or landlords, and set plenty of time aside to travel to the area and look around the properties, preferably with a friend or relative for safety. Failing that, read up about student life in the area with university guidebooks or websites and work out one or two areas you'd prefer to live in, then visit for a couple of days. Get the local papers or a copy of *Loot* when you arrive, or look in nearby shop windows for advertisements. If possible, meet the people you will be living with first, long before you even think about signing anything, as you could end up sharing with anyone from fiftysomething divorced alcoholics to young fighting couples.

It's probably easier to share private accommodation with students your own age, who have similar lifestyles and financial considerations. Think twice about sharing your housing with lots of people who are travelling their way around the world – although it's likely to be interesting and exciting there's a big chance that they will move on quickly, leaving you to rearrange your contract with the landlord, interview new flatmates or even sort out their unpaid bills unexpectedly. Another way around the accommodation problem is to book a room somewhere on a short-term basis for when you arrive, such as the YMCA, lodgings or bed and breakfast, and then house hunt during your first few days in town.

Check exactly what's provided by the university or your private landlord long before you need to travel, so that you don't end up buying or carting around anything that you don't really need.

- **Ask about bed linen and duvets, towels, pots and pans, kettles and cookers, crockery and cutlery, lighting, furniture, shelving and other storage space, laundry facilities and telephone points.**

- **Find out what the kitchen and bathroom facilities are like, including the hours that hall kitchens are open, whether you're self-catering or have access to a kitchenette, how often cleaners come round (if at all), whether the areas are secure or open and how many people you'll be sharing with.**

- **If you are bringing a car or a bike call ahead and ask about parking places, bike stands and how good the security is. You may need to apply for a parking permit.**

- **Find out what you are expected to pay on top of your rent or hall fees, how it is paid and how often. You may or may not be charged for heating and lighting, for example.**

If you're relying on public transport, it can also save you plenty of hassle later if you find out what buses, tubes or trains run nearest to your accommodation. Once you have written proof of where you're staying, seriously think about getting your belongings insured before you travel. It's one less thing to do when you arrive, and you'll be covered from the start. For more details of insurance see the chapters on Freshers' Week (Chapter 2), and Crime and Safety (Chapter 9).

GET YOUR CASH INTO SHAPE

It goes without saying that the majority of students will be on tight budgets and struggling with debt, probably feeling the pinch sooner rather than later. There are going to be several extra drains on your cash flow when you arrive, such as the enjoyments of freshers' week, setting yourself up with basic household goods and groceries and buying books and equipment for your course. Save up as much money as you can to cover these extra expenses before you leave home. To work out how much you need for the first couple of weeks, figure in the following:

The cost of getting to your accommodation from home (petrol money, tickets, taxis)

Deposits or key money for your accommodation

The most important books on your reading list

Files, paper, pens and other stationery

Getting around: bus passes, taxis home from nightclubs, buying a bike, road tax

Things for your room that you couldn't take with you

A starter pack of groceries and kitchen equipment

Going out money for drinks and entry to clubs, cinemas and concerts

Joining fees for clubs and societies

Connection fees, payphone money or mobile phone bill

Spare change for eating out, snacks and coffees

Impulse purchases of music, clothes and footwear

University fees if you have to pay them

One handy tip is to work out how much you think you'll spend on drinking, going out and other socialising. Then double this amount for a more realistic estimate. Oh yes. It might sound a bit extreme cash-wise, but it does give you the freedom to take up lots of offers and meet more people. And you always spend much more than you think you're going to on a big night out anyway.

If possible, arrange some employment during the summer holidays to help you get a little cash saved up. Try everywhere you can think of and be polite and persistent. There's always some kind of work available, so make regular calls or visits to job centres and temp agencies, or ring around large employers nearby. Perhaps family friends can help you out with some work, or you might find vacancies advertised in local papers. Make sure you're not paying too much tax on your earnings, and stick as much of it away in a savings account as you can.

It's also a good time to think about applying for your maximum amount of student loan to help meet your living costs while you are studying. Start by contacting your local award authority (not the place you will be studying at), who will send you an application form for their means-testing and eligibility assessments. English and Welsh students need to apply to their Local Education Authority, and students from Northern Ireland should apply to their local Education and Library Board; the numbers will be in the local phone book. All students from Scotland should apply to the Student Awards Agency for Scotland at Gyleview House, 3 Redheughs Rigg, South Gyle, Edinburgh, EH12 9HH, telephone: 0131 476 8212.

Anyone who applies for a student loan after 1 September 1998 is trying to obtain a type of loan called Student Support. Part, but not all, of this loan is means-tested. If your home is in Scotland and you get their application forms back to them as soon as possible, the Student Awards Agency for Scotland will then notify the Student Loans Company on your behalf, and you should have money waiting for you when you arrive to start your course. If you are normally resident in England, Wales or Northern Ireland, your award authority will send you a support notification or eligibility notice, with a loan request form on the reverse. Complete it and return it to the Student Loans Company as soon as you can at 100 Bothwell Street, Glasgow G2 7JD, telephone: 0800 40 50 10, minicom: 0800 085 3950. With a bit of luck your first payment should be transferred electronically into your student bank account by the beginning of term.

If you open a student bank account before arriving at your university, you can save yourself a huge amount of time and stress in freshers' week. Shop around for the best deals from early summer onwards, when the big high street banks start to announce their terms and offers for the forthcoming academic year. The details are published in the national press and on the websites of all the big banks and building societies, and there's more information about how to choose an account in Chapter 6.

Since I've just had a gap year, I've had a great deal of time to prepare. I've seen countless friends go to uni already and so I've been given stack loads of advice as to how to get ready. I've been working for the last year, so my affluence is somewhat better than that of students who left school in June. From that money, something like one third has actually been saved, but it's almost equal, if not above, my student loan, which places me in a comfortable position because I can pay off my accommodation and still have the full amount of my student loan to live with. I am usually really bad with money, so I'm apprehensive that I'll find myself in severe debts by the time I reach the final term, so budgeting is something I'll have to try to maintain.

One thing I'm particularly worried about is actually meeting my flatmates, and getting along with them. A friend of mine has had a torrid time for the past year as he only got on with one person in his flat and that was because he knew him from school. My personality allows me to be friendly and considerate to others, but there is always a doubt that maybe I won't like someone or they won't like me. But at the end of the day, we have to get on with it and not let it get us down too much.

Freshers' week, I can't wait for. Last year I managed to blag my way on to a few pub crawls, and some of the activities they have are simply ludicrous. But it's the time when you get to know people. First impressions count, and I hope to meet as many people as possible and make some good friends during this time. I'm expecting this week to be wild, and a non-stop party, in between enrolling and choosing modules, so sobriety is out of the question. All in all, as long as I still have some money left at the end of it, some friends, and haven't been admitted to hospital, it should be a fantastic week, and the initial highlight of the social calendar!

Gareth Charles Iestyn Stevens, about to become a first year Law student at the University of Sunderland

READY TO FEND FOR YOURSELF?

If you don't know much about handling your finances, now's a good time to find out. Learn how to make and stick to a basic budget (see the Money chapter later in this book for more details) and make sure you know how to write cheques or use bank or credit cards without getting ripped off. Get into the habit of anticipating how large your bills will be and putting enough to one side so that you can pay them on time. If you don't know how to check and pay bills, ask a relative or your local Citizens' Advice Bureau (the number will be in your local phone book or listed on www.nacab.org.uk). Most bills have a standing charge that you always pay, such as the line rental on a phone bill, and generally also have a variable charge for the units that you've used on top of this, such as the amount of gas or electricity. This will then have VAT (tax) added on top, leaving you with the total bill. Work out how you will be paying your bills and plan accordingly. For example, if the electricity in your student flat will be running on a card-operated meter, it pays to get an emergency card as soon as you arrive and keep it handy in case the power goes off unexpectedly.

Brushing up on your computer skills is going to go in your favour, lasting through university and beyond. If you can't do it already, learning to touch-type will get your assignments finished much faster, leaving you with more free time to destroy your precious brain cells down the pub. A fast typing speed can also grab you some of the better-paid and least grubby part-time jobs, doing administrative work, for example.

If you aren't already used to doing your own laundry, it's another useful skill to have before you leave home. Unless you think it's cool to be grimy and stinky, it's an idea to learn how to do a weekly wash, preferably in a way that doesn't ruin your favourite clothes. Parents or older siblings will probably be keen to help you out with advice on this, but if in doubt do something slightly strange that most people would never even consider doing – read the instructions inside the clothes, on the front of the washing machine or on the laundry detergent packet. I know, I know, it's a big ask, but this small sacrifice can work wonders and may even save your lucky pants or best pulling T-shirt. Appendix 1 contains a simple guide to laundry, ironing and general clothes care in case you get stuck.

Cooking, rather than reheating stuff and calling it cooking, is a great talent to possess. It saves you money on ready meals and takeaways, and is great for socialising and feeding friends and loved ones. If you've never even so much as boiled an egg in your life, why not pick up a few cooking tips while you're still at home? Get a few ideas from parents or guardians if they're a bit handy in the kitchen – they'll be flattered that you like their food. You don't have to be the next celebrity chef; just get together a handful of recipes that you can do simply and well and that don't need too many pans or gadgets. There are several student favourite recipes in the back of this book, plus the best ways to get spag bol stains out of your favourite T-shirt. Practise cooking a few times before you move out, to get your confidence up. Dinner at my place, honey? Oh, go on then.

Most students avoid cleaning, and that's probably because the majority of people in all walks of life hate doing it anyway. You're unlikely to be able to afford a cleaner, so you'll have to do it yourself. You might prefer to live in a hovel that looks like a council tip, of course, but do try to keep your place just above the dysentery line. If nothing else, remember that a clean and moderately tidy pad looks sophisticated, and this always makes a very good impression with attractive visitors. To save plenty of time and bother, clean up after yourself as you go. Freshly spilled pasta sauce is much easier to wipe up from a work surface than the dried-on-overnight version. Similarly, dirty crockery left overnight takes a lot more scrubbing than something you washed up before going to bed. Stick to this simple rule, and you can get away with a very light dust, wipe-round and vacuum every now and then, rather than wondering if an industrial cleaning machine might be a good idea. Check Appendix 1 for some idiot-proof cleaning tips.

FRIENDS, FAMILY AND GIRLFRIENDS/BOYFRIENDS

Moving to a new town tends to mean that you won't see so much of your family, local friends, or boyfriends or girlfriends back home. Lots of new students find this unsettling, but you can still keep in touch with everyone and make plenty of new friends at the same time too. Cheap or free ways to keep in touch include using your university email, text messages or even the free postcards that litter the entrance halls of any student union. You don't have to be on the phone to them every five minutes, though. Just check in every few days, and plan the occasional event to look forward to during the holidays or on a mid-term weekend.

You may find that some of the friends you're leaving behind can start acting a bit strangely as it gets closer to the time you're due to leave. It may be because they're worried that you'll forget all about them, or that you'll just leave them behind for something more exciting. They may also be a bit jealous of you, especially if they wanted to go to university themselves but didn't get onto the course they wanted for whatever reason. You can't do much more at this stage than hanging out with them, and promising to contact them regularly, then following up on your promise.

Boyfriends and girlfriends can become incredibly insecure if they're not going to be at the same college as you, and you may have to sit them down and talk it out with them. You both have to be realistic because long-distance relationships always need the pair of you to make an equal amount of effort. If one of you clearly isn't that committed, it's better to be honest and call it quits, rather than letting it drag on and hurting the other person more in the long run. Or you could both take the pragmatic approach, which is to see how it goes, acknowledging the fact that the university experience might change one or both of you, and that you might meet new people you are attracted to.

Mums and dads sometimes get a bit mopy or start to nag a little, especially if you have a very close family or you're the first or last offspring to leave home. They're either completely unused to it or they'll have an empty nest. Even if they're being totally embarrassing, try not to laugh at them too much or end up having an argument. Parents are bound to worry about you, it's their job, even if they are proud of you getting a university place, or if it's high time you moved out and got a place of your own anyway. Sooner or later they will get used to the idea. Phoning home or dropping a line regularly should do the trick. It never hurts to keep them sweet, in case you have to come back to them for an emergency cash injection later.

Friends who are coming with you or joining you at college can be a blessing and a curse. When everything around you is unfamiliar, a friendly face can be just what you need, and they'll feel the same way too. Think twice about living and partying in an exclusive group with them, especially if you're on the same course, because it can become very difficult to make new friends. If you're a little shy there will be no incentive to talk to other students, and it can put people off from approaching your tightly-knit social group because you look so cliquey.

THINKING AHEAD
Do you need to make any arrangements with the university or other organisations before you arrive on their doorstep?

- **International students will have extra activities laid on for them during freshers' week, to help them settle in to our strange British culture and get everyone socialising. Students can contact their** university's International Office to find out about 'meet and greet' schemes, assistance with immigration, funding issues and more.

- Mature students (anyone over the age of 21) are probably more than capable of looking after themselves, but they may wish to live with people of their own age, or they might be a bit rusty when it comes to studying. UCAS produce a handy free guide called 'The Mature Students' Guide to Higher Education', which is available from their order line, telephone: 0870 1122200.

- Students with children need to make arrangements with the university crèche, relatives or other childminders. It's also useful to organise back-up support in case of emergencies. Larger universities may have a childcare support officer and a childcare fund that makes small grants. Government support for UK undergraduate students with children includes the Childcare Grant and Dependents' Grant. Parents who are eligible should apply to their Local Education Authority (LEA) when they apply for general financial support towards their degree programme. There's more information about funding on the Department for Education and Skills website at www.dfes.gov.uk.

- Students with disabilities should find that their chosen university is keen to provide them with all the facilities they need. As well as calling up to discuss any requirements ahead of time, they can benefit from getting in touch with SKILL, the National Bureau for Students with Disabilities. They provide advice on all aspects of student life, including welfare, work experience and volunteering, and they produce a range of guides. Their website is at www.skill.org.uk, or you can contact head office at: Chapter House, 18–20 Crucifix Lane, London, SE1 3JW. Telephone or minicom: 020 7450 0620, fax: 020 7450 0650. There's also an Information Service, telephone: 0800 328 5050 (freephone) and 020 7657 2337, open Monday to Thursday afternoons.

WHAT TO PACK (ESSENTIALS AND OTHER ITEMS)

What you take with you depends on how much you like your creature comforts and how you plan on getting everything to your chosen destination. The further you have to travel, the less you should weigh yourself down with. It is hard to manoeuvre several bags and boxes around during a long journey, and it's better to stick to the bare essentials, then buy other items as you need them after you arrive.

Get yourself a small rucksack that's big enough to take an A4 notepad, and put all your essential maps and documents in it, plus a small spongebag and an alarm clock. That way you have an easily manageable pack that will get you to university and see you through the first night. It will have all your essentials close to hand in one place and be easily accessible at all times. You don't want to be rummaging at the bottom of your suitcase or in big boxes to find vital pieces of paperwork when you arrive, especially if it's late or after a long journey.

If you're driving yourself up to university or you get a lift in someone's car, do yourself a favour. Put items like stereos and computers out of sight in the boot, or at least covered up by bed linen to hide them if you can't lock them away. This should hopefully avoid inviting the attentions of opportunistic thieves. Don't leave the car unlocked and unattended while you are getting keys from the accommodation office, or putting your belongings in your room.

THE BARE ESSENTIALS

Your ID: driving licence, passport, birth certificate

Train, bus or plane tickets

Discount railcard or coach card

Your course acceptance letter

Your course reading list and other details

Accommodation office letter

Insurance documents

Campus map

Several passport-size photos of yourself

Waterproof bag or folder for your documents

Wallet, money, cash card

Bank details

Diary, or electronic organiser

Notepad and pen

Alarm clock

A few changes of clothes

Rainproof jacket or umbrella

Addresses and contact numbers for your next of kin, doctor and dentist back home

Glasses or contact lenses if you use them

Essential medication or contraception

Washbag and basic toiletries

Small first aid kit: pain killers, sticking plasters, antiseptic cream

Female students: tampons, panty liners or sanitary towels

Toilet roll or tissues

Small bag or mini-rucksack

Bed linen and bath towel (only if needed)

USEFUL

Stereo and radio, CDs or MP3 Player

Laptop or personal computer

Mobile phone (make sure it's the right tariff for you)

Hair dryer if you have long hair

Biscuits or other snacks for when you arrive

Mugs and small supply of tea, coffee and dried milk

Bowl, plate, cutlery

Enough everyday clothes to last 10 days without having to do laundry

Sports kit

Dressing gown or towelling robe (for fire drills in the middle of the night)

Multi-function penknife or Leatherman tool

Bottle opener and can opener

Small torch

Pictures, posters, photos

White tack for posters or other sticky stuff that will not damage paintwork

Electrical extension lead with circuit breaker

OTHER ITEMS

Your own lamp or other lighting

Bedspread, throws, cushions or rug

TV, video or DVD player

CD holder or record box

Cheap or disposable camera

Clothes airer or clothes horse

Sandwich box or other plastic box

Kitchen equipment: pan with lid, frying pan, wooden spoon or spatula, small chopping board and knife, metal sleve, tea towel, washing-up cloth

Hand-held calculator

Small stationery set with stapler, pins, rubber bands, paperclips, scissors

Mini clothes-mending kit

Mini tool kit with flat head and Philips screwdrivers

Books, folders, A4 notepaper

Travel iron (if you are very neat or need to look smart for your course)

Lightweight sleeping bag (for crashing on your mates' floors or travelling)

If you're staying in halls or a university-owned house or flat then be aware that you'll probably have to move all your stuff out of there again at the end of the third term. Don't take too much with you, and don't buy too much when you get there. After all of this preparation and packing, you're as ready as you'll ever be for freshers' week. Hope you packed an open mind and a sense of adventure. Fasten those seatbelts.

HOW SHOULD I GET READY FOR UNI?

Advice from the students on www.virginstudent.com

'Pack egg noodles (holy grail of finds when you need study food), aspirin, tomato sauce (will make anything taste better) and socks (you may starve but that's no excuse for smelly feet). Think I covered all basic needs there.'

'Lots of pasta, something to hang clothes on to dry, tins of baked beans and soup, CDs to make you smile, addresses and phone numbers of mates you want to keep in touch with and lots of chocolate.'

'I was always told to take a doorstop, because we had big heavy fireproof doors. A doorstop or keys rightly placed beneath keeps the door open so you don't look too antisocial if you're lounging on your bed.'

'You need to pack some clothes and a toothbrush, anything else you can always borrow from someone else. Don't forget a game of Scrabble or Twister too for those "I don't have any money again" nights in.'

'Posters so you can make any circa-1970s box (complete with brown carpet, beige walls and quaint smell) feel like home. And lightbulbs – everyone forgets lightbulbs!'

'Do not try to fit in, just be yourself and you will feel far more comfortable. There will be people you wouldn't choose as friends, but there will also be people you wouldn't meet anywhere else. Go in with your eyes and mind open. Leave your school days behind and embrace growing up.'

2. FRESHERS' WEEK

Ah, the mythical goings-on of freshers' week. It's a crash course in everything about university, minus anything to do with your chosen degree. Just as well really, because doing coursework on top of everything else would be too much for mere mortals, and might just take the fun out of things. One thing's for sure – you won't be feeling fresh by the end of it. When you arrive at your accommodation to settle yourself in you need to be ready for:

- **Doing a few chores such as checking your student loan has arrived and signing up with the health service.**
- **An insane social calendar with everything from pub crawls to joining clubs and societies.**
- **Making lots of new friends, and meeting your flatmates and the other students on your course.**

Expect long queues for everything, repetitive strain injury of your voice box from answering the same questions over and over again, reconnaissance missions at midnight to find the nearest sources of Rizlas and bog roll, and several industrial strength hangovers. Oh, and some seriously good times, plus the occasional tiny pang of homesickness.

TOUCHING DOWN ON PLANET UNI

If your folks are giving you a lift, try not to laugh hysterically when they take a wrong turn or get foxed by an unfamiliar one-way street system. Students who are driving themselves there can take their time, but stand a much better chance of getting a decent parking place outside their accommodation if they arrive early. If you've come in on the train or coach you'll probably have a few bags, so treat yourself to a taxi. There's no point giving yourself a hernia or getting all hot and sweaty lugging your belongings up the road or onto a local bus. It's going to be a long day so stay cool.

However you arrive, this is the bit where you'll be glad that you kept your maps and documents close to hand. Expect to make a few mistakes in unfamiliar terrain as you find your way around, and remember that the lost feeling doesn't last for too long, however annoying or unsettling it may be. A campus map tends to be more informative than the vast majority of passing strangers if you do find yourself lost, or trying to get somewhere in a hurry. It's helpful to keep your campus map on you most of the time for the next few weeks.

If you're staying in halls or university flats or houses, you usually have to go to the accommodation office as your first port of call, depending on your particular university's setup (sometimes you just go straight to the hall). You show them your ID and acceptance letter, and they give you your room or house number and your keys. This may sound deceptively simple, and in concept it is, but in reality the practice is best described as shambolic. Everyone turns up at the same time, and you will have to queue. Oh yes, your first queue. This is going to be fun. You come face to face for the first time with a broad cross section of people you're going to be studying, or drinking, alongside.

It can be a bit of a surprise, especially if you come from a local place for local people. Humans of all sizes, shapes, persuasions and colours jumbled in together, waiting and waiting and waiting. There's nothing you can do to get the queue to move faster, so you might as well take it easy and enjoy the experience. The Zen approach to queueing, if you like. Smile, say hello to all kinds of different students and make some small talk to pass the time. Get your new friends to hold your place in the queue while you take toilet breaks or run out to fetch a coffee. By the time you finally get your keys and directions to your accommodation, you might have found out about a party that night, or met someone off your course.

HI HONEY, I'M HOME

There may be some more hoops to jump through when you get to your hall or flat. You might need to sort out security codes for push-button locks on the front door, or a swipe card. Some halls also have telephone lines in each room where you have to sign up for a contract with the communications company on arrival. You'll also have an invitation (it's an order really) to attend an induction meeting if you're staying in halls, where they run you through essential information about security and fire escapes and so on, and you get to check out the cuties that have arrived that day. Learn the evacuation procedure for the fire alerts, including your escape route and meeting point, and rest assured that there will be at least one practice drill some time in the next few days. It is always in the middle of the night, so have some clothes nearby to throw on quickly, and bring any guests downstairs with you at the same time.

They may have laid on a social programme too, so make the most of it. Hall dwellers note that you should always be friendly and charming to hall wardens and security guards, even if they are grumpy, incompetent gits or closet nazis. You can get away with more rule bending later if they like you, but life will get very strained indeed if they think you are a fool or a troublemaker.

If one or both parents have dropped you off at your accommodation, remember to make grateful noises. It can be very tempting to wish they'd vanish immediately and stop cramping your style, but show them a little mercy. At least for half an hour or so. Most parents find it really difficult to get used to the idea that their son or daughter has finally moved out, and may get a bit mushy or even grumpy. Give them a hug or say thanks for the lift, tell them not to worry and promise to call them, then send them on their merry way. On the other hand, you may have been cramping their style for years too, so don't worry that your leaving home is going to break their little hearts forever.

FIRST THINGS FIRST

When you get to your room, be mentally prepared for the fact that it will almost certainly be bare and tiny. Get in there quickly and make it your own.

- **If nothing else, make sure your bed is made up and your washbag is at hand, so you can have a quick wash and go out, then return in a drunken stupor to a ready bed.**

- **Although it will say in all your hall literature that you mustn't stick posters or pictures up on the walls, remember that everyone ignores this order.**

- **You'll need to brighten the place up and make your mark on it, so get those walls covered with at least one or two pics, preferably with sticky stuff that doesn't ruin the paintwork.**

- **If that doesn't quite do the trick, you can always buy some cheap throws, rugs and ornaments later.**

- **If there are a few marks on the walls at the end of term three, get everyone to chip in for a sample-sized pot of paint and a brush, and the problem's solved for a few pence.**

Leave the door open while you unpack a few essential belongings so that you can see the other people who are moving in, but don't leave the room unattended. Get off on the right foot with students in your flat or corridor by smiling and saying hello, and introducing yourself. It really is that simple, just look them in the eye and be friendly, even if you're feeling shy. If you feel a bit tongue-tied, ask them about themselves: it's their specialist subject and is guaranteed to make the conversation flow more easily. Don't be the moody person who spends hours in their bedroom without saying hi. Then dig out your coffee mugs and offer to make your flatmates or corridor mates a hot drink. Even better if you've brought some biscuits and other snacks, you'll probably be feeling very hungry about now.

If you're in flats or a house, stake out some territory in the kitchen:

- **Make sure you get a convenient cupboard and drawer for your things, preferably right next to a preparation surface rather than the cooker or the bin.**

- **Don't leave too much in open hall kitchens, if it isn't nailed down some hungry drunk person or stoner with the munchies will eat it, or use it for a merry little prank of some description.**

- **In fact it might be better to keep mugs, utensils, tea and coffee, and dried or tinned food in a little box in your room. Unless you want to keep paying for new stuff over and over, without actually getting to eat or drink any of it.**

Check out the bathroom situation:

- **There's an increasing trend for self-catering flats to have tiny en-suite bathrooms in each bedroom. If so, sweet. You can be as messy as you like, and nobody's going to nick your toothpaste or shower gel.**

- **Be warned about the shared bathrooms, they get filthy pretty damn quick even if you get cleaners in regularly. You might have to clean it before you can use it, making showers easier than baths.**

- **If the showers are filthy too, treat yourself to a pair of cheap plastic flip-flops so you don't have to tread in it.**

- **As for toilets, keep extra loo roll in your room in case of emergencies and pranks, and check first before you sit down. Enough said.**

So now you're partly unpacked at least, have met your new flatmates and had the chance to grab a snack and freshen up a little. At this point pretty much everybody decides to go out with their new mates to whatever entertainments have been laid on. You will almost certainly spend a lot more than you expected to, and wake up with a hangover. But more about the partying later, let's get the housekeeping out of the way first.

NUS MEMBERSHIP

Throughout the week, you'll have to do a number of practical chores to make sure you're set up for the coming term. Expect even more queueing and smalltalk. If you've brought a mobile phone, you can at least chat to a few friends or relatives back home while you're waiting. A good place to start is by making your way along to the students' union building and joining the National Union of Students. It isn't compulsory to join, but does offer a wide range of benefits from advice on all aspects of student life to cheap beer and discounts on books and records. Take along one of your passport photos, wait in line for an eternity, and come out the other end with a lovely laminated ID card with your NUS student number on it. Whenever you're in a shop or restaurant from now on, try waving the card and asking for discount. Never hurts to ask. You'll have to show it when you go in and out of the union building too, at least until the security staff get to know your face.

YOUR COURSE

There may be a set time in the week to formally enrol on your chosen degree course. Make your way along to the faculty office, or wherever else they've set aside for this purpose, and get into the line-up yet again. These are the people you're going to be crammed into lecture halls and tutorial rooms with for at least the next three years, so you might as well get to know them from the word go. Some of them might turn out to be lifelong best friends, or even be fit. Or both. Take the opportunity to sweet-talk the departmental receptionists and secretary, for they are where the real power lies in academia. If you ever have a course-related emergency or need a special favour, these are the people you'll have to go through to get anywhere. Pick up any timetables or other course information that you need, such as a syllabus, and if there's something you don't quite understand then don't be scared to ask about it.

You could be invited to a departmental introduction, a meet-and-greet or even a wine and cheese evening. Make sure you know when it is. Turn up looking reasonably clean and not too hungover, and make a note of the names of your tutors. No matter how much they tempt you with cheap red wine, don't knock it back on an empty stomach and definitely avoid becoming completely drunk. Your inebriated antics will haunt you until the end of the course, especially if you say something stupid to a professor or throw up in the department's function room. If a terrible thirst is upon you, do what any sensible second year would do and steal a bottle of wine for later. And don't blame me if you get caught.

STUDENT HEALTH

Nobody ever expects to get ill in the first week of term, even if they have a few ongoing health problems. When it does happen it's usually without warning. That's precisely why you need to sign up with a nearby general practitioner or student health services now. Queue again, and fill in the health forms. If you do feel poorly before you've signed up, most GPs will see you as an emergency patient, but you may face a longer wait and have to fill in lots of paperwork while you're feeling absolutely wretched. While you're at it, think about signing up with a dentist if they're attached to student health or the nearby dental school. Or you may prefer to remember to arrange your six-monthly checkups for when you go home during the holidays.

GIMME THE MONEY

Two things to think about here: your bank account and your incoming money. Go to the finance office and sort out any student loans or bursaries as a priority. These cheques and money transfers could arrive late, so be prepared. Most bank managers will be sympathetic, provided you have the paperwork to show that you've taken up a place on your course and are eligible for the student loan or bursary in question. If by some miracle the money has been sorted out on time, pick up the cheque and get it straight into the bank, remembering it'll take at least three working days to clear.

If you haven't already arranged a student bank account, now's the time to get one. It's usually easiest to go for the bank that's nearest to campus or your accommodation, but shop around and look for the best deal. Think about which bank gives you the largest free overdraft and has the most conveniently placed cashtills, or offers the cheapest arranged overdraft fee to students who have gone over their interest-free allowance. When you've narrowed it down to the two banks who look the best, you can then pick the one that's offering the most generous free gift. If you're signing up, get there when the doors open to avoid yet more lengthy delays.

WHY BOTHER WITH INSURANCE?

If you haven't already arranged some insurance for your personal belongings, you should seriously think about doing so right now. Students are a general target for theft, and if everything you owned was wiped out, could you honestly afford to go straight out and replace it? Probably not. It costs students living outside London an average of £61 per year to insure their belongings during university terms (£76 inside London), which is much less than the average cost of replacement, which is estimated at around £3,000.

Although most university literature tells you not to take valuables to college, you're going to take them anyway, so I'll spare you this particular bit of totally useless advice. It's a strange person indeed who doesn't want their stereo and CDs with them when they leave home. And it's not so surprising that most students own a mobile phone, a bike, or a personal computer or laptop. They cheer you up, help you to keep in touch with your friends and get around, and allow you to pass your degree with less stress. Of course you're going to take them with you. Duh. Just leave the family jewels and your collection of fine wines at home, and make sure the rest of it is properly covered by your insurance.

Your parents' home contents insurance policy may cover you while you are at university, but check the small print carefully to see what it includes. Items such as bicycles or laptop computers may attract a premium. The National Union of Students recommends Endsleigh Insurance for protecting the contents of hall rooms and shared houses; contact them via www.endsleigh.co.uk or drop into one of their offices near to campus. One important thing to note: if your belongings are stolen from unlocked bedrooms, unattended communal areas or bags left on a table while you visit the pub toilet, the insurers will refuse to pay out. You have to show that you have taken reasonable care.

JOINING THE BOOK CLUB

If there's a guided tour of the main library go on it, because this will save you hours of hassle in the long run. Find out where the main texts for your course are kept, along with the reference books, theses by previous students, journals and magazines. It's also good to know the procedures for ordering books and papers in from other libraries, and how to get rare (or utterly useless and dull) items out of storage. Your library may also have several ways of accessing its catalogue, such as online databases and CD-ROMs. It should also have free access to subject-specific sources of information, which would otherwise be very expensive to get hold of. Work out where the photocopiers are, and whether you need to buy a copying card or pay at the desk. While you're there, sort out your library card and make a note of how many books you can borrow on it.

THE FRESHERS' WEEK ENTERTAINMENTS

Now for the fun bit. Freshers' week is about enjoying yourself and your new surroundings, and socialising like mad. The student union bar will be busy all week and the entertainments (ents) committee will have laid on all kinds of things to do. Expect anything from cheesy club nights to organised pub crawls. It depends on where you are and what the facilities are like, but you might also be treated to comedians, live bands, hypnotists, funfairs, jelly wrestling or even blind date evenings. Get along to as many of them as you can, and enjoy the atmosphere. There might also be indoor markets held at the union building during the day, with stalls selling cheap posters, second hand CDs or all types of clothes.

There will be a tidal wave of cheap beer and perhaps some free promotional alcohol on top of that. There's no point saying that you shouldn't drink it. You might also be offered a wide variety of drugs. I'll just say pace yourself, know the law and don't overdo things early in the evening or at the start of the week. Don't get into anything you can't handle, and remember you're in unfamiliar surroundings which can pose problems getting home or getting medical attention to anyone who has an accident, a bad trip or pill, or a serious dose of alcohol poisoning.

From a safety point of view, make sure you know where you're going that evening and how you're getting back to your accommodation. Avoid the temptation to walk home drunk in the dark on your own, even if it's a short walk, especially if you're female. Potential muggers and rapists can and do take advantage of the fact that students wander around alone incredibly drunk or drugged during freshers' week, or forget to lock their front doors behind them. Student-on-student theft and violence is another possibility. If another student latches onto you who makes you feel threatened or uncomfortable in any way, don't feel that you have to put up with them. Trust your instincts. Get some help from bar staff or security staff, and if necessary pay the extra and get a licensed taxi home. There's no shame in asking for help, whether you're male or female. The university may also run a safety bus to take female students back to their accommodation.

> I got involved with freshers' week during the last couple of weeks of last term. Our JCR (student union type thing) set up a committee to organise events, be contact points and generally be around to help out all our lovely freshers when they arrive at college. I'm also involved because I'm on the committee of the OxfordWelsh Society and I'll be on a stall in the Freshers' Fair. I so wish it was my freshers' week all over again – there's so much planned. There are day and evening events in and out of college including a scavenger hunt to help learn the way round college, a pub quiz, ice skating, pub and club nights and a pool party.
>
> Hannah Thomas, second year English student at Jesus College, Oxford University

YOUR NEW BEST FRIENDS

Everybody is in the same situation: they don't know each other. If you were the shy one at school, so what? You have a clean slate and nobody knows you, so be whoever you want to be. Everyone is feeling a little shy and insecure right now, you're not the only one. It's an old cliché but it's true, strangers are just mates you haven't met yet. Smile and say hello to people and strike up a few conversations, because if you start talking to someone, you've saved them the stress of having to talk to you first. You'll soon find that most people are slightly grateful when someone is friendly and takes an interest.

The conversations can be a bit repetitive at first. You may get sick of being asked where you're from, what course you're doing, where you're staying or what A Levels you took. Break out of this by asking a few open questions, where they have to think a bit about their answers and talk at length. Ask about their taste in music or films, where they've travelled, what sports they're into or what their opinion is on a recent event. You may find you have plenty in common, even if it didn't seem that way at the beginning. If you hit it off, swap names and emails or mobile phone numbers and keep in touch. Or if you really don't like them, simply say goodbye and make an excuse like needing the toilet or having to talk to someone off your course. You don't have to be rude to them, or feel like you have to hang out with them all evening either.

The people you spend time with in the first couple of days may not turn out to be the people you are firm friends with by the end of the term, but you never know. You can never have too many mates after all. Don't be fooled into thinking that you should only socialise with a small group of people who all wear the same kind of clothes, or like the same kind of music that you do. That's a bit narrow-minded and you could be missing out. If you've come to university with a few friends from back home, it's better if you don't wander around all the time like you're joined at the hip. Set a time and a place for all of you to meet up one evening during the week, so that you can catch up and share your stories. Even though it will have only been a few days, it might feel more like a grand reunion.

Platonic relationships aside, it's also a time when students meet new boyfriends or girlfriends. There's plenty of flirting, a fair amount of drunken snogging and a few one-night stands. Don't despair if you're looking for a partner and nothing materialises during the first few days, it might take a while before you meet anyone you like, that's all. There are hundreds of new people at your university, if not thousands, and you won't get to meet them all in the first week, no matter how hard you try. Female first year students might also want to watch out for prowling second and third year males, who may be circling the bar looking for fresh faces. It's impossible to say whether this is predatory behaviour or just deeply sad. Beware. They don't call it F-A-F week for nothing.

CLUBS AND SOCIETIES

Make sure you get yourself along to the Societies Fair, it could make your social life go with a bigger bang. All the university clubs and societies are represented; clubs are mostly for sports and games, and societies may be a little more intellectual or political. Or not. Chocolate Society, or Teddy Bears' Picnic Soc anyone? The sillier societies tend to be simply a great excuse for a party, and you'd be daft to argue with that. The sports clubs tend to be focused towards team games, such as football, hockey and rugby, and can be an easy way to make some close-knit friendships, communal showers aside. You don't have to be fantastically sporty to join in; the football may just be a kickabout on a Sunday morning, before you get down to the real business of a boozy Sunday lunch at the local pub or organising the club dinner. On the other hand, if you are good at it, you could end up on the first team playing against other universities, and have something impressive to put on your CV for when you graduate. There may also be a chance to try something like hang-gliding, potholing, scuba-diving, parachuting, flying or windsurfing. If you've ever wondered what any of them are like, try it now and learn for a very small fee. Unleash your sense of adventure.

The societies can cover anything from the Lesbian, Gay and Bisexual Society (LGBSoc) to the Young Conservatives group, via the Home Brew Society and the Biology Society. If there's one for your subject area, make a point of signing up. They can offer anything from moral support to work experience to a wild social life. Join at least one or two clubs and societies, and pay your subscription fee. Many people join because the person behind the desk is good-looking. And there's nothing wrong with that. Don't join too many clubs on the day though, it can get expensive, and when things get busier later in the term it may be impossible to go to all the planned activities and meetings. If you find there's one that you really like, you can get more involved by getting yourself elected as the secretary, treasurer or chair. You may also think that there's a gaping hole where a club or society should be, and if so you can drop by the student union building to find out more about setting your own group up. There may be funding, office space or other support that you can apply for.

HELPLINES IF YOU'RE HAVING PROBLEMS

In addition to your student union welfare officers, health centre and counselling service, you can call the following confidential helplines:

GENERAL ADVICE
Get Connected 0808 808 4994 (open 1 p.m. to 11 p.m. every day)

Your entire call is free and they can put you through to experts on all subjects, including safety, money, sexuality, housing and much more.

GENERAL HEALTH
NHS Direct 0845 46 47 (open 24 hours daily)

Speak to a trained nurse for advice and information about anything health-related.

EMERGENCY CONTRACEPTION
Brook Advisory Service 0800 0185 023 (open 9 a.m. to 5 p.m., Monday to Friday)

Find out what your options are, and what services are available in your local area.

FEELING DESPERATE OR DOWN
The Samaritans 08457 90 90 90 (open 24 hours daily)

Confidential emotional support for people who are experiencing feelings of distress or despair, including those which may lead to suicide.

HOMESICKNESS AND STRESS
Everything is new: people, surroundings, living conditions, rules and expectations. It's perfectly OK and normal to feel overwhelmed by it at times. Everyone is feeling the same way to some extent, it's just that some

of them are better at covering it up than others. If you're slightly nervous of meeting new people and going to new places remember that after you've done it once, it won't be new any more. It will become more familiar over time, despite it being uncomfortable to begin with. Although it's tempting to go home for a family or friends visit during the first weekend, you're probably better off sticking around and getting used to it.

Try not to go into freshers' week with expectations that are too high. Expect a few shabby buildings with stinky corridors and grotty communal areas. Expect a few surly or unhelpful staff members and long boring waits to get served. Expect a few of your fellow students to be too quiet, too noisy, or just plain old weird. Remember that making an effort is the best way to get the most out of the situation: the party won't come to you if you sleep in all day or stay in your room all evening. That way, you'll be able to cope with the less-than-wonderful bits, and appreciate the good bits too.

Self-help for homesickness:

- **Tell yourself it's perfectly normal to feel a bit homesick when you move to a new place.**

- **Hear some familiar voices: call up mates or family back home for a chat.**

- **Remember that you can't do everything at once, and nobody expects you to. Break down difficult tasks into smaller, more manageable chunks and it won't seem so overwhelming.**

- **Make your room as comfortable as you can so you have somewhere to chill out.**

- **Eat regular meals and limit your intake of caffeine to keep your blood sugar steady. This can help to prevent mood swings.**

- **Go out for a brisk walk every day for at least twenty minutes. It's a free and proven mood booster, and will also help to familiarise you with your new surroundings.**

- **Try to set a rough routine for the times you go to bed and get up. It can be a great help to stabilise your sleeping pattern.**

- **Think very carefully about getting heavily drunk or taking street drugs. They might be a temporary escape from bad feelings but tend to make them worse the next day.**

If things are getting too much for you, talk to someone about it. You can call home and speak to family or friends, and they'll probably be able to help you get it into perspective. If you confide in a new friend or flatmate, they'll probably end up admitting that they feel the same way as you do, and it's a good way to get it off both your chests. If you're feeling so anxious or depressed that you are having trouble eating or sleeping, get down to campus health or the university counselling service. They have years of experience helping students with these problems, and you certainly wouldn't be the first person to feel this way, plus it's all kept completely confidential.

UPS AND DOWNS OF FRESHERS' WEEK

Comments from the students on www.virginstudent.com

'There's a real pressure to drink yourself silly, but that goes with the territory. I'd say the high was meeting so many different types of people from all walks of life, there's nothing quite like that to open your mind!'

'The best part was meeting loadsa new people. The worst part was getting the worst chest infection ever, lasting three weeks. Being ill away from home sucks.'

'Everything was a total buzz, freshers' is just so awesome. Meeting new people, partying hard and getting easily broken into uni life really is sweet.'

'I loved exploring a big new town, but my personal low point was finding my tiny hall room had no plaster on the walls, just bare grey bricks. It made me feel a bit homesick for the first few days.'

'At the end of the day you can discover so much more about yourself you didn't know, and find other like-minded people you adore in the process too.'

'The best times were the impromptu nights with new friends in the pub. Our organised Freshers' Ball, by comparison, was rubbish.'

'I remember standing in endless queues for hours on end for university registration, faculty registration, Union registration, NUS card collection, loan cheque collection . . . then going out with people I'd just met and getting trashed.'

3. YOUR COURSE

Everyone wants to do well on their course, even if they act offhand and pretend that they don't care, the little rebels. If you're making such a huge financial investment in your future, you might as well get your money's worth, after all. At university, you're completely responsible for your own attendance, workload, learning and overall performance. While this can take some getting used to, there is also the freedom of being your own boss.

This chapter will give you the lowdown on:

- **How to hit the ground running during your first term**
- **Some of the useful skills that you need to pick up**
- **The structure of university courses and dates**
- **Getting the best out of lectures, seminars and practicals**
- **Researching and writing top-class assignments**
- **Passing those end-of-term exams with flying colours**

If you don't see yourself as much of an academic, take heart: motivated, organised and persistent students often get better grades than their brighter, but lazier, coursemates. Much of the time it is a case of working more efficiently, rather than harder or for longer.

THE BASICS

GETTING STARTED
Once the dust has settled after freshers' week, you'll gradually get more and more tasks to complete for your course. Here are some of the most important things that you'll need to get sorted out right from the beginning:

COURSE CONTENT
Your department should provide you with a course guide, hopefully a comprehensive one that gives you a very specific idea of what topics will be covered, the skills you're expected to pick up, and how your work will be assessed. Have a good look through it before you file it. Keep this in a safe place because you will need to refer to it often, especially around exam time. Some of the best course guides also contain names and contact numbers for staff and useful organisations

TIMETABLE
Make sure you have the most up-to-date version of your study timetable, with all the times and places of lectures, seminars and practicals listed. Be

aware that these are often altered at short notice because of staff or venue changes. It is best to attend everything on your schedule, at least at the beginning of term, so you can find out what's truly compulsory. Keep a copy of your timetable with you whenever you're on campus, and have one stuck to the wall near your desk at home too.

YOUR STUDY AREA

Make the area around your desk as work-friendly as possible. In addition to your study timetable, pin up a list of your term's assignments and deadlines so you know what work is outstanding and how long you have to finish it. Have your textbooks to hand, plus a dictionary and anything to do with improving your study skills. Your course content guide and administrative paperwork should be filed nearby for easy reference, along with lecture notes and other research for the subjects you're starting to study. Make it a pleasant and comfortable place to sit, without too many distractions. If your accommodation is too noisy, full of gorgeous babes, or otherwise not conducive to learning, you may end up doing most of your studying in the library. In which case, you still need to keep an area in your room that's reasonably well organised, and devoted to storing notes and papers, and so on.

BOOKS

You will have been given a book list that probably looks gigantic, divided into main texts and other texts. The good news is that you don't have to buy everything on the list. However, the greater the number of main texts that you own, the better you are likely to do in your studies. Look at your course guide and discuss it with a tutor or students in the years above you, and don't rush out and buy the whole lot the moment you arrive. If it's an essential textbook where most of the chapters are covered during your course then definitely buy one for yourself, and make sure it's the latest edition. If it's only one or two chapters that are truly helpful then photocopy them in the library. Lesser texts can be bought second-hand at bookshops, at fairs or through notice boards in your department, or from academic websites, so long as they are not too out of date.

EQUIPMENT

Depending on your course content, this could be anything from white lab coats and goggles to art equipment. Make sure it's all necessary before you buy it, and don't be tempted to skimp on safety equipment. Sometimes there is a standard pack that you have to buy from your department, otherwise you may be able to pick things up second-hand or share them with other students.

FILING

Get into the habit of sorting out your paperwork regularly, and keeping it in clearly labelled files that are easy to locate quickly. Use different files for each module or subject, and for administration and other paperwork. Yes, this is a boring task, no point lying about it, but it does stop your hard work from getting lost or mixed up with other stuff, and saves trouble later, at times when you might be rushed or stressed. If you're short on shelf space, a few box files can be stacked up neatly by a wall for extra storage.

RESOURCES

You will have probably wandered into the library at some time during freshers' week, but if not, now's the time to pay it a visit. You also need to find out where the computing centre and other computer terminals are located, and what hours they are available. You may also need to check out other resources such as design labs and studios, language labs or study skills centres.

COURSE AND TERM STRUCTURE

Knowing when to turn up, what to stay sober or conscious for, and what gets you the most points towards your degree can only go in your favour.

TERMS AND SEMESTERS

Some universities use a two-semester system, and others work to a three-term structure to divide up working time and holidays. At the moment these vary from university to university, but as a very rough idea:

- **There will be an autumn semester beginning approximately at the end of September and ending around the end of January, plus a spring semester starting around the beginning of February and ending mid-June. Each semester has a short break within it.**

- **OR There will be three terms, with approximate dates of end of September to mid-December, start of January to end of March, and end of April to mid-June. The terms have different names, according to the institution you're studying at.**

COURSE STRUCTURES

The average university degree will earn you the qualification of Bachelor of Arts or Science, and takes three years to complete (or four if you're studying in Scotland). Sandwich degrees have a year out working in industry and can take four years to complete, and degrees such as medicine take five years. There's more information about courses with work placements in Chapter 7. Language courses often require at least one semester at a university abroad. Someone who is studying dual (or combined) honours is taking two subjects within the same degree, rather than doing two degree courses simultaneously.

More and more courses are becoming modular, i.e. they are broken down into separate units, allowing you to choose between different areas of study. When picking modules, consider how useful they will be after you graduate, how much they interest you as a general subject area, and how well you think you'll be able to perform in them academically. When your timetable is put together, double-check it to look for clashing lectures and exams. If you decide you don't like a particular module, aim to change it to a different one as soon as you can (see notes about changing courses at the end of this chapter).

MAKING THE GRADE

If you're planning on doing well in your degree (of course you are, ahem), then it can be a bit of a numbers game. You need to know how you're being assessed, and how many marks each activity is worth towards your final grade. This distribution of marks varies between degrees, and can be split unevenly between exams, continuous assessment of coursework, practical work and perhaps a final year project or dissertation. It pays to do the most work on areas that will gain you the largest proportion of marks, and perhaps spend less time on areas that have a lower weighting. If you find that you don't traditionally do well in one form of assessment, say sitting exams, then you could decide to work extra hard on everything else you're assessed on, in case you go to pieces in the exam room at the end of term.

Some courses don't count anything from the first year in the final class of degree, but note that if you mess up your first year it may affect your predicted marks and affect the way that staff regard you. Students who do very well academically are awarded first-class degrees (or 'firsts') and may also be awarded special prizes or distinctions, and students who score slightly below this are awarded '2.1'. Below this students who score slightly less are given a '2.2', and students who score lower than this either pass their degree with a 'third', or fail the course. It's worth knowing exactly how many marks you require to get into each category, and checking your marks from time to time to see if you are on track.

OVERSEAS STUDY

Part of your course may involve studying abroad, most often during the first semester of the final year. This can be a fantastic opportunity to immerse yourself in the language and culture of another country, but it also means that you are far away from your university and have less support from your British tutors than students who stay within the UK. It's a big challenge, looks good on your CV, and increases your opportunities for travel during the holidays. There can be heavy competition for places, and grants and other funding may be available, so if you're interested then start looking at your departmental website and ask around the staff as early as you can.

Your department may have direct links with other universities around the world, or may be matched with them via initiatives such as the Socrates–Erasmus scheme, which is aimed largely at helping students study within the European Union. This is administered in the UK by the UK Socrates–Erasmus Council, Research and Development Building, The University, Canterbury, Kent, CT2 7PD. Telephone: 01227 762712, fax: 01227 762711, website: www.erasmus.ac.uk.

PEOPLE

STAFF/UNI STRUCTURE

The staff structure at university can be confusing to an outsider. You have the administrative staff and the teaching staff, and some of them may have both administrative and teaching roles. The figurehead of the university is the chancellor, and although they may look very grand and important in their gown and other regalia, their job is largely ceremonial. The real head honcho is the vice-chancellor, who is responsible for everything to do with the running of the university. Below them in the administrative pecking order there are various staff such as the registrar, followed by deans (who oversee each faculty, or broad subject area), heads of department (who oversee divisions within each faculty) and a variety of support staff. The top academic people are the professors, and below them are senior lecturers, lecturers and tutors. All of them conspire to make your life difficult by providing things for you to study, when you'd much rather be watching daytime television.

YOUR PERSONAL TUTOR

When you arrive at university, you are assigned a personal tutor. There's often a meeting arranged so that you can meet them for a chat during your first few days of term. They are supposed to be your first port of call for any major issues to do with your general welfare or academic progress, but the relationship can be pretty variable. Some tutors arrange regular meetings or social events for the students in their care, and take a very active interest in their welfare, while others are more laid-back, waiting for students to contact them first. It's quite common to have little or nothing to do with your personal tutor throughout your whole degree course, but it's also good to know that they're there in case you need some extra support.

LECTURERS AND TUTORS

These are the people who are responsible for teaching you, setting and marking coursework, supervising dissertations and projects, and so on. Some of them still fall into the stereotype of tweedy, dusty old codgers who are blessed with brains the size of a small planet, yet have no idea about the trials and pressures of modern life in the real world. Do not be fooled by this appearance. If you think you can pull a fast one over them or palm them off with a lame excuse, they've heard it all before and you're unlikely to get away with anything. Unless of course, you are one of their star pupils. Most lecturers and tutors are real human beings who work long hours and are under pressure to meet or exceed their departmental targets for research, in addition to teaching the undergraduates. They're also juggling shrinking budgets, growing families, and many other personal pressures. It's no wonder that most of them respond best to students who don't give them heaps of attitude, appear to be taking an interest in the subject, and get their work in on time. You'll probably find that some staff are more approachable than others, or that you get along with certain teaching styles better than others.

Teaching staff are an invaluable resource, and unless you are the biggest pain in the arse they've ever met, they want you to get good grades and pass your degree with flying colours. If, like thousands of students, you are lectured to in large groups, it can be hard to feel any kind of connection to the academics. You may think that they are all rather unapproachable, but don't let that put you off. Drop by their office briefly from time to time to get your face known, or email them with a few quick questions, and you'll start building up a rapport which will be useful in a number of ways. They can lend you books or suggest the best research to be reading, saving you hours hunting it down in the library, and possibly going off on useless tangents. You can also make appointments with them to discuss essay structure, research skills or your general academic progress, and they might tip you off about subjects that turn up in exams. If things aren't going so well for you, it's easier to get help sorting yourself out when you know the staff already, and they know you as the kind of student who is normally reasonably conscientious. Staff you hit it off with could eventually provide you with glowing references when you start applying for employment, or help you set up projects for postgraduate study.

SUPPORT STAFF

Your departmental receptionists and secretaries are your first port of call when you need to make appointments, complain about lecturers not turning up, hand in your coursework, ask about lost property or fill in any administrative forms. Most of them are decent hard-working people, but you might be unlucky and find the place is ruled by an old dragon. No matter how tired, grumpy or unreasonable they might be, always go out of your way to be nice to them. At the very least, try not to say or do anything that will get their backs up because you will find it takes you twice as long to get anything done. If you want something done, it's better to be polite and persistent rather than getting shirty, and it never hurts to say thank you or pay them the occasional compliment. Even if you don't mean it.

COURSEMATES

The other people in your year can be a motley crew, but sometimes that's part of the fun. Make an effort to talk to everyone, even the people who look a bit boring or uncool. Some of the students who seem quiet at first turn out to have an amazingly dry sense of humour, and even the brash noisy ones can have insightful and reflective moments. Yes, even the beer-swilling, raw-meat-eating rugger buggers, well, a few of them anyway. You're all in it together, so make the most of it. There's a strong chance that the close friends you make on your course will still be your close friends long after you've graduated. Even if you don't think you have much in common with your coursemates, there's no harm in being on good terms with them. After all, if it's a specialised or vocational course, you may well end up working with them or bumping into them for many years to come.

Hopefully you'll end up with a happy atmosphere and a healthy amount of socialising. Unfortunately, there may be one or two difficult people to deal with, but that's just life. Some courses can have a highly competitive atmosphere, and occasionally students resort to dodgy tactics to get ahead of their peers. They may spread gossip, refuse to let you borrow their notes if you've been off sick, 'forget' to tell others about important course information, or deliberately hide textbooks from other students in the library by filing them on the wrong shelf. It's all rather sad and childish, and smacks of insecurity. Stay positive and don't stoop to their level, and concentrate on doing your personal best. If you're helpful to others, most of them will eventually repay the favour.

USEFUL SKILLS
Many of these skills are useful long after you have graduated, in everyday life and the world of employment. Picking them up early on can only make things quicker and easier for you.

TIME MANAGEMENT
This is the balancing act where you have to decide on the right amounts of work and play. If you want to do well in your degree then you have to work your social life around your lectures, tutorials and study periods, and not the other way around – sad but true. However, prioritising in this way does not have to mean all work and no play, far from it. You can build in regular space for your ferret fancying, tandem skydiving and pole-dancing lessons, no problem. Most students who manage their time well use a seven-day timetable that covers their waking hours for the whole week, similar to their course timetable, but including the weekends and evenings. They also tend to be good at remembering to note everything down in their diaries or personal organisers, and they know how to say 'no' when they are overloaded with things to do. It's unrealistic to expect that you'll become an instant expert in time management; it takes a while to learn how long it truly takes to write a decent four-thousand-word essay or research a paper for next week's tutorial. Start by making a rough estimate based on your best guess, and try to be flexible.

When you're making a timetable, in addition to your academic activities include the following: lunch breaks, long journeys, clubs and meetings, exercise time, part-time paid work, time with friends or partners. If you go out clubbing on an average Thursday night, it's unrealistic to expect that you'll be studying hard in the library at 9 a.m. on Friday morning with a banging hangover after a 'full' four hours of sleep. Unless you're still dreaming. Allow yourself some time for the occasional lie-in and some space for just chilling out. Having some time for doing absolutely nothing is essential for unwinding, reflecting on what you've learned recently, and coming up with new plans and ideas – or staring out of the window and smoking, whatever you prefer. For more about time management, read *Get Everything Done and Still Have Time to Play* by Mark Forster, Help Yourself, £6.99.

MOTIVATION AND ATTITUDE
Naturally you will find some of your study topics more interesting than others, or you will respond better to the way some subjects are taught. It's

easy to stay motivated when you're enjoying what you're learning about. If it's a subject you find difficult you will have to work harder to gain a better understanding of it. Wherever possible, try to see this as a challenge rather than a chore or a struggle, and imagine yourself triumphing over it, rather than being crushed or weighed down by it. Look forward to a sense of achievement when you've won your battle or overcome this obstacle. If it's a subject you don't struggle with, but just dislike or find uninspiring, try to plod along with it and reward yourself every time you attend a lecture or do an hour of private study. If you suspect it might just be the teaching that's dull, get a mate to take lecture notes for you and use the extra time to find out about the subject in another way. You might prefer to find an interesting or unusual textbook that catches your interest, or to look at your department's online resources. If you find your course dull or difficult to understand most or all of the time, this is a sign of impending trouble. You may be better off changing courses, or could be in need of extra support from your tutors.

NETWORKING

Not just for yuppies, you know. Networking is using the people around you as a resource for finding out or passing on information. Your mates are a network, for example. Get used to chatting to all kinds of people about your course or anything that inspires you, because you never know what they might come up with. You may find new tips for studying, useful book recommendations, offers of help or new contacts for work or further study. For the second part of the equation, be prepared to help others out in return. Networking with your coursemates can be a way to get notes for lectures you couldn't attend, or to be told about the changed date or venue for an exam that you might otherwise have missed. It's human nature to chat and pass on a little gossip, so it might as well work in everyone's favour. After you leave university, you may find that contacts from your student days turn out to be invaluable in the world of work.

WRITTEN ENGLISH

No matter what your degree subject is, you need to present your written work in good English. Using the correct spelling, grammar and punctuation helps you to communicate your ideas in the best way possible, and it makes you look more eloquent and intelligent. The spelling and grammar checkers on computers can be of some use, but make sure you're always using the British English version, not American English, and don't rely on them too much. They often miss words that are incorrect for the particular sentence you're writing, especially if they are correctly spelled words that would fit in a different sentence. For example 'their' and 'there' are commonly mixed up by some writers, but this error might not be picked up by a spellchecker. An examiner would notice it, though. The final check through of a piece of writing has to be done by a human, that's *you* if you hadn't guessed already. Buy a dictionary and don't be scared to use it as often as necessary. Don't go overboard with the long words, it's better to use plain English most of the time.

Most students know deep down if their written English is slightly shaky. If that includes you, now's the time to brush up on it and improve your presentation skills. Get into the habit of looking up words in a dictionary whenever you're not quite sure of their spelling or exact meaning, and you'll soon find it increases your vocabulary. Try buying one of the smaller and friendlier books about punctuation and grammar, and keeping it handy when you're working at your study desk. If you are having trouble reading and writing, and have the slightest suspicion that you may be dyslexic, speak to your student support services or contact the Adult Dyslexia Organisation's helpline on 020 7924 9559. You may qualify for extra help with your studies. If your first language isn't English and you aren't too confident when writing or speaking in it, spend as much time with native English speakers as you can, and keep studying the language. International students may have access to free English classes, especially at the start of term. It can also help to get English friends to check your essays and projects before you hand them in, so try bribing them with home cooking or copious quantities of beer.

There are several useful books that can help your writing skills, including *Basic Written English* by Don Schiach, John Murray, £5.99, which contains skill checks throughout the book. If your spelling keeps tripping you up, invest in a copy of *Basic Spelling* by Michael Temple, John Murray, £4.99, and if your grammar could use a little help, get *Good Grammar* by Graham King, Collins, £5.99. Keep them by your desk for those times when you get stuck with tricky words and phrases. If your course has lots of jargon then invest in a subject dictionary. These are available for biology, law and so on.

EXTRA CLASSES
Increasing numbers of people are arriving at university who don't enter via the traditional GCSE and A-Level route. If you do well at interview, you may also be accepted onto courses such as medicine without the traditional Maths–Physics–Chemistry A-Level combination. Should this apply to you, don't be surprised if you're offered optional or compulsory extra classes in anything from study skills to extra physics. In addition to this, most universities offer a wide range of free extra tuition to all the students who are quick enough to snap up the places. There are often several helpful classes or short courses on offer from freshers' week onwards, which should be advertised in your welcome pack or on notice boards in the students' union building, the library or the computing centre. Larger universities may have a learning centre that co-ordinates most of these. Take your pick from basic computer skills, relaxation techniques, critical thinking, essay-writing skills, using the library efficiently and much more. If your university doesn't have these on offer and you think you could benefit from them, you could always ask if they'd be willing to lay some on. If that's not possible, you may find similar subjects on offer at low cost in the town library or nearby adult education centre.

EMAIL
Every undergraduate student should be given a university email address. You can use it when applying for work experience or doing research to prove

that you are who you say you are. However, be aware that computer services staff may be able to monitor the content of emails that you send and receive, so watch what you're doing and keep your dodgy dealings confined to personal free webmail addresses. Boasting about your drug intake, offering stolen exam papers for sale to your classmates or sending joke porn pictures around might not be the brightest idea. Many tutors and faculty offices now use email as their main method of disseminating important information, such as timetable changes or assignment details, so check in regularly to see if there's anything urgent you might have missed. If you're unused to email, ask the staff at the computer centre to help you get started. They will help you with your username and password, and show you how to read, store and reply to your emails. You can also get tutorials in using email efficiently, where you learn about setting up online address books, sending out bulk emails to several people on a mailing list at the same time, the etiquette (or netiquette) of sending people emails, and ways to avoid or deal with spam (unwanted and unasked for emails that sometimes contain harmful computer worms or viruses).

WORD PROCESSING

If you are a complete computer-phobic, tough luck mate, you'd better get used to using them. It is becoming increasingly rare for students to be allowed to hand in handwritten assignments. This is because, in theory, a word-processed document is much easier to read than your caffeine-crazed four-in-the-morning last-minute scrawly handwriting. You could type it using a typewriter, but that makes it impossible to go back and add things or take them away from the text, like when you spot a massive typing error in the first sentence of your fantastic essay. Oops. And you'd have to remember to photocopy it before you handed it in, just in case your tutor's hamster ate it or something.

Even people who've been using word-processing software for years make mistakes when it comes to university assignments. Unless it's an art or design project, let your words do the talking. Use an easily readable simple font such as Times New Roman or Helvetica, in a size such as twelve point, and use plain white paper, forget all the fancy stuff. Leave a decent-sized margin to allow whoever is assessing your work to make notes and comments, and use the spacing that your department asks for. For example, if they ask for double-spacing, you need to format each paragraph so that there's a wide gap between all the lines of text. Good presentation may gain you marks either directly or by indirectly making the marker think that you're more sophisticated or professional. Either way, it's an easy way to give yourself an advantage without even having to resort to cheating.

BACKING UP

Always, always keep an extra copy of anything you're going to hand in for marking. Unlike most areas of life, it definitely pays to be utterly paranoid here. Ask around any group of final year students and there will almost certainly be a horror story of a virus chewing its way through an essay document an hour before it was due in, or a computer being stolen that had four months' worth of research for a final year dissertation on the hard drive. The trauma is made infinitely worse by having no backups. You'd be surprised at how many sensible, intelligent people forget this basic safeguard, and end up having a big headache trying to piece something back together before their deadline.

If you're doing any work on a computer, get into the habit of saving it as you go along. If you're working on something all evening, remember to save it whenever you get up to make a cuppa or go to the loo, or when your mum phones up to make sure you've been eating your greens and saying no to drugs. And don't tell me you're fine because you're working on a Mac and it never crashes, because pride comes before a fall, my friend.

As well as saving your work regularly, make several copies of it, and keep copies of drafts of larger bits of work. How you save your copies is up to you: burn it onto a CD, use an old-fashioned floppy disk, send it to yourself in an email (so long as it isn't so big it overloads your mailbox size limit), or even rent a little space in an online repository who will store your data for a fee. Print out a few hard copies (paper versions) every now and again too. If you're using discs and CDs, make sure you have a copy that isn't stored next to the computer, or it could be lost during a burglary, fire or flood. Or any other biblical plague you'd like to mention.

SPREADSHEETS
Getting to grips with spreadsheets such as Microsoft Excel can be of use to all students. The trick is to learn the basics of using them and not to be daunted by all the advanced functions that you will never need to use. At their simplest, they are grids that present facts and figures, in an organised way, that you can easily print off. You can set them up to do your sums for you automatically, such as a running tally of this month's personal budget, or the average lifespan of some rare form of snail. The more scientific your course, the more you're likely to need to use spreadsheets, so get yourself booked onto a free course if you can.

STATISTICS
Any course that expects you to conduct experiments will also require you to collect data and present the results. If you're not a maths genius, don't worry – unless you're studying maths, in which case you're in deep trouble. Statistics can be pretty straightforward most of the time, and you don't need to learn pages of theory or memorise theorems for most degrees. Doing your stats tends to fall into two main categories: descriptive and comparative. Descriptive stats get you looking at a bunch of results and finding ways to describe them as a whole. For example, you may want to find the 'average' value among, say, body weights in a sample of a hundred cattle. How do you describe average? You can look at the mean (add all the weights up and divide by the number of cattle), the median (take the centre point halfway between the lightest and the heaviest), or the mode (the weight category with the largest number of cattle in it).

Statistics can also be used to see whether a sample group of measurements is likely to reflect 'real life', and generally speaking, the larger the sample size the more likely it is that you've got a realistic set of results. One thing to note is that statistics can never be used to 'prove' anything absolutely, they just show that your theory is very probably true. You can also use statistics to compare groups; for example, do the science undergraduates at your university have higher IQs than the arts graduates? (I'm not even going near that one with a ten-foot pole.) This is when you need to apply tests like t-tests and chi-square tests, and a small and simple book about statistics comes in handy, such as *Statistics Without Tears: An Introduction for Non-mathematicians* by Derek Rowntree, Penguin Science, £8.99.

RESEARCH

Being able to find the library is a good start, but you also need to know how to find and evaluate useful materials, in between eyeing up the most attractive second year undergrads.

THE LIBRARY

Get to know the library well, starting as early in the first term as you can, to save time later. You can take a guided tour with a librarian, or there may be handouts available that explain the layout. Look out for the help desk, the general reference area, the journals and periodicals, books that relate to your course, the stacks where older books are kept in storage, and areas where they keep DVDs, CD-ROMs, videos, audio tapes and so on.

The library will have an electronic catalogue of books that you can search using keywords, author or editor names, subjects or titles. The systems libraries use to classify the books can vary, and it's worth finding out how yours works, but generally books on a similar subject are stored near to one another. The main library catalogue will also tell you the names of periodicals and journals in stock, but won't include the titles of the individual articles inside each edition. If you get stuck, ask a librarian: they can tell you quite quickly where everything is and what they stock, and they can also teach you about using the catalogue and making other searches.

Often-used or expensive books are reference only, so you can't take them out of the library. They may be shelved in an open reference area or you may have to sign up to use them by the hour. You will have to photocopy the information you need, so get yourself a photocopying card. The remaining books are either short-term or long-term loan books, and can be taken home. Short-term loans often incur heavy fines if you forget to bring them back on time.

Periodicals and articles may be listed in an online database, on CD-ROM or in a large printed catalogue. Find out how to search each of these by title, author, keyword and subject. If the articles are online or on a CD-ROM, they may also have links to similar articles. Newspaper and magazine articles may also be kept in stock, either in paper form or sometimes on microfiche if they are older.

In addition to your main library, your department probably has its own library or resource room where you can borrow books and other items. You may also wish to use other nearby libraries such as the large public library in town.

HOW TO RESEARCH

Research, evaluation and analysis, and critical thinking are all important skills that you need to do well in your degree. When you're given a coursework assignment or you want to find out more about a subject you're having lectures, tutorials or practicals on, it can sometimes be hard to know where to start looking for the information. Here are a few tips for starting your research:

- **Get started by doing some background reading, rather than narrowing it down to a particular subsection straight away.**

- **Look through your textbooks, course outline and lecture notes to get a basic overview of the subject, noting down any useful references. Talk to lecturers, librarians and other students to get ideas, and try initial internet searches.**

- **Browse the library catalogue, noting any relevant subject headings or photocopying important parts of main texts. Look at similar books on the same shelf to see if they might be useful too.**

- **Go through the library's reference section for anything that may be relevant, from subject-specific dictionaries to general encyclopaedias to 'Who's Who' biographies.**

- **Take away your preliminary material, browse through it, and write brief notes on anything that looks interesting. Take a break from the material for a day or so, if time allows, to get it into perspective. Then jot down a plan of what you want to write and which research materials you need to get hold of.**

- **When you've decided what you're looking for, go back to the library and search for specialist books, journal articles and any other useful information in other formats such as video or newspaper articles. Read through online abstracts to see if articles are relevant to your work.**

- **Check recent journal or magazine articles within your subject, as they may not be in the catalogues yet.**

- **Keep an eye out for other work that is frequently referenced in what you're collecting, either in the main text or in bibliographies. It may be helpful to get copies of this work too.**

- **You may find useful items in the catalogue or databases that are out on loan or kept in different libraries. If you think you're going to need them, get them on order as soon as you can, as they often take a while to arrive. You may have to pay a small fee for the service.**

- **Start to evaluate the material you have collected, and be flexible. You may find it prompts you to do some additional research in one or more areas.**

CRITICAL EVALUATION OF MATERIAL

It isn't enough to take articles or books out of the library and memorise them, or quote parts that look interesting. You have to be able to summarise what the authors are saying, and evaluate their research and analysis to see if it's been correctly carried out and has logical conclusions. If you can gain these skills, and keep working on them, you stand a much better chance of getting a first or a 2:1, whatever your subject. Start by gaining a brief overview of the material, by reading the first and last paragraphs of the chapter along with the subject headings. If you're reading a research article, read through the abstract, any subject headings, the results and the conclusions. This should give you an idea of whether or not the material is suitable for what you're trying to study. Then go back and briefly skim-read through the whole thing to give yourself the gist of their area of research, what the author is trying to prove, how they tried to prove it, what their results were, and how they interpreted their results. Then read it through once more, looking carefully at all the details.

Ask yourself the following questions:

- **Are the researchers experts in their field? Is the article or chapter in a well-known and respected publication? Has the work been reviewed by other respected experts before publication?**

- **Have the researchers carried out the study in a logical way? Could their results be biased due to the way they have set the study up?**

- **What theory are they trying to prove or disprove?**

- **Have they recorded any measurements properly?**

- **Have they carried out the correct statistical tests?**

- **How have they interpreted their results? When you look at the results, do the conclusions they have drawn from them make sense?**

- **What other theories are they drawing upon when they make conclusions from their results? How much do you know about these other theories? Are they logically sound?**

- **Are their arguments rational and unbiased? Have they deliberately or accidentally ignored any important information?**

- **Do you understand any jargon they may have used?**

When you're reading new research and information, keep this checklist handy, and try to keep an open mind, at least to begin with. At the start, try to ignore your personal beliefs, prejudices, opinions, traditions and any received wisdom that you may have heard. See if the researchers have come up with work that is consistent and coherent, and if you can apply their model to real experiences. Look at their style of argument: does it flow well, make sense and avoid emotional appeals to the reader? You may find that some parts of their work are done well, but other areas have weaknesses. Being able to spot the difference is invaluable when you're writing reviews and essays, because you need to compare different schools of thought and possibly argue for the one that has the most weight behind it. For more depth in this subject, try *Critical Thinking for Students: Learn the Skills of Critical Assessment and Effective Argument* by Roy Van Den Brink-Budgen, How To Books, £9.99.

INTERNET RESEARCH

As well as being a fantastic source of pictures of naked ladies and men, the internet can be a helpful way to gather information for your coursework – so long as you know where to look and how to look.

Start by looking at your university, library or departmental website to see if they contain course information or recommend any online resources. You may find that there are well-known online databases specific to your subject. For example, the Medline database is a helpful source of medical research findings and other health-related information. You can also search for general background reading using search engines or directories.

SEARCH ENGINES

Search engines are tools that automatically search the whole internet for web pages that contain specific words, phrases or images. Examples include www.google.com, www.hotbot.com, www.ask.co.uk and www.altavista.com. They each work in a slightly different way, so to use them most efficiently, go to the home page and click on the link for 'help' or to do an advanced search. Many of them operate using Boolean searches to enhance your query, and if so this will be explained in the help section. For example, typing the word 'AND' between two other words means that the search engine will only look for web pages that contain both of those words, 'OR' will find pages that contain either word, and 'NOT' means that it will find only pages that contain only the first word and not the second. You can also use 'wildcards' to search for partial words by replacing certain letters with asterisks (*), so searching for 'philosoph*' will expand your search to include: philosopher, philosophers, philosophy, philosophies, philosophical and so on. You can find exact phrases with some search engines by putting the words inside quotation marks, so looking for "University Survival Guide" should bring up exactly that, rather than pages with the words 'Guide', 'University' and 'Survival' scattered randomly throughout the text.

DIRECTORIES

Directories classify web pages by placing sites in different categories under specific subject headings. You can browse through them using their main key, or use a search box to bring up a list of possible subcategories. They may be very generalised, such as www.yahoo.com and www.ipl.org, or specialise in covering only one main subject area.

Preliminary searches for background information often bring up too many web pages rather than too few, and it's useful to get the hang of using engines and directories efficiently to help you to narrow down the search. If you're looking for something topical, try searching the websites of newspapers and broadcasters such as www.guardian.co.uk, www.ananova.com and www.bbc.co.uk.

When using the internet for research, be aware that a very large percentage of the information you're looking for is not going to be published online. This is for a number of reasons, including copyright laws and financial considerations. Internet research is therefore not the only background work that you need to do. Always consult lecture notes, textbooks, people and other resources as well. Another point to be aware of is that anyone can publish just about anything they like on the internet, within reason, so when you're looking at the content of a web page, ask yourself a few questions:

- **Is this up-to-date information? When was this page first published and has it been updated recently?**

- **Is this obviously biased information, or is there a hidden agenda? Is it written by a political group, a company who stands to make financial gain from it, a religious group, schoolchildren or a bunch of cranks?**

- **What are the credentials of whoever wrote it? If it's from a leading authority, such as a leading academic, a regulatory body for a particular industry, a government research agency or a well-known journal, this has more weight than a personal web page.**

- **Are any facts and figures correct? Do they tally roughly with other research in the area?**

As you continue with your search, you can add useful sites to the favourites section in your web browser, print off the page, copy down the web address (or URL) of the pages, copy and paste the words on the screen into a text document, or temporarily save a copy of the web page to look at later. However you save or bookmark the information, remember that if you want to use it in any assignments you'll have to reference them properly and include a copy of the URL in your bibliography section. Do not just use huge chunks of the text word-for-word, unless you put them inside quotation marks to show that it's not being illegally passed off as your own work.

ATTENDANCE REQUIRED

What do you mean, I can't lie in bed watching *Trisha* every morning? Oh no! If you're going to haul yourself out of bed at some ungodly hour, you might as well make the most of your lectures, tutorials, practicals and so on.

LECTURES

Lectures are a formal method of teaching, where students cram themselves into sweaty overcrowded lecture halls and members of the teaching staff bark vital information at them until everyone in the audience has fallen asleep. The number of lectures you have each week varies widely from course to course, and the two most common lecture-related grumbles are that all of yours seem to start at 9 a.m. when everyone else gets a lie-in, or that your lectures are strangely timetabled so that there's one in the morning and one at the end of the afternoon, leaving you stuck on campus for hours. They aren't going to rearrange the timetable for anybody, so you have to grin and bear it.

Attendance at most lectures is compulsory, and they sometimes pass around a register sheet. Most of the time it's in your interest to attend as many as you can, as it can be an excellent short cut to finding out the most important information for your studies, and there may be essential administrative or academic announcements that you wouldn't otherwise hear about. Having said that, some lecturers are better than others at being entertaining, or getting the facts across, and some subjects are simply more interesting than others. If you can't attend a particular lecture, ask someone in advance if you can copy their notes afterwards so that you don't miss out too much. Some students even take it in turns to attend particularly boring lectures, and pool the information every few days or so.

There is a certain amount of etiquette to be considered when attending a lecture. Firstly, if you haven't washed or slept in a while, are drunk or are running more than ten minutes late, stay away. This is because you will disrupt everybody else in there and make them dislike you intensely, and you'll probably nod off anyway. While falling asleep in lectures is a grand student tradition, do please remember that if you're feeling dozy you should slouch down in a seat at the back of the room so you can't be seen, and if you're a loud snorer, forget it. Go home or buy yourself a strong coffee.

Asking questions is another point of etiquette – if there's a word, concept or phrase used at the beginning of the lecture that you're not familiar with, ask the lecturer what it means or how it is spelled so you can look it up later. Chances are that nobody else understood it either. Don't keep bombarding the lecturer with questions throughout their talk, it can disrupt the flow of the lecture and annoys the audience by making the whole thing drag on for too long. It doesn't make you look particularly keen or clever, and nobody likes a would-be smartarse getting in their way when they're dying for a tea or ciggie break. Write your extra queries down and catch the staff member after they've finished, or bring them up in a tutorial later. If you've struggled badly with the topic, ask them to suggest a simple but comprehensive text that would make it clearer.

Quality note-taking will help you with everything from research to exam revision, so get into the habit early on.

- **Note the date and the subject when you start, to help with your filing, and keep your handwriting as neat as you can. There's no point in taking notes if you can't read them or find them later.**

- **You don't have to write down everything the lecturer says, just try to summarise the main points, but do write down any quotes and references word for word in case you need to use them later. Take a moment to understand what's being said, rather than trying to copy every single word.**

- **There may also be simple diagrams that you can copy down that make the subject easier to understand, but don't feel that you have to make exact copies of everything that's presented on overhead projections.**

- **Use subheadings and bullet points to break up the text as you go along, and make sure you include any references or recommended reading even if you have no intention of ever searching it out (you might change your mind later).**

- **Sometimes lecturers provide their own printed set of notes for students, which can be very helpful, but feel free to add your own comments to them as you go along.**

- **Rather than hand writing it all down on paper, some students will prefer to tape their lectures or type them up onto a small laptop or palmtop computer. This can be especially helpful if you write slowly or have difficulties with your hearing or vision, and there may be extra support available from your department with this. If sound recording appeals, make sure you have extra tapes or battery power as backup in case something goes wrong, and check with your lecturer to see if they mind being taped or not.**

Taking in the information given to you during a lecture is a form of passive learning. In order to make the most of it, you need to reinforce what you have learned and carry out some active learning too. When you go back to your room or to the library, read through your notes again to see if they make sense and add a few more comments to them if necessary. It may help to use coloured pens to underline or highlight key words or sentences, or write sections out again more clearly if your handwriting is hard to read. For the active part of the equation, work on your own initiative and check the notes against other sources of information, and carry out any recommended reading. When you have a good idea what's going on within the topic, make a few summary notes or key points in your own words for quick reference later. Then file everything in the right place.

TUTORIALS AND SEMINARS

These are meetings between tutors and small groups of students, often held regularly throughout term time. There may be teaching, discussion of theories or results, feedback on your essays or practicals, or small presentations by the students. Tutorials can be a useful environment to gain a deeper knowledge of your subject or raise issues that you don't fully understand from your lectures or private study, and can help you work out how well you're doing and what you need to do to improve. It may be tempting to skip these sessions in favour of an extra hour in bed or the latest edition of *Hello!* or *Heat* magazine, but your attendance or absence is usually noted and it feeds back to your department eventually. Just go to them.

When you know what the subject of the tutorial is going to be, make sure you have read ahead at least a little and have made a few brief notes to help you get the most out of it. Make notes as you go along, and try to make at least one intelligent-sounding comment during the seminar, or ask one or two probing questions. At the very least, ask the tutor to suggest a couple of good references for further reading, so that you look as though you're awake and interested in participating. Before you leave, make a note of anything you have to prepare before the next tutorial and remember to figure it in to your study timetable. For more about maximising your study time, try reading *The Study Skills Handbook* by Sheila Cottrell, Palgrave Macmillan, £10.99

PRACTICALS

Most courses with vaguely scientific content will have practicals at some point, and the more scientific it is, the longer and more regular they tend to be. Students may be expected to work alone, in pairs or in groups, usually in a laboratory. You should be given a handout or booklet in advance to explain exactly what you need to do, and what equipment you will need. As there is always some scientific principle or other behind it, or you're supposed to be replicating some famous experiment or learning a specific skill, it might help to read around the subject a little to see how your results are supposed to look before you start. You will be expected to provide a written report at the end of most practicals, so be prepared. Ask about the format that your department wants you to write your reports in.

Practicals are easier if you get there early, and get your hands on the necessary equipment and materials before they run out. Keeping a calculator and ruler on hand is useful too. Go through the instructions carefully and see if your supervisor has anything important to add before you get started. Then work out how long each step of the process should take, and get on with it, taking note of any safety instructions. Try not to blow anything up or dissolve it in strong acid unless you're specifically asked to do so. If you're working in pairs or groups, make sure everyone is doing a roughly equal amount of the work and knows which tasks they're in charge of, or chaos will reign supreme and it will take far longer to get home or to the canteen afterwards.

Take notes as you go along, preferably neatly in a bound notebook or in the practical booklet, and not on loose scraps of paper that can easily be lost. If there are any periods where you're waiting around for a while, start writing up the practical to save time later when you'd much rather be down the pub. You may be expected to hand them in on the day, or hand them in later as a longer report, perhaps to be followed by a discussion of the results. When you're marked for practical work and report writing, you get points for carrying out instructions properly, finishing and handing in on time, recording and presenting your results in the right format and interpreting or evaluating the results in accordance with the relevant literature. If results don't fit into an expected pattern, students often fiddle them to make them fit, but it may earn you more points to give a thorough and comprehensive list of suggestions for why it all 'went wrong'.

FIELD TRIPS

This is where a group of students is sent out to see or learn something first-hand, in the company of a harassed tutor or lecturer, for a day or sometimes longer. For example, if you're studying archaeology you could be sent to several digging sites, or biology students could be sent to sites of special scientific interest to find out more about rare and protected species. If there is some kind of learning outcome or project work to hand in when you get back, write everything down as you go along, and keep any relevant sketches or diagrams safe. Otherwise, use the trip to gain some orientation or general experience within the working environment.

Find out in advance if you'll be travelling out of the country in case you need to renew your passport, because this can take a while to come through. Be prepared for both rain or shine when you pack, and remember to take some beer money along with you. The atmosphere tends to be relaxed and enjoyable, and if you're feeling a bit jaded about the subject you're studying it can perk up your interest in it again. It's a great opportunity to bond with other people on your course, and there's always a strong social element if you're going to be away from home for a while.

ASSIGNMENTS AND EXAMS

ESSAYS

Essays can make up a significant proportion of your degree marks, so it pays to have good essay technique. With a little planning you can write well-crafted essays that will earn you higher grades, perhaps taking some of the pressure off you at exam time. Start researching early before somebody else takes the main texts out of the library, preventing you from using them, and photocopy sections of main texts to take away with you if you don't need the whole book. If you're having problems at any point, ask for help as soon as you can, and try not to request an extension unless it's absolutely necessary. Being organised from the start means that you won't end up with a poorly researched and barely understandable essay that you have to write in a panic in the small hours.

To avoid some of the commonest mistakes:

- **Write down the essay question word for word and make a careful note of the date it is due in and how many words it should be in length.**

- **Study the question, and look closely at how it is worded. For example, if it says 'discuss . . .' then you're being asked to show all sides of an argument and give critical evaluations of them all. If it says 'outline . . .' then you need to summarise all the important points of this specific subject and so on.**

- **If the essay title mentions the names of researchers, authors or philosophers then you'd better make yourself a mini-expert on their work with some background reading before you start.**

- **If you don't understand the question (this is more common than you might think) then don't be embarrassed, have a quiet word with the tutor and ask them to explain it fully.**

- **Ask about the assessment criteria for the essay and use these as a checklist.**

The next step is to research your essay:

- **See what there is about the subject in your main textbooks and lecture notes to give you a good idea of where to go next. Make a few rough notes and move on to internet searches and journal articles.**

- **As a general rule of thumb, if a journal article is cited by many other journal articles, it is probably a well-known and respected piece of research. However, be sure to read it critically and be certain it is up to date.**

- **Wherever possible use a mix of classic and current research to bring your essay to life, give a sense of history and show that you have read widely around the subject.**

- **Read through any photocopied articles briefly to get a rough idea of how useful they are, then go through them again with a highlighter pen or add comments. This will save time when coming back to important points later.**

- **Add more points to your rough notes as you go along, and you should find that a plan for your essay starts to develop.**

- **Most essays have the following structure, but you may have to be prepared to be flexible: an introduction where you outline the main points that you are about to discuss, a longer arguments section where you discuss the relevant research in the field and the differing opinions within it, a brief summary section where you evaluate the research and give your conclusions based on the evidence, and a references or bibliography section.**

If you have done your research well but still feel confused about the arguments you want to include in your essay, get in touch with your tutor or lecturer as soon as you can and take your notes in with you. Ask if there are any other reference books you could borrow or if they think you've missed anything out. Show that you have done some work and taken the initiative already, and that you don't expect them to do the hard work for you.

Once you've done your reading, note taking and planning, you need to decide on your section headings and how long each section will be. Then you have to start writing:

- **If you find it hard to get started, pick the section that interests you the most to work on first.**

- **Keep your writing style clear and simple to show that you understand the principles behind various arguments, and use the correct terminology.**

- **Don't try to make your sentences overcomplicated to look more intelligent, it can end up looking too fussy or just be difficult to read, and your ideas may be lost on the reader.**

- **Don't keep repeating the same things again and again or waffle to make up the word count, it won't get you any extra marks and will annoy whoever is marking your work.**

- **Show critical thinking, and back up comments and opinions with the relevant research.**

- **When quoting large passages of text or reporting speech, always remember to use quotation marks and credit the writer or speaker, or you could accidentally be guilty of plagiarism (passing someone else's work off as your own).**

- **As you write, update your references section to save time at the end – it often takes longer to set out than it does to write the whole of the rest of the essay.**

Take care with your presentation and make sure you're laying the essay out as your department has requested, or you can lose valuable marks. Make sure your name is at the top of the paper, or your student number if it is going through an anonymous marking scheme, plus the exact essay title or question. Stick to the word count, which you should mention at the start or end of the text, and lay out your references in the bibliography using the exact ordering system that your university wants you to use. When you've finished, take a break from it for a while if possible, and come back to read it through again later when you might decide that something needs rewriting. Look for mistakes in spelling, grammar and punctuation, and make sure you really have answered the essay question. You could also get someone else to read it through for style and errors, to give you more perspective. When you're sure it looks right, print out a good quality copy of the essay and hand it in, keeping a copy of your own. A simple plastic wallet can help to stop the paper from getting crumpled up, and keeps the pages together without looking too fussy, or you may be asked to staple it all together.

ON CHEATING

Don't even think about using copies of other people's work and then passing it off as your own. It's plagiarism. Sooner or later you will get caught out and rest assured it will get you into a whole lot of trouble. You could even get thrown off your course. Don't cut and paste essays from cheat websites – your lecturers probably know about them already and if someone else on your course turns in an identical one then you're both in for a nasty surprise. By all means look at what other students have written in previous years to see what's considered to be an excellent essay, but do your own research and thinking, and at least make sure it's all in your own words.

REVIEWS

Writing reviews has much in common with essay writing, but rather than answering a question using facts or quotes from a variety of sources, you're making an evaluation of a single piece of work. This could be a book, a journal paper or even a television documentary. You will have to read it or watch it thoroughly and write a brief description of its key points, then discuss the accuracy or validity of the research or ideas contained within it, and follow this with your conclusions. Where possible, refer to several books, articles or other resources that evaluate the material you're reviewing. Include sources that disagree with one another, or represent a more modern branch of thought, and if the weight of argument supports one way of thinking more than the others, note this down too. As with essays, you need to keep to the word count, present it well and use the format that your department prefers. List all of your references, including the relevant chapters of any books you've used.

FINAL YEAR DISSERTATIONS OR PROJECTS

These are long, long pieces of work where you're supposed to be showcasing your research and analytical skills, and they may carry a high proportion of your marks for the year. It could be about anything from the life and works of Jane Austen to the effects of giving psychology students beer before their lunch. Not every course expects its students to do one, but if you're one of the unlucky students who have to, arm yourself with a copy of the department's guidelines and start looking around for a supervisor with a good reputation. A good supervisor makes all the difference: they can help you to choose the best area to study (with realistic limits), help you use the best methods of analysis for your results, show you how to recruit volunteers, sign your application to the ethics committee if necessary, proofread your drafts and generally keep you motivated. If possible, aim to pick a fairly narrow topic that's interesting and that you can cover well.

Copies of most final year dissertations end up in your faculty office or the library, so have a look at a few of the best ones before you get started. Dissertations tend to take the form of an extended essay. It's a lot of writing, commonly around eight to twelve thousand words, and the more backups you make of it the better. A good piece of work will usually have an abstract at the beginning, where the results and conclusions are outlined briefly in a paragraph of text, and a section at the end that suggests further work that could be done as the result of carrying out the dissertation project. That's in addition to the usual introduction, a review of the relevant literature, original research, and a discussion of the findings, plus a very large bibliography. After marking, your dissertation is bound, either in the department or professionally, then shelved forever where it prettily gathers dust and serves no useful function for the rest of its natural life.

For a good idea of what these projects are all about, look through a copy of *Research Survival Guide* by Ann Marttinen and RN Doordan, Lippincott Williams and Wilkins, £15.00, or *Research Made Real* by Mark Walsh, Nelson Thornes, £10.75.

PRESENTATIONS

Student presentations seem to cause more lost sleep than any other academic activity, apart from all-night parties and exams. Perhaps that's because it's only the extroverts and exhibitionists among us that truly enjoy having to stand up in front of a group of our peers and start chatting away. Most of us are secretly afraid of boring our audience senseless or of making fools of ourselves in front of our classmates. Fortunately it doesn't have to be like that. With good preparation and a few presentation tips, you'll be doing fine.

- **To start with, make sure you know what your topic area is, when your presentation will be and how long it is supposed to last. Most of them are only around ten minutes or so, which isn't too long.**

- **Read around your subject thoroughly, and decide exactly what you want to cover during your talk, and in what depth.**

- **Prepare your 'script' by writing it out in full and reading it out at a medium pace while timing yourself. If it's too long or too short, you may need to remove or add facts.**

- **Include one or two jokes at the beginning to perk it up if you like, or start with an interesting question, and make sure the different elements of your talk flow smoothly.**

- **Try making a few cards with the main points of your talk on them, so that you can look up more at your audience when you're talking but the points will always be there for easy reference if your memory fails you.**

- **Once the timing is about right, ask a flatmate or friend to listen to you while you read it out and tell you what they think. This will give you some valuable feedback and practice in speaking in front of an audience, albeit a very tiny and matey one.**

- **The more you practise the less intimidating it will feel and the more you'll gain in confidence.**

Then think more about your presentation skills. Your voice is the best place to start: stand up straight when you're speaking to allow yourself to breathe properly and project your voice. Take a couple of slow, measured breaths before you start, and remember not to rush your words. Work out how much you will need to speak up so the people at the back of the room can hear you, and vary the speed and tone of your sentences to avoid sounding monotonous. If you find yourself talking too quickly, slow yourself down by counting to four in your head after finishing each subsection, before starting on the next one. Make eye contact with the audience, and try to look like you're enjoying yourself.

If using a projector or slides will enhance your talk, then do so, keeping your visible text to no more than five simple lines or bullet points per page or slide, and making your diagrams look as professional as you can. You can even provide handouts if you like, but resist the temptation to hide behind them. After your conclusions or summing up, ask the audience if they have any questions, then all you have to do is muddle through them as best you can, and it's all over. If you do go a bit red or you stammer a little, you certainly won't be the only one. You'd be surprised how sympathetic most of your audience will be, and in the unlikely event that you do really mess it up, your friends will forgive you. It will soon be forgotten. Just getting through it will earn you some marks.

EXAMS

Sitting exams is probably the worst torture known to studentkind. You're under pressure to succeed, and if you've been slacking off with the studies (and, let's face it, most of us do from time to time) it can be a nasty shock when you work out exactly how much you need to do to catch up. Here's how to make the most of the remaining time that's available to you, and how to cope with the stress.

PREPARATION

This is essential if you want to succeed. Start by making a revision timetable, using the relevant areas of your course outline as a guide for all the topics you're expected to know about. Make sure you can cover all of the main areas in the time you allow yourself for each topic, and aim to leave some extra time at the end for troubleshooting or relaxing before the exam. Double-check with your tutor and departmental office about the subject of the exams, how long each will last and what format the exams will take. Will you be writing essays, or long- or short-answer questions, or will it all be multiple-choice? Ask them to provide you with past papers, to get an idea of the kind of questions they're likely to ask, plus the correct answers. Make sure your work area is tidy and comfortable, with enough light to allow you to read comfortably, then make sure your notes are in order and your textbooks are to hand.

REVISING

Start by skim-reading through your notes to refresh your memory, then read them through again more thoroughly a couple of times to make sure you understand them properly. If you haven't done so already, start to make brief summaries of the most important points. Some students like to use file cards for this because they are a convenient size. Don't put too much on one card, keep it simple, and feel free to use colour coding or diagrams if they help to make more of an impact. You should end up with key concepts, facts and figures, theorems, equations, foreign verbs and tenses, or all of those important names, places and dates at your fingertips. Keep looking at your summary notes or cards to help you to memorise them, either by keeping them in a small box or sticking them onto a convenient wall at eye level.

You can also make up mnemonics to help you to remember more complex sequences of facts. These are phrases or funny rhymes, the ruder the better, where each word or letter corresponds to each fact you need to remember. A simple example is the phrase 'Richard Of York Gave Battle In Vain' where the first letter of each word is the same as the first letter of each colour of the rainbow as it appears in order (Red Orange Yellow Green Blue Indigo Violet). Experiment with making up a few mnemonics on your own until you come up with something that really helps those facts to stick in your brain. Different people respond to different modes of learning, so you may need to gear your revision to words you can read, diagrams or images you can look at, or recordings that you can listen to. Experiment to see what works for you, or try a combination of all three.

Another good way to help yourself revise is to test yourself after you've done your work for the day. You can write your own questions, use past papers or look new ones up online. There may also be a few questions in some of your textbooks. See how well you score, and look for the areas where you need to improve your memory or your understanding. If you are approaching end-of-year or final exams, your timetable may include tutorials in exam technique or mock papers to fill in, plus useful feedback. If these are available, attend them if you can.

If you don't stick to your timetable, or you don't make a timetable of any kind, you could end up doing lots of last-minute revision. It goes without saying that this is not the best way to learn, and it's definitely the most stressful, but all is not lost. Work out the most important subject areas and prioritise them, and skim through your notes and textbooks for the rest of the information. Hopefully this will refresh your memory, and you'll realise that you do remember a significant amount of it already. Try not to read too much unfamiliar material late at night or in the morning before an exam – you probably won't take the information in and it can make it harder to remember other information you have recently learned.

EXAM STRESS

This gets to everyone to some extent, even if they are very good at covering up their nerves, but at least the exam period doesn't last forever. There are several practical ways to reduce your stress levels in the run up to exams, so make the most of as many of them as you can.

- **One simple measure that people often forget is taking short regular breaks. This can be a chance to watch your favourite soap on TV, get some fresh air or make a hot drink. It calms you down and also helps your brain to remember facts more efficiently.**

- **Bigger breaks such as an occasional meal with friends, or a trip to the cinema, need to be figured into your timetable too.**

- **If you have revised well and stuck to your timetable, make sure you give yourself a few rewards, such as a bar of chocolate or a magazine or CD. It will help to cheer you up a bit, and remind you that you're making progress.**

- **Treat yourself well, and make sure you eat regular balanced meals to keep your energy levels up.**

- **Try to get to bed at a reasonable time, and avoid coffee or strong tea late at night, because you need your rest when you're under pressure.**

- **Taking regular exercise is a good idea because it will improve your mood and help you to sleep better.**

- **You might also benefit from using a relaxation tape or learning some breathing exercises to help you calm your nerves.**

Student welfare services are geared up to help students who are suffering from exam stress, and often offer extra counselling or relaxation classes around exam time, so make the most of them if you're feeling the strain. If you can barely sleep or are feeling sick with worry you should think about seeing your GP too, even if it's just for reassurance.

Remember that although alcohol or cannabis can make you feel calmer temporarily, they may interfere with your sleeping pattern and can affect your short-term memory. What was I saying? Oh yeah . . . The night before the exam, avoid last-minute revision of new material if at all possible, and pack your bag with everything you need so you're not rushing around in a panic the next day. Always include extra pens or pencils, just in case one runs out unexpectedly, and set out some old comfortable clothes that won't irritate you if you're a bit hot and bothered. In the morning, get up in plenty of time to eat some breakfast and make your way to the exam hall without rushing.

THE EXAM

Whatever the type of paper you're sitting, there are a few basics to remember. When you arrive at the exam hall, it's normal to feel a rush of adrenaline. Don't expect to go in there as cool as a cucumber; after all, a little nervous tension can improve your performance and sharpen you up. Take a couple of long, slow breaths, and tell yourself that you probably know a lot more than you think you do right now!

- **The first few minutes of the exam are where you should take your time, even if you feel like racing off into the paper.**

- **Read the instructions slowly and carefully, and work out exactly what they want you to answer.**

- **If you have a choice of questions then make sure you know how many of them you need to answer before the end of the exam.**

- **Make a plan where you divide up your time between the questions, allowing extra time for ones that are worth more marks.**

- **Build in a few minutes at the end for checking and double-checking what you have written.**

If you're doing essays, write a short plan at the start of each answer. Include brief notes on the main points the examiner is likely to look for. You can cross it out when you're happy with each finished essay, but if you do run out of time, a good plan will pick you up several marks. When you start writing the essay, use neat handwriting and stick to your plan, checking that you're answering the question that has been asked. Keep an eye on the time, and move on to the next question even if you haven't finished the first one. Five completed plans and half-finished essays will probably score you better marks than three perfect essays on their own. If your paper consists of short- or long-answer questions, stick to key concepts or 'buzz words' in your answers, and don't overwrite by adding waffle. If you feel stuck at any point, move on to the next question you feel you can answer well, and go back to the difficult ones later. Again, stay aware of the time, and don't spend too long on any one question.

Multiple-choice papers often have several similar possible answers for each question, and you may find it helps to cover up the possible answers while you read the question first to avoid confusion. The correct answer will hopefully pop into your head, and then you can read through the options to see which is the closest. Watch out for tricky or ambiguous language among the possible answers, and take the time to read them slowly and carefully. Only then should you put something on the answer form. Multiple-choice answer papers are sometimes marked using an automated system, so use the right kind of pen or pencil and follow the instructions. Make sure you know if your department is using negative marking (where points are deducted for each wrong answer) or not. If they aren't, then make a guess at all questions where you're not sure about the answer. If they are, don't even think about guessing, you could end up with a score of less than zero on your paper.

IF YOU'RE FEELING PANICKY DURING AN EXAM, TRY THESE TIPS:

- **Remember the sensation of anxiousness is being made worse by breathing quickly and shallowly. Take a long, slow, deep breath and hold it for a count of three, then slowly exhale. Repeat this a couple of times and you should start to feel a little bit calmer.**

- **If you're allowed to take a water bottle into the exam with you, try taking a few slow sips, and loosen any clothing that's too tight.**

- **It can also help to concentrate all your attention on something to take your mind off any unhelpful panicky thoughts that might be going around your head. Try focusing on the pen you're holding, the terrible hairstyle of the person sitting in front of you or the view out of the nearest window.**

- **The first few minutes of an exam tend to be the most stressful, so it should get easier as you settle in.**

MISSING EXAMS

If you think you will be unable to take one or all of your exams, let the university know straight away. If you are very unwell, or are suffering from the recent loss of a loved one, for example, then the university should give you special consideration. Get a medical certificate from your GP or the hospital as soon as you can, if one is needed. You may be able to take resits the following term, depending upon your course or the rules of your department.

EXAM AFTERMATH

When an exam is over, unwind, say hello to your coursemates and catch up with them. You may have all been shut away revising for weeks on end. Avoid exam postmortems where people pick through the paper or go on and on about how they've probably failed. These don't help anyone and they can drag you down or make you unnecessarily anxious. Keep it upbeat and have a laugh. If it's your last exam of the season then it's time to party and let off some steam. You've earned it.

When the results come back, check to see if they're the grades you were expecting. If you scored much lower than you thought you would, speak to a tutor immediately and get some feedback. Occasionally marks are added up wrongly or electronic marking systems fail, but if you've ruled that out then you have to face up to your mistakes and learn from them. Improve your study technique or exam technique and do your resits, or make the points up by getting better marks for your attendance, essays and projects. If you got the grades you were aiming for, congratulations!

For my finals, I had nine exams over two weeks, plus another later on in the month, which was a bit much. That's the price of not having to do a dissertation though! I read through my notes (some of which I was digesting for the first time), condensed them by rewriting the important bits and then I typed them up. I also drew some funky diagrams, which make the details easy to remember. Always remember to keep organised too, typing up your notes over the months saves you from deciphering your notes come summer from a half-ripped notebook with tea stains! I spent most of my waking hours in the library at my usual place, not too loud but not too quiet as well. I spent entire days on single modules, so I'd be doing enough revision, minus meals and general dossing about and procrastinating.

It was really nerve-wracking in the run up to the exams, as I'd spent half of the last term involved in sabbatical elections, then most of the Easter holiday on a massive 4000-word essay. But there's always lots of pressure during exams, especially finals, and this was no different. I still managed to clock up the odd night out and some field hockey practice to keep me sane. My exams were quite difficult, as three-hour exams just bored me (I tend to resort to twiddling my thumbs for five minutes before I actually start), whilst I never had enough time to finish the one and a half hour ones, no matter how rushed and scrappy my writing. But, I've heard they marked our final papers a bit more generously than previous years so that gave me some solace!

After I finished I went on holiday to California for two weeks. When the results came out a friend and I went along to this low-key buffet dinner, and they posted the results on a wall. I actually passed! I have never been so scared and then suddenly so happy about 2 numbers separated by a decimal on a piece of A4 in my life.

Matt Ng, just graduated in Combined Science at the University of Lancaster

---

HAVING PROBLEMS?

CHANGING COURSE

It's quite common to wonder if you're doing the right course or not, especially at the beginning of your first year. Think long and hard about this, and make sure it isn't something else like homesickness, disliking your accommodation or generally feeling down in the dumps. Most students go through phases of feeling like this, but often settle in as the term goes along. However, you may decide that you genuinely dislike the university that you're at, or the course you're taking.

Learning at university is different from any other study you've done before, and it can take a lot of getting used to. Generally speaking though, if you're taking the wrong subject, the course content will be almost uniformly uninspiring to you, even when you do your own private study, or you'll find that you're struggling to get your head around any of it. The course might also be in the wrong format for you, and perhaps you would be better off with something more or less traditional, or with a different proportion of work experience and so on. Perhaps you're currently doing a choice of module that you don't get along with.

When you've decided exactly what you dislike, you need to think about something positive you'd like to replace it with. Do you want to stay where you are but change a few of your course modules, do the same subject at a different location, a different subject at the same location, or is university just not for you altogether? Don't just bump along becoming more and more demotivated, and get terrible grades, or drop out without an explanation. Talk to someone about it as soon as you can, such as your personal tutor, and discuss it with trusted friends or reasonable relatives.

If you want to stay within the university system, find alternative courses that cover a subject that inspires you, taught in a format you can respond to best, in the location that you want. Find out if there are places available this year or next, and whether they will take you on. UCAS is a good place to start if you want to change location, and your personal tutor may also be able to make suggestions about options within your current university, or make calls on your behalf. Phone up tutors on these courses or drop round to see them. If you find exactly what you're looking for, contact your local education authority to see if you can rearrange your funding. The earlier you change, the more likely it is that they'll be able to help you, and make sure you get it in writing if you are told you're eligible. After this, make an appointment to see your head of department to find out about their course transfer rules or any forms you need to fill in. You may have to continue on your course for a while longer before you can leave. Be aware that when you start the new course there will be lots of catching up to do, and it may be easier to take some time off and start again at the beginning of the following academic year, depending on how much you've missed.

In all honesty it was not the course that was specifically the problem, it was the university itself. Without wanting to sound like some 'working-class hero' as a local student I was just never made to feel like I fitted in. Lots of people said I made little effort but in actual fact I worked very hard at forging friendships that never went anywhere. One of the main contributory factors to my unhappiness was the rule that freshers have to 'live in' in their first year. I was required to uproot myself and move a mere 10 miles away from my friends and family. I suppose I felt from the second Mum and Dad dropped me off that I didn't fit in.

Anyway, the course itself was interesting. We could take modules from different departments and through this build a tailor-made degree combining our interests. Through this I was able to study history, economics, sociology, philosophy and education. The main drawback of the course itself was that combined honours students were often left with little choice regarding modules. The course director was wonderful, he helped as much as he could by contacting departments and pestering them to give more help to his combined honours students. Essays and projects were often due at the same time from up to four departments and tutors were not very understanding of combined honours students' needs! There wasn't anything I could do. The workload was high and I already felt my very presence there to be undermined. By the middle of my second year I was losing interest in university life. Somehow it felt more appropriate to just lie in bed and wish everything would go away.

In the end I was feeling so low that I approached the university counselling centre and they were marvellous. For the first time I actually felt like my feelings regarding university were validated. I finally realised that being unhappy at university in order to gain a degree was not what being a student is all about. I decided to leave. This decision was really hard for me because my parents were so proud of me for getting a place at such a prestigious university. My mum in particular couldn't hide her disappointment, but I think once I explained things to them they could understand my motivation behind what I did. After the Easter holidays I wrote a letter to my course tutor, my college Master and my college tutor explaining the situation. Within a few days I received a letter from my LEA asking me to confirm that I had withdrawn and I signed a few forms. I felt liberated. But I didn't know what to do next! I looked at a variety of degrees involving social work but I didn't have the right experience. I began to look at Open University, and I begin my new course in February. Many people can't believe that I gave up my dream of studying at Durham University so easily, but it wasn't an easy decision. In the future I hope to work within the social sphere – perhaps working with the victims of alcohol and substance abuse.

Simone Turnbull left her Combined Honours in Social Sciences degree at the University of Durham in 2003.

FALLING BEHIND WITH WORK

It's almost compulsory to get behind with your studies from time to time. There's a certain camaraderie when you know that most of your coursemates are going to be up all night trying to get that assignment in before the deadline. If you're late with all or most of your assignments, you're not doing your self-directed study and your attendance is poor, then you aren't going to get good grades. You may even get called in to explain yourself to your exasperated head of department.

The main cause of falling behind is simply not being organised enough with your time. It takes a while to settle into a routine, and sometimes you mess up your time management abysmally while you're learning the ropes. Sooner or later though, you will have to take responsibility for it, no more excuses. If this sounds like you, take a long hard look at your weekly timetable, and motivate yourself to get on with what you need to do. You may decide that your part-time job is eating into your study time, you don't go to the library enough or your social activities are leaving you too knackered to function on most days of the week. You may have to make some unpleasant decisions that mean you'll have less money, or less time with your mates or loved ones. Once you've sorted out your hours of study, remember to figure in enough extra time for catching up. Doing additional study on top of the usual amount can be unpleasant and tiring, but it's worth it if you want to get a decent qualification when you graduate. Prioritise anything that will gain you a large proportion of marks towards your final score, or has compulsory attendance or a compulsory pass mark.

If you are struggling with the work itself, rather than the time you've allowed for it, then think about why that might be happening. Are you doing enough preparation work before lectures, seminars or practicals? Are you doing the recommended reading and making good notes, plus a little research of your own? If you can say yes to both of these questions, then you're struggling in spite of your best efforts and you need to speak to a tutor urgently. It may be something you can sort out by improving your study skills, or going back a step and studying the absolute basics of your subject. Universities tend to be more sympathetic to students who ask for help before they start failing their subjects, rather than afterwards. The longer you leave it, the more it gets on top of you, and the harder it is to turn things around.

PROBLEMS WITH ACADEMIC STAFF

Under the students' charter, you are entitled to expect a minimum standard of teaching and general conduct from staff. It's natural for certain students not to get on with certain lecturers, simply because of a personality clash. Lecturers and other staff are only human, and it's not surprising that some of them get a bit ratty when they're overworked and underpaid, and have to listen to yet another pathetic made-up excuse for why you didn't prepare your presentation for this week's seminar. Don't push your luck, and remember that a little politeness and respect go a long way.

Having said that, if you are being repeatedly subjected to abusive comments, they're not turning up when they're supposed to be teaching you, or your essays have been left unmarked all term, then you have grounds for complaint. Keep a note of what's happened, what was said and how long it has been going on. If it's an issue that's affecting all or most of your year group, try to make a joint complaint along with everyone else who is affected. Raise your concerns via a senior member of your department, a personal tutor or an NUS representative. Wherever possible, just state the facts, without making any personal comments.

If you think a member of staff has singled you out for unfair treatment because of your gender, race, sexuality or religion, then keep a record of any prejudiced remarks that have been made and try to get witnesses to come forward. There are several organisations that can advise you, from the LGBSoc officer at the Students' Union to the Commission for Racial Equality (www.cre.gov.uk, telephone: 020 7939 0000).

Sexual harassment from staff is occasionally a problem, and it may be subtle or overt. Many institutions also have strict rules banning staff from dating their students, to prevent problems such as sexual harassment and coercion. Don't put up with any behaviour that makes you uncomfortable, tell anyone who is behaving inappropriately that their actions are unwelcome, avoid being left alone with that person wherever possible and be sure to get some moral support while you make a complaint.

DISABILITY
One in ten of us has some form of disability, but our society is not always as clued-up about the matter as it should be. Things are improving as awareness increases and more laws are put into place, and most university staff are more than willing to give their students some extra support, although some campuses have more available resources than others. Wherever possible, remind the university well ahead of time that you're likely to need things such as improved physical access, permission to tape lectures, additional teaching materials, extra time or a separate room for dictation during exams and so on. Practical advice, support and a variety of other information can be gained from SKILL, the National Bureau for Students with Disabilities. Telephone or minicom: 020 7450 0620, fax: 020 7450 0650, website: www.skill.org.uk. Information Service, telephone: 0800 328 5050 (freephone) and 020 7657 2337, Monday to Thursday afternoons.

OUR EXAM TIPS

Seasoned advice from the students on www.virginstudent.com

'Best bet is to just knuckle down, keep yer head up, and most important, CHILL. If you stress, it gets harder. Just work steady, and relax every now 'n' then.'

'Read the rubrics when they are released, know if you're allowed a text/dictionary/calculator and prepare accordingly.'

'Start revision *early*, at least a couple of weeks before your first one; ideally more like 3–4.'

'Remember to plan for breaks, meals and *Simpsons* episodes.'

'I became a library geek but strangely enough so did everyone else, including very fit boys! The library turned out to be the social scene and I learnt a lot just from random comments with people I bumped into off my course who I never really spoke to before.'

'If you're reading and nothing is going in, stop – do another subject. Take regular breaks every hour or two.'

'Only study with friends if you are going to work. If you end up chatting you're not getting anywhere.'

'Get a good night's sleep before the day of the exam, don't bother revising the morning before. Stay calm, eat something before you go in.'

4. HEDONISM

Doing a degree is about much more than passing exams, but you knew that already, right? Of course you did. University is an all-round experience, and no way are you supposed to sit up all night every night, studying on your own. It's party time, baby. Get out there and make the most of everything that's on offer. Meet, greet, snog, be entertained and expand your horizons. It's tempting to push your own boundaries as far as you can, go out late every night or try everything twice. As with all things, there's a fine line between harmless fun and overdoing it – whether physically, legally or financially. Trust your instincts, let common sense kick in from time to time, and you should be fine.

This chapter looks at:

- **Entertainment: what's on offer, and making your own**

- **Sex and dating: chatting up, going out and sexual health**

- **Alcohol: cheap drinking, hangovers and safety tips**

- **Drugs: the law, effects of drugs, and first aid information**

HEDONISM ON A BUDGET
Celebrity lifestyles are always plastered all over the media. They're snapped in the latest designer outfits, slurping champagne and falling out of hot new restaurants and clubs, or jetting off to exclusive resorts. I'll break it to you gently, this isn't possible on a student budget, unless your daddy is an ageing rock star or a generous high-flying businessman. You can still have a rich social life, but you have to make a few compromises. If you want a big blowout at the weekend, you'll have to stay in for a few nights during the week to save money, and make cutbacks elsewhere. If you want the designer wardrobe you'll have to make friends with the designer, or buy just one or two decent items in the sales. Want to holiday in the South of France with the beautiful people? You'll be hostelling or camping. You can also make your money stretch further by developing good blagging skills:

- **Be charming, polite and friendly. People will want to have you around and will do favours for you, or make allowances. The more friends you have, the more friends you can make.**

- **Be cheeky. If you don't ask, you don't get. Invite yourself to parties. You can get free tickets, free drinks, free food or free taxis if you ask at the right time in the right way.**

- **Always ask for money off. Flash your NUS or ISIC card wherever you go, or barter to save money on clothes or other goods that are slightly shop-soiled but fixable.**

- **Plan ahead. If there's a club you want to get into at the weekend, call up during the week to say you're having a 21st birthday party, or fib** and say you're someone who works for a record company and you want to check the place out.

- **Offer to help out. Sometimes you have to give before you can take. Max out your staff discount if you have a part-time job.**

- **Work your contacts. Make the most of any friends or distant relatives who work in useful trades or shops, or who can get you freebies or goods at wholesale or warehouse prices.**

Tip: Don't blag off your mates too much. Be inventive, have your fun and get on as many guest lists as you can. Freeloading and blagging from commercial concerns are fine if you're a student, in fact it's a respected art form. It's also OK to let your friends feed and water you from time to time, but eventually you must repay the favour, or you'll find that you start losing mates or gain a bad reputation as a bit of a leech. Buy a round occasionally, or at least pay for your own beer when you go out. If you're invited to meals or parties, do the decent thing and bring something to drink, even if it's own-brand lager from a budget supermarket. If you want to be invited back, that is.

ENTERTAIN US

STATE OF THE UNION
Most students' union buildings lay on a wide range of events all year round, mostly at low prices. Depending upon the facilities you can expect live music, comedy, club nights, big screen sport, karaoke or cinema. You can take a gamble and watch some up-and-coming bands who might just turn out to be the next big thing. There may also be special themed parties laid on such as casino nights or indoor beach parties, or celebrations for Valentine's Day, Halloween or Christmas. Clubs, societies and larger halls of residence may also host music or film nights. These are all good opportunities to try something new, and allow you to meet different people throughout the year. Like the gorgeous people you somehow missed during the first weeks of term. Check notice boards around campus for what's on when, or look out for posters and flyers in the union building.

YOU'VE GOT BALLS
Don't you scrub up well? Balls or formals only happen once or twice a year, so they're big blowouts. It's a night of debauchery and revelry, where much chatting up goes on, and many rumours are spawned. They're probably the only time that you're going to need formalwear too, and if you're lucky they're held in a classy function suite or posh hotel, and include a decent meal. It's a major expense, but it's also the stuff that memories are made of, so you might decide it's worth splashing out on. Many students hire or borrow their outfits for the evening – there's no need to buy a pricey 'black tie' or tuxedo outfit or a ballgown that you'll never use again. Make sure that you or one of your friends takes a camera along, even if it's a disposable one. It's great to have a record of what everyone looks like when

they're all dressed up, and how it all degenerates throughout the course of the evening. And you may be able to use the pictures for blackmail purposes later.

RAG WEEK
These are fundraising weeks full of strange and silly activities for charity, organised by the university's rag team, if your uni has one. It can include anything from a parade through the centre of town, to sponsored activities such as sitting in a bath full of custard, dressing as a giant baby and being pushed around in a pram, or abseiling down the town hall. If your college does anything for rag week, you can get involved yourself or sponsor and cheer on your mates.

A NIGHT ON THE TOWN
If you're living in or near a large town, there will always be a wide range of leisure and sports activities available. Many clubs do cheap student nights with bargain drink offers, and there's something for most musical tastes. See if you can get student discount wherever you go; a wide range of restaurants, cinemas and theatres have at least one night of the week where they are cheaper for NUS members. Afternoon showings of films and plays tend to be cheaper at the start of the week too. Most of the large cinema chains have student areas on their websites containing special deals, email newsletters, competitions and complimentary advance screening tickets. Students may get free entry to some art and historical exhibitions, so ring first or look in the local paper for details if you fancy getting all cultural. Big music and sports events aren't the best places to get in cheap or for free, but sometimes you need a treat, especially if it's your favourite band or the greatest team in the world playing. That's my team, not yours, obviously.

The social life is pretty good. There are bars on campus and a bunch of communities you can join, as well as extra curricular classes, such as dancing and playing musical instruments. Everything is really well advertised and some of these extra curricular things give you points on completion towards your degree. There are bars in the student village too, which lets everyone get to know people that they might not have on their course or living in their flat.

Also, I'm in uni in Swansea and it's got brilliant nightlife there – supposedly the best in Wales. There's the Mumbles Mile, which is – as the name suggests – a whole mile of pubs and clubs, and then there's all the pubs and clubs in the city centre. As far as social interaction goes, there are areas of the library and study halls for group work and getting to know one another, as well as a big selection of canteens and seating areas to hang out in.

Catherine Reohorn, first year Law and Psychology student, Swansea University

---

GETTING INVOLVED
If you want to be invited to more parties, meet big bands or be on guest lists all over town, start by doing some relevant paid or voluntary work in the

field of entertainment. Train up to do the sound or lighting for student union events, help out by lugging band equipment from van to stage or become one of the people responsible for booking the acts. Or you can learn how to project films, sell tickets on the door, work behind a bar in a pub or club or be an usher or wardrobe assistant in the local theatre. If you're more of an extrovert, you could form a band and support bigger acts that come to town, or do some DJing. Some students go even further and arrange their own club nights or other events. Don't expect to get paid much if you're starting out as a performer, but do expect a few perks, like the occasional free ticket and after-show party invitations.

FESTIVAL SEASON

The long summer holidays make it easy to get to most of the British music and arts festivals. Events such as Glastonbury are so popular now that tickets sell out on the first day of sale, so you may have to employ sneaky tactics to make sure you get yours. Get everyone you know to write in for the maximum number of tickets, and ring up as soon as they go on sale. If you end up with more than you need, you'll have no problems selling spare tickets off. Failing that, you may have to settle for buying day tickets and staying off-site in the evenings. If you're driving down, set off as early as you can to avoid traffic jams and other snarl-ups, and remember that your car will probably be blocked in for the duration of the festival.

Camping out tips:

- **Don't take anything too expensive to a festival, including fancy tents or other posh camping equipment. Keep valuables like cameras with you wherever you go, or take a disposable camera.**

- **To make the most of a festival, arrive early and find a good spot to set up camp. It's also easier if you let most of the crowd leave on the last day before you start packing up.**

- **Arrange a meeting point in advance with your friends. Remember that mobile phone reception can be poor to non-existent.**

- **Make your tent easy to find. Remember what field you've parked it in, and what landmarks are nearby. You could also tie a balloon or flag to your tent, or spray graffiti or draw on the canvas.**

- **Decide what bands you want to see but be flexible, sometimes acts clash or your friends don't want to watch them with you.**

- **You are a captive audience while you're on site, expect to pay extra for food, drink and other items, or bring things with you. Have some munchies in your bag when you arrive.**

- **Almost without exception, the toilets will be disgusting. Be mentally prepared for flies, piles of poo and sewage running under the doors. If possible, get up early and use the toilets in the morning while they are relatively clean.**

- **Think twice before buying drugs from dealers at festivals.**

- **Plan for all kinds of weather. Take a clear plastic sheet and waterproofs along in case of rain, warm clothes, and either some wellies or plastic bags to tie around your shoes. Also bring light clothing, sunscreen, sunglasses, a hat and sandals, in case of a heatwave.**

- **Useful items include: small rucksack or shoulder bag, water bottle, loo roll, matches, mini-torch, multifunction penknife, painkillers, condoms, sticking plasters, wet wipes, and plastic bags or a large cotton square to sit on.**

- **You aren't on your own if you're having difficulties. Make the most of festival stewards, first-aid facilities, chillout areas or the Samaritans tent.**

Keep up to date with the music press and festival websites such as www.efestivals.co.uk, for news about cancellations, available work and who's been booked to play.

DIY ENTERTAINMENT

Sometimes you have to make your own amusement, like your grandparents did during the blitz. Only a bit more up to date, of course. It's the perfect way to see your friends without spending a small fortune on entry fees and overpriced bars, and it's a much better option than staying at home on your own feeling sorry for yourself when you're skint. Throw a house party or a dinner party, or turn up to someone else's, or arrange an evening in or out that costs next to nothing.

HOUSE PARTIES

These can get badly out of hand if you don't plan them carefully, so think ahead. Pick a night all your flatmates agree on, decide how many people you want to invite and think about security issues. If you want it to go with a big bang then choose a theme such as a James Bond night, a cocktail party, a bad taste fancy dress or a Halloween party. If your guests have to bring their invitation or dress in a particular way, this should weed out gatecrashers.

Long before the night of your party, speak to your neighbours to warn them what you're planning. Invite them, or at least promise it won't get too raucous. It's best to have parties at the weekend if you're living in a residential area. A little consideration goes a long way, and could be the difference between the police getting called or not. When it's party time, clear away any breakables or expensive items like tellys and videos. If you have lockable rooms or cupboards, use them. It only takes one dishonest guest or gatecrasher to ruin the night, so take care. If it's likely to be an old-fashioned housewrecker of a party, clear out your fridge and kitchen cupboards, and move as much out of your living room and bathroom as you can. If it isn't nailed down, someone will nick it or use it to have a food fight. Think about fire exits and clear everything out of your corridors.

Now you can set the scene for the party. If you're doing a themed party, stick up your decorations. Get as many ashtrays as you can and put them all around the place for the smokers, and make sure there are big bins for the empty bottles and cans. Sort out your lighting, but be very careful with candles: they can easily get knocked over by passing drunks. Decide what's happening with the music, and whether or not you want to borrow or hire a sound system. Either make time slots for people to DJ so they're not fighting over the decks, or make a big collection of MP3s, burned CDs or party tapes (then hide your music collection).

All that remains is to fix up the drinks and snacks. Make sure your guests know that they'll need to bring some alcohol with them too. You can buy a bulk pack of cheap cans or bottles of beer at the supermarket, and some cheap mixers like lemonade and cola, and maybe make some punch, without spending too much money. Get the beer chilling in the fridge, or use a bath full of cold water if you need more cooling space. If you're making cocktails, stick to just one or two simple recipes so you don't need to buy too many ingredients, or make cocktails that have the same spirit base such as vodka or white rum.

If you're making punch, make plenty of it and don't make it too strong. People drink it like fruit juice and you'll soon be finding your guests falling over or being sick. Keep an eye on the punch in case some idiot thinks it's funny to spike it with extra alcohol or drugs.

- **Scrub out a large saucepan, or a new bucket or washing-up bowl, and add a ladle.**

- **Start with the booze: a bottle of any spirit, or two bottles of fizzy wine, or bottles of plain white or red wine mixed with some brandy.**

- **Then top it up with a few economy packs of chilled fruit juice, soda water or lemonade.**

- **Throw in some chopped apples and oranges and give it a stir.**

- **As the level goes down on the punch bowl, top it back up again with alcohol and mixers.**

Make sure you have plastic cups for people to drink their wine, punch or spirits out of, for when you run out of glasses. Have something handy for opening wine and beer bottles too. Corkscrews and bottle openers have a habit of getting lost at house parties, but you could try tying them onto a long piece of string that's attached to a table leg or cupboard door handle. Put some nibbles out to soak up the booze. You don't need to go crazy: some tortilla chips, a six-pack of crisps or family-sized bag of peanuts will do.

Guests tend to arrive as the pubs close, so pace yourself. If possible, bribe someone beefy to be the door person, to keep out passing strangers and other unwanted gatecrashers. After that's done, just relax and enjoy the evening. If you're the host or hostess, you get to chat to all your guests and chat up anyone you like the look of. For some reason, and it doesn't matter who you invite, you will always end up with a girl crying on the stairs about something relatively minor, a couple shagging in your bathroom or a bed that isn't their own, and a fresh-faced young man who can't handle his beer and bores everyone stupid talking about politics before puking into a plant pot. If your party goes well, you will be the party king or queen and the envy of your friends for the rest of term. Sometimes they even take on legendary status.

When the party's over, most people get the message and clear off home. If they don't, you have a number of options: play quiet and miserable music, turn the lights on and tell them to sod off, or rope them into the end stages of Operation Cleanup:

- **Get someone to walk around the whole place once or twice during the evening with a bin bag asking the guests to get rid of their empty bottles and cans, to keep the mess down and reduce the risk of spills.**

- **Keep a mess kit handy: rubber gloves, paper towels, wiping-up cloths, cleaning fluid, carpet stain remover, plastic bags and air freshener.**

- **If you do get drink on the carpet, blot it up gently but quickly with kitchen paper then rinse with clean water, rather than scrubbing at it which rubs it further into the floor. Don't put salt onto red wine splashes, salt can fix the colour permanently into carpets, upholstery and clothes.**

- **Have a quick run round the house after the party and collect up empty glasses and leftover food, then get all the ashtrays together and make sure there are no burning cigarette stubs dropped anywhere. It won't take long, and makes the party aftermath less difficult to cope with the next morning when you have the worst hangover.**

DINNER PARTIES

Invite a set number of guests, and make sure you have enough chairs and plates for them all. You can cook a Sunday lunch or an evening meal, but don't feel that you have to splash out on expensive ingredients to keep them all happy, they're mainly coming over to hang out with you and the rest of their friends. Choose simple recipes that you can make in bulk, and if in doubt make something vegetarian – it's cheaper and just about everyone will be able to eat it. Try making big pies, stews, curries, bakes or casseroles. Make the food go further by adding extra pasta, rice, potatoes or home-made garlic bread. Puddings are normally more popular than starters, because most students don't make desserts when they're rushing around and making meals for one, and nearly everyone has a sweet tooth. If you only have a small oven, don't serve three hot courses, or you'll end up having to borrow cooking space from your neighbours. Ask your guests to bring starters, nibbles, puddings or wine to keep the costs down and to get everyone involved. Student dinner parties may sound highbrow and sophisticated but they are typically drunken affairs, so always make sure you have a few extra beers or bottles of wine hidden away.

PAUPERS' NIGHTS

Even when you're down to your last few quid, you can still have a social life. Get your friends round for a big bowl of pasta in front of your favourite TV show, or have a film night where you watch a classic video or all chip in to hire a couple of the latest DVD releases. Squeeze as many people onto the sofa as you can, and sit the rest of them down on the floor on some cushions. You can even buy some corn kernels and make your own popcorn for a few pence. Ask around to see if anyone has board games or a couple of packs of cards, and arrange a games night. Gamble for pennies or matchsticks, and take bets on how long it will take for someone to suggest a game of naked Twister or strip poker. If you want a night on the town, find out if anywhere nearby needs a rent-a-crowd, and will provide free entry and at least one free drink. Go and be culture vultures at a gallery opening, a free gig in a music store, a book signing or the newest club night in town.

TRAVEL

The world is your oyster here, even if you aren't loaded. You can snap up last-minute package deals, travel independently on a shoestring or fit some local exploring in around working holidays or international exchange placements. If fortune smiles upon you, one of your friends may have a relative who owns holiday property abroad, and all you'll have to do is pay for your transport and pocket money if you get an invite.

Think about all of the places you'd like to visit. Talk to people who've already been there, or ask for other recommendations. Make a hit list.

- **Take out travel books from the library such as Rough Guides, Time Out Guides, Lonely Planet books and so on. Go on to travel websites to find out more about budget travel in these countries and special events you might want to attend. Swap tips on message boards with other travellers.**

- **Save up as much as you can, and work out how much spending money you'll need when you're off travelling. Set a budget and stick to it.**

- **Ring around travel agents or use the internet to compare prices of flights, ferries and package tours. STA Travel specialise in travel for students.**

- **Sort out vaccinations, visas and decent insurance long before you go.**

- **Check with the Home Office about political hotspots you need to avoid.**

- **Get yourself a youth discount card such as an ISIC card or a Euro <26 card. An outlay of a few pounds gets you discounts on cultural and sporting events, cheaper accommodation at some hostels and reduced prices on some consumer items.**

When you're travelling:

- **Have the time of your life and make new friends. Don't be scared to go a little off the tourist trail.**

- **Keep emergency numbers for health, insurance, next of kin and the nearest British Embassy to hand. Have a photocopy of your passport with you in case the real one is stolen.**

- **Keep a diary or an internet blog, or take photos to remind you of your travels. You don't need to buy and carry around expensive souvenirs.**

- **Make an attempt to speak the local language, and respect the traditions of the country you're in.**

- **Keep in touch regularly with friends and relatives over email or the occasional phone call.**

You don't have to go outside Britain every time though. It's good to get out of town every now and again to visit friends within the UK at weekends, go to summer music or arts festivals, go hiking and admire some beautiful scenery or do a few touristy things closer to home. Recommended reading includes *The Virgin Travellers' Handbook* by Tom Griffiths, Virgin Books, £14.99. It's aimed at students or anyone thinking about a gap year.

SHOPPING

Nearly everyone likes books, films and music, even if they're broke. They can all be bought at discount from big stores that have student days or other deals. If you know somebody who works at one of them, quietly try to get them to make your purchases as part of their staff allowance from time to time, but be discreet or you'll get them sacked. Enter competitions to win tokens or freebies, share things with friends or take out CDs, DVDs and novels from the local library for free or for a few pence. Downloading most films and MP3 music files is illegal for copyright reasons, but at the moment very few prosecutions have taken place and the i-Pod reigns supreme, with friends and fans swapping the contents of their MP3 collections. There are a few record company websites where tracks are available legally, either cheaply or for free.

The NUS have special deals with certain music, food and clothing chains, so check what's currently on offer before you hit the high street. If you want new clothes, buy them in the sales, as seconds or samples, from discount stores or out-of-town cut-price retail 'villages' such as Bicester shopping centre. If there's something special you want, it might have to be a birthday or Christmas present from a kindly relative. Start nagging early.

SEX AND DATING

Although it might not seem like it at the time, your years at university may give you the easiest opportunity ever to meet attractive people and chat them up. Don't believe me? The union bar, all the entertainments, your course, clubs and societies, charity fundraising activities, bookshops, supermarkets near campus, and even the university library can be right for romance. Honest. There are blind date events as part of some union entertainments programmes, free university-based romance and friendship websites, and speed dating evenings arranged specifically with students in mind, all to help you if you're a bit backwards in coming forwards. Don't be shy now.

CHATTING UP

Got your eye on someone? Get in there before someone else does. The key to chatting someone up is confidence. Look at someone who's skilled at it, the person who gets all the girls or all the boys, and you may well find they *aren't* the best-looking person in the room. They're confident, and they've practised their pulling technique. If you don't have confidence, you can increase it or fake it, so have a go. Clean yourself up a bit, wear clothes that suit you and make you feel comfortable, and focus on your best bits. Practise generally being friendly, and make an effort to smile and make more eye contact with people. Then you're ready to go out on the pull and start talking to someone you fancy. If you have chosen a target for your affections, try not to calm your nerves too much with excessive quantities of drink or drugs. Although you might feel more confident this way, you risk coming across as a gibbering boozy idiot, or a letch. One or two drinks, fine, eight or nine drinks, less fine. If you *are* a gibbering boozy idiot or a letch, you're on your own, mate, I can't help you. Otherwise:

- **Don't build it up too much in your head. If it doesn't work out, be philosophical about it, there are plenty more fish in the sea. No really, there are.**

- **Check them out from afar by making eye contact and smiling, then holding eye contact for a few seconds before looking away. Then repeat the process a few more times. Don't stare at them scarily without blinking for the whole evening.**

- **If anyone knows your 'target' already, get them to introduce you. Subtly. 'My mate fancies you' is the kiss of death if you're hoping to chat someone up.**

- **If nobody knows them, you have to be brave. If they've been holding your gaze and smiling back, go over and start talking to them. So long as they look single.**

- **Ask an open question (something that needs more than a 'yes' or 'no' answer), or introduce yourself and ask them their name, or pay them a compliment about something they're wearing.**

- **Chat up lines rarely work unless they fancy you already or it's an incredibly clever line.**

- **To keep the conversation flowing, ask them a few questions about themselves. It shows you're interested in them, and they're going to know all the answers too. Unless they're really really dumb – in which case they'd better be very gorgeous or you should walk away.**

- **Try to find things that you have in common. Talk about something you've done recently, or about things you both might love or hate. It's surprising how many couples have bonded over a shared love or hatred of certain foods or types of music.**

- **While you're talking, think about your body language. Keep up the eye contact and move in slightly closer. If they move back or keep looking away, back off a bit. It's generally a good sign if they move in closer,** touch you lightly, mirror your posture, stick their tongue down your throat or grab your bum.

- If things are going well, suggest meeting up at a particular time to have coffee or go to something you both like. You don't have to call it a date. Swap phone numbers or emails.

- If it didn't go so well, chalk it down to experience and move on. Keep it light-hearted even if you feel disappointed or you'll look like a bad loser. Maybe you decided you didn't fancy them so much when you got talking to them. Their loss anyway.

THEY SAID YES, NOW WHAT?

Some poor fool has agreed to see you again. You get to meet up with them while you are both sober, which can be a scary prospect. Call them when you said you were going to call them, and not first thing the next morning. Play it slightly cool to begin with. If you're nervous you can go for the safe option, and meet up somewhere low-key like a café during the day. Or you can go for the thrillseeker's option: an action movie, a theme park with big rides, or even the shark tank at the local aquarium. That should shake it up a bit. Get to know them better, talk about your interests, flirt like crazy and hope for the best. If they're flirting back then that's great, but make sure they feel the same way about you before you move in for a big snog. Sometimes people give out mixed messages when they just want to be friends, and even the best of us can read the signs wrongly on occasion. If they're only after friendship, at least you've made a new friend. It's disappointing but it's not the end of the world and you do have to respect their decision. If things go well though, there will be more of a spark, and they'll want to see you again.

DINNER AT MY PLACE?

Fancy restaurants are out, but cooking someone dinner is a tried and trusted student seduction technique. If they accept your invitation, double-check to see if they have any special dietary requirements such as vegetarian food or a violent nut allergy, and then set a date and time. If you aren't much of a cook, find a decent recipe and practise cooking it, or ask a chef-like friend for help choosing or cooking the meal. It's best to go for two courses, starter and main, or main and dessert, followed by coffee. Present it well, maybe with some fresh basil or other herbs on top. Don't make the meal too rich or fatty because indigestion is about as unsexy as it gets, and it means you won't be able to lie down for hours. If in doubt, go for something simple using good quality fresh ingredients. Pick up some wine that costs more than £2.99 per bottle for once.

Set the scene by kicking out your flatmates (bribe them if necessary), then finding matching glassware, crockery and cutlery, and fixing up some music and low lighting. You might get lucky after dinner, so straighten out your bedroom and put your best pants on too. The idea is to look as though you're incredibly sophisticated and can throw a meal together out of almost nothing, so do most of the cooking before your guest arrives and then tidy everything away. Add the finishing touches calmly in front of them. Hand them a drink and make some chitchat while the dinner cooks, and keep the conversation flowing during the meal. Don't be too precious about your cooking – if it ends up burnt, laugh it off and ring up for a takeaway.

GETTING IT ON

Yes, yes, yes! Time to get sexy. This is the right time to point out that sex is not compulsory, no matter how it may seem. It's only for consenting adults who both feel that the time is right to get physical with one another. There may be pressures such as wanting to be like your mates, doing it to stop someone from dumping you or being desperate to lose your virginity, but frankly they are all pretty stupid reasons. Only have sex if you both want to. In fact, it never hurts to ask the other person if it's what they really want to do, especially if drink or drugs have been consumed earlier. Quick reality check: sex with a new partner can be incredibly nerve-wracking and exciting, but it's not like the movies. Most couples find it takes a while to feel relaxed and work out what feels good, and what their partner likes. Keep a sense of humour with you at all times, and try not to have your expectations too high at the beginning. Also, it's unrealistic to expect your partner to be psychic, sometimes you have to ask them for what you want, or ask them what they're in the mood for. While you're talking, someone should bring up the subject of safer sex, preferably while you still have your underwear on. The sobering statistics of sexually transmitted infections and unplanned pregnancies should be enough to have everyone thinking, 'actually, there's a big chance something *could* happen to me.' If someone isn't mature enough to talk about safer sex then they aren't mature enough to be having sex, full stop. Use condoms with a new partner for safety and peace of mind. Keep your condoms within easy reach by your bed, or carry them with you if you think there's the slightest chance of getting any hot under-the-duvet action.

If you have a roommate, getting a new girlfriend or boyfriend can be tricky. It's probably best to come to an agreement at the start of term about having privacy if one of you gets lucky. Having someone walk in on you unexpectedly while you're mid-shag tends to put most people off their stroke, unless you're living in an alternative reality that's uncannily similar to a porn movie. Stick a 'do not disturb' sign on the door, send them a text message in 'code', or whatever it takes. Then they can turn around and go for a walk for an hour or two. Or a more realistic three and a half minutes, whatever.

ONE-NIGHT STANDS

These can be anything from a horny sexual adventure to a drink-fuelled disappointment. If you're not in a committed relationship there's nothing to stop you having a night of passion if that's what you want. We aren't living in the Dark Ages any more, so if you're both completely up for it then play safely and have a good time. If you pick somebody up in a club or pub, it may be difficult to work out exactly how old they are so make sure they're over the age of consent. Also remember that your partner has every right to change their mind about having sex at any point, and you need to respect that completely. Tell a friend where you're going, rather than disappearing off and worrying your mates.

The morning after can be very awkward, especially if you can't remember their name or only one of you wants to get together again. Whether you make a silent getaway or not is up to you, and largely depends on how unattractive they are while they're snoring. The decent thing is to wake them up and say thanks for a great evening, but you have to go now. Mind you, who does the decent thing? If you're both awake, and you have no intention of seeing them ever again, don't feel obliged to give them your phone number and pretend you'd like to meet up sometime. They might hound you for weeks before they get the message. If you're both students at the same university, be aware that gossip can start circulating pretty quickly, especially if there has been any unpleasant behaviour.

SEXUALITY AND EXPERIMENTING

It's quite common for students to wait until they have moved away to university before coming out as gay or bisexual. They can benefit from support from the Lesbian, Gay and Bisexual Society and its welfare officer, having a few more open-minded people around, or a large local gay scene. If you're thinking about coming out, there's no need to rush, and you don't have to announce it to the whole world at the top of your lungs, unless that's your personal style. In which case, go for it. You may prefer to start by talking it through with a helpline such as your local LGB switchboard, or telling one sensible and trustworthy mate, then taking things from there at your own pace.

Uncertainty about sexual preferences is more widespread than you might think. For example, around 10 per cent of the calls to the general advice helpline Get Connected are from young people aged under 25 who are confused about their sexuality. Don't be in too much of a hurry to stick a label on yourself until you're absolutely sure. It may help to talk it through with a counsellor in complete confidence.

It goes without saying that the university years are a time when all kinds of people are exploring their sexuality and experimenting. Straight people try same-sex relationships, gay people try heterosexual relationships and so on. A consensual one-off snog or fondle with someone doesn't define your sexual identity, unless you have a 'eureka!' moment and realise that it's the kind of sex that you prefer. On the same note, if a particular sexual activity doesn't appeal to you then this doesn't make you a boring old prude. You don't have to do anything to impress others.

COUPLED UP

Many long-term relationships that start during university end up with people moving in together, having kids or getting married. It's a good place to meet someone. So long as you both make an effort to see your other friends and keep up individual interests, you're not likely to miss out on the social life. Make sure you don't turn into the embarrassing snogging couple who rarely, if ever, come up for air, and make their mates feel like gooseberries.

Leaving home and doing a degree can broaden your horizons, and it considerably changes many people. A long-distance relationship with somebody from your hometown may well feel the strain, especially if they stay based at home and don't go to college themselves. If you want things to work out, you both have to be honest with one another and make an equal amount of effort to visit each other and stay in touch. Bear in mind that your feelings for each other could change into a platonic friendship over time, or either one of you could meet someone else and develop strong feelings for them instead. There's no accounting for chemistry.

I've been with my boyfriend since before I went off to university. We've been together for two-and-a-bit years and now live together in a rented house with one other housemate. Being at uni has put a strain on the relationship occasionally. In his first year at uni I was still doing my A-levels on the other side of the country, but we still saw each other at least once a week. Most of the students I know seem to be shagging around; in fact, I don't know anybody who's in a relationship like ours, except for our housemate.

I don't feel like I'm missing out on anything – I got the shagging around and getting pissed out of my system while I was still in sixth form. I think what I've got now is much, much better. If you want to go on the pull, Newcastle's a brilliant place for a night out so take your pick. The union's incredibly cheap and cheesy, so I hardly ever go in to avoid all the drunken letches, but if you're looking for a place to pull a pisshead then that's the place to go!

Ellie, second year European and International Politics student, Newcastle University

BREAKING UP

Not every relationship is going to last forever, and if you're not happy with the way things are going then it's best to get this out in the open. There's no point in keeping someone hanging on if you don't feel crazy about them, and there's no point putting up with someone who doesn't treat you properly, or acts towards you in an offhand or indifferent way. The worst way to break up with someone is by insulting them, telling them in public that they're dumped, or by being gutless and hiding behind a friend or a text message or email. It's usually easiest in the long run if you tell them face to face (or over the phone if it's a long-distance relationship) that things simply aren't working out, and you want to finish the relationship. You don't have to stick the boot in or be spiteful, you may even be able to stay friends.

Breakups may feel devastating even if they are civilised, or you may have a sense of relief. There's no harm in taking it easy for a few days, or letting your mates come round to cheer you up. Have a good cry if you want to, or get it off your chest with someone who's a good listener. Put photographs and souvenirs away, and go out and try to enjoy yourself. It takes a while to get over a bad breakup, especially if it was a long or intense relationship, but it does get easier with time.

COULD YOU BE PREGNANT?

No method of contraception is 100 per cent perfect, and accidents can happen. If you're worried about being pregnant, buy a pregnancy test from a chemist or go to see your doctor for free testing. The latest over-the-counter test kits are very accurate and most can be used from the first day that your period is due. There may be no signs that you are pregnant, or there may be any of the following: tiredness, increased need to pass urine, missed period, breast tingling or soreness.

If you do find out that you are pregnant, your legal options are to continue with the pregnancy and raise the baby yourself, give the baby up for adoption or terminate the pregnancy (provided certain conditions are met). This can be an incredibly difficult decision and you could benefit from some unbiased counselling. On the other hand, if you are not pregnant, it might be time to reconsider your contraceptive options to reduce the risk of further scares.

CONTRACEPTION

For anyone who's having heterosexual sex, contraception is essential if you want to avoid pregnancy. Having unprotected sex only once could be enough to cause a pregnancy. Is it worth the risk? Contraception is free, after all. No method of contraception is totally reliable, but some are better than others. Many clinics suggest using condoms plus another method (such as the combined pill) to be doubly safe, and to avoid sexually transmitted infections. Your main options are:

Condoms: Sheaths made of latex or polyurethane that cover the penis during sex. Must be rolled on carefully when the penis is erect, and before the penis touches the other person's body. Although condoms are strong, they can be damaged by sharp nails or jewellery, or anything oil-based such as hand cream or petroleum jelly (e.g. Vaseline). Sold in a variety of shapes and thicknesses, they can be lubricated, flavoured or contain spermicide. There is also a female condom that can be worn inside the vagina. Condoms are the only contraceptives that also protect against most sexually transmitted infections. They are easily available from chemists and supermarkets, or can be obtained free from health centres and family planning clinics.

Combined contraceptive pill: Pills containing oestrogen and progestogens that prevent the female body from releasing eggs every month. Most brands are taken daily for 21 days, followed by a break of seven days, during which there is a 'withdrawal bleed' that's like a period. Sometimes given to treat painful periods or acne, as well as being a contraceptive. Not suitable for smokers, small risk of high blood pressure and blood clots in the veins. May be made ineffective by vomiting or diarrhoea, so use additional contraception such as condoms until you're protected again (usually takes five days, but check the instructions in your pill packet).

Progestogen only pill (POP): Pills containing progestogens, which have several different actions to prevent pregnancy. Must be taken at the same time every day to be most effective. May be made ineffective by vomiting or diarrhoea.

Contraceptive injection or implant: Contraceptive hormones that are injected into the female body, or placed surgically under the skin. Useful for women who can't take the combined pill, or who keep forgetting to take their pills regularly. Can cause irregular bleeding.

Intra-uterine device (IUD or coil): Most IUDs are only suitable for women who have already had children. They are metal or plastic devices, sometimes containing hormones, that are placed inside the womb to prevent eggs from implanting and causing pregnancy. Can be effective for up to five years.

Cap or diaphragm: A barrier that's placed inside the vagina to prevent sperm reaching the cervix (the neck of the womb). Used with spermicide for extra protection. Has to be inserted properly before sex, and left in place for several hours afterwards.

Natural methods: The woman carefully measures natural changes such as variation in her body temperature, to work out the days she is most fertile. The couple then abstain from sex during these times, or use another form of contraception such as condoms. These methods take a long time to learn, and are only suitable for women who are incredibly organised, and have supportive partners.

EMERGENCY CONTRACEPTION

If you've had unprotected sex in the last five days and are worried about the risk of pregnancy, you may still be able to get emergency contraception, provided you get to a doctor or family planning clinic quickly. The post-coital pill (sometimes called the 'morning-after' pill) is effective up to 72 hours after unprotected sex, but the sooner it is taken the more effective it's likely to be. It can be prescribed free by GPs or family planning clinics, or bought over the counter at certain chemists. Follow the instructions carefully, and if you have sickness or diarrhoea after taking them, speak to the person who prescribed them to see if you need to take another set. An IUD (a 'coil') can also be inserted to prevent pregnancy, up to five days after having sex. Both these methods prevent an egg from implanting in the womb, rather than causing an abortion.

GPs, Brook Advisory Service and the Family Planning Authority (fpa) can all give advice about contraception and emergency contraception.

Brook Advisory Service helpline: 0800 0185 023, open 9 a.m. to 5 p.m., Monday to Friday.

Contraceptive Education Service provided by fpa
Tel: 0845 310 1334 (England), 028 90 325 488 or 028 71 260 016 (Northern Ireland), 0141 576 5088 (Scotland), open 9 a.m. to 7 p.m., Monday to Friday.

SEXUALLY TRANSMITTED INFECTIONS (STIS)
It's been estimated that around one in ten sexually active young people is carrying an STI, and many of them aren't even aware of it. You don't exist in

some kind of protective bubble while you're at college; if you're sexually active you're at risk of catching sexually transmitted infections, no matter how healthy or 'nice' your partner looks. Posh girls get chlamydia too, you know. It's often impossible to tell who has an STI just by looking at someone, they may have no symptoms at all. Although many infections can be cleared up with antibiotics, there's currently no cure for herpes and HIV, and if certain bacterial infections go undetected for long enough they can cause infertility, abscesses and other serious health problems.

There are only a few ways to reduce your risk of exposure to sexually transmitted infections. The first two are total abstinence or monogamy, where both partners are completely faithful to one another and are certain they're disease-free. If these options don't appeal, the only other choice is to practise safer sex and use condoms with every partner. Infections are so widespread nowadays that it simply isn't worth risking your health.

Some STIs to be aware of:

Chlamydia: Very common bacterial infection. May be passed on during vaginal, anal or oral sex, or transferred to the eyes after touching the genitals. Women often have no symptoms, but there may be vaginal discharge, increased need to urinate or painful urination, pain inside the pelvis, pain during sex, irregular periods or bleeding between periods. Men may have no symptoms, or have discharge from the penis or a burning sensation when they urinate (pee). Treated with a course of antibiotics. If left untreated, it can leave women infertile, or increase the risk of ectopic pregnancies (a medical emergency where the pregnancy occurs in the fallopian tubes instead of inside the womb).

Genital herpes: Common viral infection. Passed on during anal and vaginal sex, and the similar cold sore virus can also be passed onto the genitals. After infection there may be flu-like symptoms, and blisters develop around the anus or genitals. The blisters burst to leave painful sores that take around two to four weeks to heal, and are highly infectious. There may be pain when passing urine. There may be further milder attacks later. There is no cure, but tablets or cream can be prescribed to help shorten the attacks.

Genital warts: Common viral infection spread by skin to skin contact during vaginal or anal sex. Can cause small white or pinkish lumps or cauliflower-shaped lumps on the penis, scrotum, anus, vulva or vagina, or infected areas that are flat and invisible to the naked eye. Warts may be painless or itchy. Depending on where the warts are, they can be removed at the clinic with special paint, freezing, or laser treatment. Never treat them yourself at home. It may take several treatments to get rid of them completely. Some strains of wart virus are possibly linked to cervical cancer, so regular smear tests are important.

Gonorrhoea: Common bacterial infection, passed on during oral, vaginal or anal sex. There may be no symptoms, but women can have a yellowish or greenish strong-smelling discharge, or pain or burning when they urinate. Men can have a yellow or white discharge from the penis, or have inflammation of the testicles or prostate gland. Either sex may have irritation or discharge from the anus, or perhaps a sore throat. Treatment is with antibiotics. If untreated, women can develop fever, pelvic pain, infertility and increased risk of ectopic pregnancy.

Hepatitis B and C: Viral infections that can be passed on during sex or by sharing needles. They affect the liver and there is no known cure, but in some people the body can fight it off. There may be fever, stomach upsets, weight loss and yellowing of the skin and eyes (jaundice). If the disease progresses, there may be liver damage such as cirrhosis, and increased risk of liver cancer.

HIV: Viral infection that can be passed on during anal, vaginal or oral sex, by sharing needles, or from pregnant mother to baby in the womb or in breast milk, or unchecked blood transfusions. Although relatively uncommon in the UK, the rate of infection is increasing among the straight community, and it isn't going to go away. HIV (human immunodeficiency virus) weakens the body's immune system so it can't fight off infections. Eventually it can cause acquired immunodeficiency syndrome, or AIDS, a specific group of serious illnesses. There is no cure for HIV, but there are treatments that can delay the onset of AIDS.

NSU: A condition that affects men, usually caused by bacteria such as chlamydia. Its full name is non-specific urethritis. There is burning or stinging when passing urine, or a discharge from the penis. It can be treated with antibiotics, but sometimes the infection can flare up again after treatment.

Pubic (or 'crab') lice: Tiny parasitic insects that attach to body hair, especially in the groin. Passed on during sex or by sharing infected bed linen or towels. They feed on blood and leave tiny black droppings behind, and cause itching. Can be treated with a special shampoo or lotion.

Scabies: Tiny mites that burrow into the skin, causing an itchy rash, sometimes around the genitals. Passed on by close contact such as sharing a bed, or during sex. Treated with special lotion or cream.

Syphilis: A bacterial infection passed on during vaginal, oral or anal sex, or from direct contact with sores. Initial infection causes a painless sore (a chancre) in the genital area. If left untreated, this can be followed by flu-like illness, mouth ulcers, a rash, or warty growths on the genitals. It then appears to vanish, but may silently attack the body for many years causing brain damage, heart damage or miscarriage. Treatment is with antibiotics.

Trichomonas: Tiny parasite passed on during sex or, rarely, by sharing wet towels or hot tubs. Often no symptoms, but may cause genital discharge, or pain when passing urine, or during sex. Treated with antibiotics.

If you suspect you might have a sexually transmitted infection, get it checked out right away. Don't hang around hoping it will disappear on its own – it might seem to have healed up but you could still be carrying the infection. Try to ignore feelings of embarrassment, and get some medical attention. You can visit your GP, or go to the nearest GUM (genito-urinary medicine) or sexual health clinic. Many of the people who attend GUM clinics are simply getting a clean bill of health at the start of a new relationship, rather than worrying about symptoms. The number for the GUM clinic will be in your local phone book. Treatment is free and 100 per cent confidential, and you don't even need to give your real name if you don't want to.

If the clinic prescribes you some antibiotics, you must finish the course, otherwise the infection could come back. You will also need to abstain from sex until the clinic gives you the all-clear and tell your partner so they can be tested too. Different antibiotics at specific strengths are needed to treat certain STIs: don't be tempted to tell your GP you have a chest infection to get some antibiotics to secretly treat an STI, you will probably get the wrong treatment. They've seen it all before, so you might as well be honest.

You can call the Sexual Health Line free on 0800 567 123 for more information on sexual health (including HIV), or ring your local clinic.

OTHER COMMON SEXUAL PROBLEMS

Thrush: This is an infection caused by a yeast called *Candida albicans*. It lives naturally in small amounts on human skin, but certain conditions allow it to start growing in large amounts, causing symptoms. It can be passed on to a partner during sexual intercourse. In women thrush causes itching, soreness of the vagina and vulva and whitish lumpy discharge. It's treated with pessaries (special tablets placed into the vagina) and cream, both available from the chemist. Men may have itching, redness or discharge on the head of the penis or under the foreskin, and can be treated with thrush cream. Anyone who has repeated thrush infections should go to their doctor for tests and stronger medication.

Cystitis: This is a bladder infection that mainly affects women, where there is pain when passing urine, and sometimes cloudy or dark urine, back pain and a need to pass urine more frequently. It can be caused by bacteria from the bowel or friction from sex. During an attack of cystitis, it helps to drink lots of water to flush out the bladder, and take painkillers. To make the urine less acid and keep bacteria in check, you can add a teaspoon of bicarbonate to every pint of water, or add sachets of anti-cystitis medication from the chemist. If the symptoms last longer than a day or two, or there is blood in the urine, go to see a GP. You may need antibiotics and need to rule out STIs. Men who get cystitis should always seek medical attention.

Loss of libido: Levels of desire naturally increase and decrease over time, so there's no need to worry if you have periods where you don't feel horny at all. If it goes on for weeks or months then get yourself checked out by your GP to rule out depression, stress and hormone disturbances.

Erectile dysfunction: This is where a man can't get, or keep, an erection. It can happen to any man, and is most likely to be caused by too much alcohol, or stress. The stress can be caused by anxiety about performing well sexually, or by anything else such as arguing with a partner, or exam or money worries. Most of the time it's nothing to be concerned about, but a quick checkup to rule out physical illness is advised if it continues. Counselling can be very effective for reducing the psychological stresses that lead to erectile dysfunction.

Premature ejaculation: PE or 'cumming too quickly' affects more than 10 per cent of younger men. It tends to improve with age and experience, and the man can learn distraction techniques or other methods to help him last longer. Sometimes using thicker condoms, or condoms that contain a desensitising gel, may do the trick. If that doesn't work, there are treatments a doctor can prescribe.

ALCOHOL

Drink can be friend or foe, depending on the circumstances. On one side it's available at most social events and can be a mood enhancer, and it's kind of a food too because it contains calories. You drink toasts with it when you're celebrating. It can be delicious, and it may be healthy to drink moderate amounts of alcohol as you get older. On the other hand, it's a drug that can make you so drunk you do stupid things or become a target for violence, poison you or give you a bad hangover, or become part of addictive behaviour. Be the boss of your own boozing habits.

CHEAP DRINKING

University is not the best time to get a taste for champagne or Château Lafitte. It's all about getting value for money when you're drinking at home or going out. The union bar always has cheap beer on tap, plus regular promotions. Companies pushing new drinks target student bars with two-for-one offers or sometimes give out free alcoholic drinks. Many bars in town have happy hours, or you may find that buying pitchers of beer or cocktails works out the cheapest. Generally, the most cost-effective drinks are draught beer and cider, followed by wine. Spirits and mixed drinks such as cocktails tend to be more expensive. If you're going out drinking in the evening, you could wait an hour or two and have a few drinks at home first, or go somewhere that does drinks offers. Hunt down cheaper pubs and clubs that are student-friendly, and think twice before you blow all your cash in a trendy style bar.

Drinking at home and at parties tends to cost less, especially if you try a few of the supermarket beers and wines to see if you like them, and buy in bulk with friends. Ask a relative to buy a supermarket plonk guide for you as a Christmas gift, so you stand less of a chance of buying stuff that tastes like vinegar or meths. If you know anyone who can get you cash-and-carry prices, or who is going to France to get bargain wine, suck up to them and don't be afraid to beg. Do remember that a large stockpile of alcohol in your house will automatically suggest a party to you, and the chances of you rationing it out over the course of the term are pretty slim. Some students also make home-brew using kits, or ferment their own wine from fruit, potato peelings or other leftovers. Sometimes it turns out to be pretty drinkable, but it's equally possible that you're going to end up with a glassful of rocket fuel or a dose of the shits. Caution required.

PACING YOURSELF

Many students pride themselves on their ability to hold their drink without falling over or being violently sick. You don't have to be a hardened drinker to do this. There are several measures you can take to save on embarrassment, money, stomach lining and hideous hangovers. For example:

- **Let the hard drinkers have a headstart. Join them later in the evening.**

- **Eat something a while before you go out to line your stomach. A sandwich, a pizza or even a glass of milk can help. You won't get drunk as quickly.**

- **Don't buy rounds. It will save you money, and let you drink at your own pace.**

- **Drink the occasional pint of water during the evening to slow down your drinking and reduce the dehydrating effects of the alcohol.**

- **Spirits, alcopops and cocktails are often stronger than you think. Drink them slowly or stick to beer.**

- **Have your drink on the table in front of you where you can always see it, but don't hold it in your hand all the time – it makes you drink faster.**

- **Drink a pint of water when you get home to reduce the risk of a hangover.**

Many students drink far more than the recommended weekly amounts of alcohol. Government guidelines suggest that men drink no more than 28 units of alcohol per week, and that women have no more than 21 units per week, although some doctors think this is too high. One unit of alcohol is half a pint of ordinary strength beer or cider, a small glass of wine or a single measure of spirits. A standard bottle of alcopop or pre-mixed drink usually contains one and a half units.

DRUNKEN BEHAVIOUR

Being drunk can seriously affect your judgement. It can result in a few funny stories or comedy pratfalls, or it can be downright dangerous. Exercise a little common sense. Wherever possible, don't let your friends walk home alone drunk at night, drink-drive or get into a car with a drunk driver. Alcohol can make utter mingers look attractive and cause even the most sensible person to forget to use a condom. It can also make you a target for physical or sexual assault, or make mild-mannered people become violent and aggressive. The last thing you need is a conviction for drink-driving or being drunk and disorderly, or a broken leg from falling downstairs. Pranks such as stealing road signs and emergency lighting from roadworks, or defacing portraits or statues of your university's founder, may seem hilarious at the time, but they might come back to haunt you later. If you're not hurting anybody and you don't get caught, it's probably fair game.

HANGOVERS

If I could do one thing to make the world a better place, I'd seriously think about abolishing hangovers. They are evil. Following the 'pacing yourself' tips above can seriously reduce your risk of having a hangover, but you might still be unlucky. Hangovers are a mixture of dehydration, the effects of toxins known as congeners, and low blood sugar. Get your fluids back up by drinking flat cola, isotonic sports drinks or diluted fruit juice, and take a couple of painkillers and hope for the best. Some people are more prone to hangovers than others, unfair but true, and some students are able to bounce back from them quicker than their friends. Many people swear by their own special hangover cure, such as a long hot shower, a walk in the park or a big greasy fry-up, whatever it takes. A 'hair of the dog', starting the day with another alcoholic drink, works by making you drunk again, but rest assured that hangover has merely been postponed – it's best to avoid this one.

ALCOHOL POISONING

Alcohol is a drug that works by depressing the functions of the nervous system, and in large amounts it acts as a poison. Many students are hospitalised due to alcohol poisoning every year, and a few of them die. It can also cause permanent brain damage. Poisoning often follows a sudden bout of binge drinking, where too much alcohol is consumed too fast. Look out for your friends. The signs of alcohol poisoning include:

- **Confusion and aggressiveness, or unconsciousness**
- **Vomiting**
- **Fits (seizures)**
- **Slow or irregular breathing**
- **Low body temperature, bluish or pale skin**

If you think someone might have alcohol poisoning, don't leave them alone, and don't put them to bed to sleep it off. They could choke on their own vomit or die because of hypothermia, irregular heartbeat or suppressed breathing. While they are unconscious, their blood alcohol can continue to rise due to drink that's still in their stomach or intestines. Don't offer them coffee or other stimulants or get them to walk around, these can all make things worse. Don't try to handle an aggressive person on your own either, stay with them if you can but get some help. If you're worried about the possibility of someone having alcohol poisoning, be safe rather than sorry and call 999 for an ambulance. If you're wrong you could feel slightly embarrassed for a day or so, but if you're right you're probably saving their life.

SPIKED DRINKS

It's essential for both male and female students to be aware of spiked drinks. They have been used to assist robbery and sexual assault, and in some cases the attackers are fellow students. Attackers may be alone or working in pairs or groups. Over thirty different substances may be involved in drug-assisted rapes, the most common one being alcohol. Various other chemicals have been used to drug the victim, and these have been added to food, soft drinks, alcoholic drinks or hot drinks such as coffee. The drugs take effect quickly, causing drowsiness, vomiting or unconsciousness, and the victim often has no memory of the attack.

There are a number of precautions that can be taken to avoid spiked drinks:

- **Don't accept drinks of any kind from strangers. It doesn't matter if this makes you look slightly rude, a decent person will understand.**

- **Wherever possible watch your drinks being poured.**

- **Don't leave drinks unattended at any time, even if you have to go to the toilet.**

- **Buy bottled drinks and keep your thumb over the top of the bottle.**

- **If your drink looks, smells or tastes unusual, don't take another sip. This also applies if the level of your drink changes – something could have been added to it.**

- **Keep an eye on your friends and their drinks too.**

- **Signs of having your drink spiked include nausea and vomiting, or a sudden sensation of drunkenness that's far too strong for the amount of alcohol you've had to drink.**

- **If you or your friends start to feel unexpectedly sick or drowsy, take action immediately – you may not have long. Tell a trusted friend the drink may have been spiked, and if you're in a pub or club tell the security staff too.**

- **If you suspect your friend has had a drink spiked, call an ambulance and don't leave them on their own.**

There's more information about spiked drinks and drug-assisted rape in the Crime and Safety chapter in this book.

DRINK PROBLEMS

Heavy drinking throughout your late teens and early twenties can set a dangerous behaviour pattern that lasts for many years. Alcohol can cause both psychological and physical dependency (addiction), and may lead to liver damage, a wide range of personal and social problems and even death. Someone who is developing alcohol dependency may fall into one or more of these patterns:

- **Tolerance: needing to drink more and more to get the same effect**

- **Alcohol becoming their priority over friends, partners, work, study and other interests**

- **Becoming stressed, upset or angry if they can't get a drink**

- **Physical withdrawal symptoms such as shakiness or sickness**

- **Drinking to avoid withdrawal symptoms, possibly drinking in the morning**
- **Hiding the amount they drink, or lying about it**

About 15 per cent of young people show some signs of alcohol dependency, with males four times more likely to be affected than females. If you are being affected by your own or someone else's problem drinking, it can be a great help to have some skilled counselling. Try talking to Drinkline on 0345 320202.

DRUGS

Around 50 per cent of young people admit to having tried at least one recreational drug, most commonly cannabis, and an estimated 500,000 Britons take ecstasy on an average weekend. Drug culture permeates large sections of society in this country, including the student population. Many students never take drugs, some dabble for a short period and then stop, and others go on to become regular users.

There's no point in me getting all preachy here and saying that everyone who takes drugs is going to get ill, die, go mad, become a junkie or get arrested and thrown in prison. However, I'm not going to kick back and show you how to roll a perfect joint either. There are several genuine risks related to drug use, and bad things can happen to just about anyone, however careful they think they're being, because the effects are unpredictable. Drugs are not compulsory, and if you don't want to take them then a polite but firm 'no thanks' should do the trick.

Various people talk a lot of rubbish about drugs, and it can be hard to know which information to trust. There are political interests, personal interests and financial interests on all sides, and users and dealers who claim to be experts on a particular drug could be passing on myths too. If you're thinking about taking drugs, make sure you have a clear picture of what you might be getting yourself into first. Read around the subject with a critical eye, understand how the law works and get an idea of the physical and mental effects. Whether you choose to take drugs or not, it doesn't hurt to be aware of the problems that can arise, or how to help someone who is in trouble.

Certain factors increase the risks of drugs. For example:

- **A history of mental illness**
- **Physical health problems**
- **Being in unsettled or unfamiliar surroundings**
- **Going off alone to use drugs**
- **Buying drugs from strangers**
- **Using needles, especially shared ones**

- **Mixing different drugs**

- **Taking large amounts of drugs in one go**

Mixing drugs increases the chance of something going wrong. Some drugs are stronger when they're added to other ones, and certain combinations can mask the symptoms of an overdose, overheating or being on the edge of a collapse. A number of prescription drugs such as anti-depressants, decongestants and Viagra can lead to fatalities if they're mixed with certain recreational drugs. As a general rule, alcohol doesn't mix well with most other drugs, and neither does heroin. Although not strictly mixing drugs, smoking cigarettes while using sleep-inducing drugs can lead to house fires.

DRUG FIRST AID

If someone is unwell try to find the first-aid person if you're in a club, and if in doubt always call for an ambulance. Someone who is showing signs of panic and anxiety should be led away from crowded areas, loud noises and bright lights. Talk to them in a gentle voice and reassure them that it's going to be OK. Get them to breathe slowly. If you can't get through to them at all, send another person off to get help.

Overheating can happen as a combination of hot clubs, drugs and dehydration. The signs include dizziness, tiredness, cramps in arms and legs, dark urine and difficulty peeing. Sit someone who looks overheated down in a cooler, quiet place, and get them to sip a pint of water very slowly. Splash a little tepid water on their face or neck or wipe them down with a damp towel. Don't cool them down too fast or they could end up in shock.

Someone who collapses should be treated as an emergency. Try to rouse them gently but don't shake them hard. If they don't come round, call out for help and loosen any tight clothing they're wearing. Check to see if they are breathing. If they are breathing put them into the recovery position on their left side with their right arm and leg bent, making sure their head is back and their airway is open. If they are not breathing then they need mouth-to-mouth resuscitation. If you don't know how to do this, put them into the recovery position and wait for the first-aider to arrive.

DRUGS AND THE LAW

Most people think that the term 'supply' means dealing, or selling drugs in large amounts. It also includes selling tiny amounts of drugs to friends, or giving them away for free. Having drugs on you or at home is classed as possession, and that includes storing or carrying them for someone else. If you are found with a large amount of drugs on you, if it's more than the arbitrary amount that the police would describe as 'for personal use' then there's a chance you could be charged with 'possession with intent to supply', which carries more serious penalties. Driving under the influence can be applied to drug-driving as much as drink-driving, and if caught, you will be charged accordingly under the Road Traffic Act 1988.

Things you should know:

- **Passing drugs among friends is classed as supply by the police, even if no money changes hands.**

- **Allowing people to take drugs in your house can get you a conviction, even if you don't take any drugs yourself.**

- **Your uni may take a strong anti-drugs stance and throw you off your course if you get caught with drugs.**

- **A major drug conviction can mess up your employment prospects and freedom to travel.**

CLASSES AND PENALTIES

Some substances are covered by The Misuse of Drugs Act 1971 and others are regulated by The Medicines Act. Class A drugs include ecstasy, heroin and LSD, and the maximum penalty for possession is seven years in prison and an unlimited fine. Maximum penalty for supply is a life sentence and an unlimited fine. Class B drugs include amphetamines. The maximum penalty for their possession is five years in prison and a fine, and supply can bring up to fourteen years in prison and a fine. Class Cs include mild tranquillisers and anabolic steroids. Possession of drugs such as temazepam can get someone up to two years in prison and a fine, but for most Class Cs possession may be permitted if it's for personal use. There can be up to five years in prison and a fine for supply. These are of course the maximum penalties, and they don't tend to be applied to first-time offenders or people caught with tiny amounts of drugs for personal use. If caught with drugs and the offence is possession only, the most likely outcome is a police caution or a fine, but this can vary from area to area.

GETTING SEARCHED OR ARRESTED

On the street you can be stopped and searched if police have a reasonable suspicion you're carrying a controlled drug. They can check your outer clothing, but can't do an intimate search or make you remove your hat in public. It's a bad idea to resist a physical search, you could be injured or prosecuted. Anything you say can be used in evidence against you later.

If you are arrested, you have the right to notify someone of your arrest, and to consult privately with a solicitor. Do not discuss your case with the police until your solicitor arrives. Try to stay calm and remember they cannot keep you locked up indefinitely. The police may also decide to search your home.

THE DRUGS

CANNABIS

What is it?: Leaves or tips of the *Cannabis sativa* plant, containing active ingredient THC. Sold pressed into dark brown blocks as hash, as chopped up leaves or buds, or occasionally as hash oil.

Alias: marijuana, weed, hash, grass, dope, draw and many more

How is it used?: Mixed with tobacco and smoked as a joint, smoked in a pipe, or sometimes mixed with food and eaten.

Effects: Users feel relaxed, happy and quiet, or giggly or talkative. Effects start quickly and last from an hour to a few hours. Someone who has been smoking heavily may have red eyes, a dry mouth and an attack of the munchies.

Risks: Users can become paranoid or anxious, or may feel sick. Heavy use may affect short-term memory. Smoking any drug can harm the lungs and heart.

Legal: Currently Class B, but due to be downgraded to Class C in early 2004. Oil is Class A.

AMPHETAMINE

What is it?: A group of synthetic stimulants. Can be up to 95 per cent impure, cut with anything from vitamin C to scouring powder. Sold in wraps as an off-white, greyish or pinkish powder that may contain small crystals or look putty-like, or as small white prescription pills.

Alias: speed, whizz, 'phet, sulph, uppers

How is it used?: Snorted, rubbed onto the gums or swallowed. Some forms may be smoked or injected.

Effects: Users feel energetic, wide awake and chatty for a few hours. After use there may be a comedown with feelings of depression.

Risks: Irritability and aggression, difficulty sleeping, paranoia and psychosis. Overdose. Addiction. Dangerous mixed with anti-depressants and alcohol. Injecting drugs makes overdose more likely and increases risk of HIV and hepatitis infection.

Legal: Class B, unless prepared for injection when it becomes Class A.

NITRITES (POPPERS)

What are they?: Yellowish liquids called alkyl nitrites that are sold in small bottles.

Alias: poppers, amyl, or by brand names such as TNT, Thrust, Rock Hard

How are they used?: The vapours are inhaled. Used in clubs or during sex.

Effects: Cause a short-lived head rush lasting two minutes or so, often followed by a headache. May cause dizziness, light-headedness or weakness.

Risks: Highly poisonous if swallowed, can burn skin or cause collapse, flammable. Unsafe for anyone with a heart or lung condition, or blood pressure problems. May make users forget about safer sex.

Legal: Classed under the Medicines Act. Possession is legal but supply is an offence.

LSD

What is it?: Lysergic Acid Diethylamide, a hallucinogenic drug. LSD is sold dotted onto squares of paper, often with pictures on them, or in the form of tiny tablets or capsules.

Alias: acid, trips, tab, tabs, blotter, or named after the pictures on the paper (rainbows, strawberries etc.)

How is it used?: Blotting papers are licked, tablets are swallowed.

Effects: Takes around 20 minutes to an hour for effects to be felt, can go on for 12 to 20 hours. The experience, or trip, varies from person to person and can include sensations of time slowing down or speeding up, and distortions of colours, sounds and shapes. They can be funny or enjoyable (good trips) or highly unpleasant (bad trips).

Risks: Panic or paranoia can happen, especially in unfamiliar surroundings. Bad trips can't be predicted, and can be very frightening or last for hours. Users can injure themselves accidentally or deliberately. Flashbacks, where part of the trip is relived, can happen weeks or months after taking acid.

Legal: Class A.

MAGIC MUSHROOMS

What are they?: The most common type are *Psilocybe semilanceata* mushrooms that grow naturally in fields in Britain. Picked fresh or sold dried.

Alias: 'shrooms, mushies, majicks, liberty cap

How are they used?: Eaten raw, cooked, or made into tea.

Effects: After about 30 minutes a trip begins, lasting up to nine hours. Users may feel giggly and happy, and sounds, colours, shapes and time may feel distorted. The effects depend on the mood of the user and how much is taken.

Risks: Picking the wrong type of mushroom and being poisoned. They can make mental health problems worse. Bad trips, diarrhoea, flashbacks.

Legal: Possessing raw mushrooms is not illegal. If they are prepared for use, for example by drying them or making tea, they are Class A.

ECSTASY

What is it?: Pure Ecstasy is MDMA (3,4 methylenedioxymethamphetamine), a stimulant with very mild hallucinogenic effects, mainly sold in pill form, or as powder or capsules. Newer pills contain less MDMA and are more likely to contain other drugs such as PMA or 4MTA.

Alias: E, pills, doves, XTC, or named after pictures on pills (mitsubishis, rolexes etc.)

How is it used?: Usually swallowed, sometimes snorted or smoked.

Effects: They take 30 minutes or so to take effect. Users feel energetic, euphoric and more in tune with their surroundings, music and other people.

Body temperature can increase, and jaw muscles tighten. Effects last around 3 to 6 hours with a gradual comedown.

Risks: Anxiety, panic attacks, paranoia, epileptic fits. Dehydration, overheating and collapse, death. Dangerous for people with heart and blood pressure problems, asthma or epilepsy. Long-term effects uncertain, but may include memory loss and depression.

Legal: Class A.

SOLVENTS (AEROSOLS, GASES AND GLUES)

What are they?: Volatile chemicals found in a variety of products, including some paints, aerosol cans, lighter fuel, glue, cleaning fluids and many more.

Alias: inhalants, glue, gas

How are they used?: Fumes are sniffed from liquids on rags, in jars or bags. Gases are inhaled directly.

Effects: Similar to drunkenness but lasts for a shorter period. Users become intoxicated, euphoric and dizzy. Some users report hallucinations.

Risks: Headache, rashes, vomiting, blackouts, death from choking and irregular heartbeat. On average six people die from solvent abuse every month in the UK.

Legal: Not illegal to possess.

COCAINE

What is it?: A stimulant drug made from the leaves of the coca shrub. Sold in wraps, looks like a whitish powder.

Alias: coke, charlie, sniff, powder, gack, snow, toot

How is it used?: Chopped into lines on a flat surface and snorted up the nose. Sometimes made into a solution and injected.

Effects: Users feel wide awake and extra confident. Raises body temperature and makes the heart beat faster. Effects last around 30 minutes.

Risks: Psychological dependency, damage to the inside of the nose, heart attacks, overdose. Can cause anxiety, depression and sexual dysfunction. Especially dangerous when mixed with heroin, as a 'speedball'. Overdose more likely when injected.

Legal: Class A.

CRACK

What is it?: A smokeable form of cocaine. It's sold in small lumps or rocks.

Alias: base, wash, stones, rock

How is it used?: Smoked in a pipe, glass tube, or on tinfoil.

Effects: Similar to cocaine but more intense and more short-lived.

Risks: Cravings, addiction, overdose.

Legal: Class A.

TRANQUILLISERS
What are they?: A group of over 50 prescription drugs that have a sedating or calming effect. Includes tablets and capsules such as Valium, Mogadon, Rohypnol and temazepam.

Alias: downers, benzos, jellies

How are they used?: Tablets are mostly swallowed, but sometimes they are prepared for injection.

Effects: They depress the nervous system and slow body processes down. Users may feel calm, sleepy or relaxed.

Risks: Psychological and physical addiction. Overdose when mixed with alcohol, memory loss. Injecting may lead to gangrene, loss of limbs or death.

Legal: Class C. Possession is now an arrestable offence if a user does not have a valid prescription.

HEROIN
What is it?: A drug made from morphine, which is extracted from the opium poppy. Medical grade opiates tend to be white powder, street heroin is brown or brownish-white in colour.

Alias: brown, smack, H, horse, skag, gear

How is it used?: Smoked, snorted or prepared for injection.

Effects: Feelings of warmth and comfort, relaxation or sleepiness. Can also cause sickness and vomiting.

Risks: Constipation, overdose, coma, physical dependency. Infections and abscesses from injecting and sharing needles.

Legal: Class A.

DEPENDENCY
When a user becomes drug-dependent they have a strong desire for the drug, often needing to take increasing amounts to get the same effect. When the addiction is psychological, there can be strong cravings for the drug, or a belief that they need the drug to cope with everyday life. If a drug is physically addictive there are withdrawal symptoms when the drug is stopped such as shaking, flu-like symptoms, stomach upsets or hallucinations. When an addictive pattern develops, it can cause serious problems with relationships, work and money. Many users give up drugs on their own, but others prefer to have the support of their doctor or from a specialist organisation.

DRUG AND LEGAL ADVICE

RELEASE
Charity that can provide legal advice and support if you are arrested.

Helpline: 020 7749 4034, open 10 a.m. to 6 p.m., Monday to Friday.

TALK TO FRANK
General information and advice about all street drugs

Helpline: 0800 77 66 00, open 24 hours every day.

DRUGSCOPE
Information sheets and independent up-to-date research about all drugs.

Website: www.drugscope.org.uk, telephone: 020 7928 1211

THE BEST NIGHTS OUT AT UNI

Party along with the students from www.virginstudent.com

'The best nights out are spur of the moment ones, where you just pop out for a quick drink but end up out all night. Big planned nights out are quite often a disappointment because you worry so much about it all going well.'

'I like house parties and birthday parties the best, always the most fertile ground for meeting the babes. So long as it's not at my house and I don't have to clear up the mess afterwards!'

'Balls and things like that don't always work out. They are usually really expensive. Tickets, drinks and outfit can still add up to a rotten time, in my experience anyway.'

'Random spur of the moment pub crawls down White Ladies in Bristol. Utter madness!'

'I'm giving up with the organised approach this semester except for one night, which includes bowling so has to be planned. Apart from that it's a case of union with mates and the phrase: "What ya wanna do now?"'

5. HOUSING

Home sweet home, at least during term time anyway. You always need a place to lay your head, cook your pasta and set up your stereo, wherever you end up. It's important to choose the right kind of place and to get good value for money, because accommodation costs are the single largest yearly expenditure for students. The average term-time rent over one year is currently estimated to be £2,814 inside London, and £2,003 around the rest of the UK, which is a huge chunk of your student loan.

The main types of student accommodation include:

- **Halls of residence**
- **University houses and flats**
- **Privately rented shared houses and flats**
- **Places students have bought themselves or with parents**

HALLS

A large number of first year students decide to live in halls of residence. Most of them are near to the university campus and charge their fees at the beginning of every term, rather than a monthly rent.

Pros	Cons
Very sociable with lots of other students nearby	If it's catered you may not like the food or find the serving hours convenient
Rent may include food and bills so it's cheaper or at least easier to budget	Can be noisy when you're trying to sleep or revise
Facilities such as staff/common rooms, launderette, cleaners	Rules and regulations may annoy you
More safety features than most private housing	Small basic rooms can have a 'rabbit hutch' feel
Close to campus and other facilities	

WHAT UNIVERSITY HALLS ARE REALLY LIKE

Hall facilities, layouts and décor are highly variable, to say the least. In recent years there's been a move towards self-catering, with less than 40 per cent of accommodation now providing meals. There are still some enormous buildings that house hundreds of students, with several rooms on each open corridor, plus shared bathrooms and toilets, and kitchenettes.

These types of halls tend to have a staffed security entrance, and include lighting and heating in with their fees. It's now more common to find bigger buildings split into blocks and further subdivided into self-contained flats, or several low-rise blocks of flats arranged around a communal area. There's usually a launderette on site, and some payphones, but the larger halls come into their own with facilities because they're more likely to have telly or games rooms, or a bar.

Rooms tend to be small, and contain a single bed and a sink. Some of them are 1970s monstrosities with beige walls, knackered plywood furniture and threadbare brown carpets, but others are light and airy and have their own en-suite bathrooms. No arguments about who peed in the shower or used up all the bog roll then. Standard issue items include: a desk with lamp and chair, a wardrobe, a chest of drawers, a pinboard, a bookshelf, an easy chair, a bin and perhaps a bedside table. A few rooms in older halls are shared, so students have to learn to get along with their roommate, and his or her sleeping, shagging, washing and hangover habits. Most places have cleaners who come into communal areas at least weekly, and some hall cleaners empty bins and vacuum bedrooms. In rarer cases, there might be a laundry service that provides clean bed linen. It pays to be on friendly terms with hall staff such as receptionists, security people, wardens and the manager, so make an effort to be pleasant from the beginning and you may get away with a few misdemeanours later.

The first few weeks are hectic as all the residents arrive and settle in. Hall events are laid on, such as film evenings or pub crawls, and everybody drinks too much. Expect much flirting and a fair bit of running up and down corridors in the small hours of the morning, and drunken door-knocking. Some bedrooms or kitchens morph into the neighbourhood boozer, dope den, sleaze pit or gossip centre. There may be some pranks, like some bright spark setting off the fire extinguishers or squirting shaving foam under doors. And perhaps the occasional pile of vomit in the reception area. While it's all good fun at the start, nerves can get frayed as time goes by, unless people learn some consideration for their neighbours. It helps to keep the noise down, at least after a certain time in the evening. That includes shouting in corridors, loud TVs and stereos, and last but not least the carnal lust stuff. Your neighbours aren't jealous because they're not getting any and you are, they're pissed off because you woke them up with moaning, grunting and heavy breathing.

Although out-and-out robbery is more common in privately rented housing, pilfering is rife in halls. Some people think that because they don't have very much money, they have some god-given right to help themselves to anything that isn't nailed down, conveniently forgetting that other people around them might be worse off. Expect food to go missing from communal fridges, cutlery and crockery to mysteriously sprout legs and wander off, and tea and coffee to drink itself. Or simply buy food in small quantities and keep important things in your room. If you do catch someone blatantly stealing your stuff, don't let them get away with it. Give 'em hell.

RULES, REGULATIONS, DISPUTES

Some halls are stricter than others. If your hall has a single security entrance, there tend to be rules about who you can or can't let in, having parties, or overnight guests. You're normally expected to sign people in and out, and give warning of who is staying with you. If you're in a low-rise block of four flats with your own front door and no security staff, they can't stop you from doing much at all, unless neighbours or cleaners make a complaint. Problems with neighbours or flatmates can be sorted out amongst yourselves, or through mediation with hall wardens or the students' union. If you're asked to move out because of something you've done, you may not have too many legal rights, depending on what type of place you're living in. If you wish to dispute their order, you'll need specialist advice from your student advice centre or a specialist organisation such as Shelter.

PRIVATE HALLS

These are halls of residence that are built and run by private companies, but are normally let to students under regulations that are imposed by the university. The number of private halls trebled in 2002, so expect more in a town near you soon. Research from the National Union of Students suggests that rent increases are more frequent in private halls. Public service union Unison say that students in private halls may end up having to pay higher rents, and for more weeks of the year, although the quality of rooms overall has improved. The main contractors are Jarvis, Unite, Opal and Servite, although there are a few smaller companies in the market too.

RENTING PRIVATELY

Pros	Cons
Rent is slightly cheaper than most hall fees	Can be further away from campus
	Some student landlords are dodgy
More privacy and fewer noisy people around	The bills can pile up
Freedom to come and go as you please and have guests	May be too quiet during holidays

WHAT SHARING IS REALLY LIKE

Most students rent rooms in large shared houses with a group of their friends. These places are usually at the cheaper end of the market, often in slightly dodgy parts of town, and can be very basic or unfit for human habitation. There may be no communal areas apart from a kitchen, if the landlord decides to rent out the living room as an extra bedroom. Hopefully you get on well with the people you live with and socialise together, although there are occasionally squabbles about various household issues. As a general rule, the more people you have living in one place, the quicker your kitchen and bathroom will get cluttered up and dirty, and most students aren't big on cleaning. Living in privately rented accommodation allows you to have more freedom with your general lifestyle, whether that just means getting up at 4 p.m. to eat cereal and watch children's television, or to have a massive house party. In return there are more responsibilities, such as looking after your living space and sorting out all the household bills.

WHO TO LIVE WITH

Obviously start with people you like and take it from there. You're going to be seeing people off-duty and at their worst when you live with them: bleary-eyed and grumpy at breakfast, hungover or ill, moaning about studies and money, heartbroken after relationships end, or at breaking point around the exam period. Easy going, fairly considerate people you have something in common with are the safest bet. Think carefully about living with all the party people; you might have a whale of a time at the beginning, but it can wear you and your bank balance out and everyone needs the occasional quiet moment. Don't move in with people who seem spiteful or bitchy, or are bullies, because rest assured they'll become much worse when you're stuck at home with them, and frankly nobody needs the hassle. Although a tidy place is more relaxing than a dirty one, try not to live with an obsessive cleaner because they'll probably start clearing your meals away before you've finished eating them, or throwing your treasured possessions out because they don't like the look of them. It might be worth giving quiet flatmates a go if they seem pleasant enough, perhaps they'll come out of their shell later, and if not then at least they'll be easy enough to ignore.

FINDING A PLACE

Once you've decided who you're going to live with, give yourself plenty of time to find a place. Start looking in early spring if you can to get the pick of the best places. If it's a large group, sit down and decide what everyone can afford, the areas you'd consider living in and what kind of place you want. Think about the number of bedrooms, communal areas, the kind of heating you'd prefer, washing machine, storage space, parking and so on. Make sure everyone agrees on what you're going to go for. Be prepared to look around for a while to find somewhere suitable, and try not to get rushed into last-minute panic decisions – there's often something better around the corner. It's true that some university towns have a shortage of suitable accommodation, but others have plenty of places. Get an idea of the average cost of rented housing in your town from older students or the students' union, and ask where the best areas in town are to look. Your university may own a number of shared houses to let out to its students, which may have the benefits of controlled rent and good safety standards, so it's worth asking if there are any of these available.

Start your search by looking at the university accommodation service or notice boards, the local paper, internet accommodation sites like www.bunk.com or www.accommodationforstudents.com, or asking around older students for recommendations of landlords they think are decent. There may be adverts in shop windows in the areas you've selected, if you go there for a look around. Perhaps you'd like to put an advert up yourself, saying what kind of house or flat you're looking for. The environmental health office at your local council might be able to provide you with a list of approved landlords, and so could your uni. You can also try accommodation agencies, but look for ones with a good reputation and never be persuaded to pay any money upfront. Accommodation agencies can only charge you a fee for finding a place *after* you've accepted one of the houses on their list.

If you see something that looks promising, follow it up quickly and ask for as much advance information as you can. Check the location of the place on a map, and if it's in an acceptable location, arrange a viewing. Get as many of your group as you can together to view properties that sound good, but don't worry if you can't all make it. The others can go along later after the advance party have expressed their interest to the agency or landlord. Follow these safety tips before you go out to view any property:

- **Never go there alone, always go with someone else.**

- **Try to go during daylight hours, which will also give you a better view of the property.**

- **Tell someone exactly where you're going and what time you expect to be back.**

- **If you get a bad feeling about the landlord or whoever is showing you around the place, trust your instincts and leave.**

Things to ask:

- **What bills are the tenants liable for? What do they normally cost?**

- **Is rent charged at half rate or full rate during the holidays?**

- **How much is the monthly rent and the deposit, and are there any other expenses or fees to pay?**

- **What kind of heating and hot water supply is there?**

- **Can you talk to the current tenants? What do they think of the place, and the landlord?**

Important things to look for when viewing a place:

- **How near the place is to shops, banks, sports and entertainment facilities, and public transport.**

- **Parking spaces or somewhere for safe bike storage.**

- **The feel of the local area. Are the streets well lit and would it feel safe at night? What are the neighbours like?**

- **The whole house or flat. Look at everything, including each room, inside storage areas and cupboards, the state of the roof tiles and guttering, back of the house etc.**

- **The size of every bedroom. Is there a tiny little box room that nobody will want?**

- **Strong front and back doors with decent locks on them, and secure windows. Garden gates and passageways that can be locked and closed off.**

- **Signs of damp or mildew, such as a musty smell, peeling-off wallpaper or black spores on walls or inside cupboards.**

- **Draughty doors and windows, or cracked windows.**

- **Signs of rats, mice, slugs or cockroaches, such as droppings, holes in skirting boards, slime trails or dead insects.**

- **Gas safety certificates for all gas appliances, carbon monoxide detectors.**

- **The state of the electrical wiring and appliances, and the number of plug sockets in each room.**

- **Easy exit in case of a fire. Does the landlord provide smoke alarms and fire extinguishers?**

- **State of repair of the kitchen and bathroom. Does anything need fixing? If so, get the landlord to agree in writing to a timeframe for the repairs.**

- **What's included in the rent, such as crockery, pans and cutlery. If the kitchen doesn't have a freezer or a washing machine can you persuade the landlord to get them?**

- **The general state of the furniture, mattresses, carpets, curtains and paintwork.**

- **Telephone landline and sockets, and internet access. Can you get broadband in this area if you need it?**

- **What any garden is like, and whether you're responsible for the gardening or other outside areas.**

SIGNING UP FOR A PLACE

Once you've found a suitable house or flat, you need to sign a contract and find a deposit. The contract is an agreement where both you and the landlord agree to certain behaviour, and it's legally binding so read the small print before signing anything. You can't get out of it unless you can prove the terms in it are unfair or you've been a victim of fraud or misrepresentation. If there's anything that seems unreasonable or hard to understand, get it looked at thoroughly by the university accommodation office or your local Citizens' Advice Bureau. Your contract will probably be an 'assured shorthold tenancy', lasting for at least six months, and most commonly for twelve. Check whether it's a single or joint tenancy agreement. If it's a single tenancy each person is only liable for their share of the rent and bills, but a joint tenancy means that if one of you moves out or defaults on the rent, the rest of you can be charged for the money.

Check your contract for the following:

- **The start and end dates of the contract**

- **The amount of rent each month and the deposit. Rent is most commonly paid one month in advance, but it may be more.**

- **Fees or interest if you're late with the rent payments (don't sign if these are high)**

- **What the landlord is responsible for (repairs, decorating, water rates etc.)**

- **The landlord's full contact details**

- **What your notice period is if you want to leave before the end of the contract**

Once you've all signed the contract, you should be given your own copy before you move in. Keep it somewhere safe, away from the mice, mould and damp, in case you need to refer to it later. An oral contract is also legally binding, but it could be hard to prove in court, so get a written one instead if you can.

The inventory is a list of everything in the property, and when you are given one make sure you check thoroughly around the house to see if it's correct. Don't sign anything if items of furniture are missing or already damaged etc., as you could be charged for them later. If you aren't shown an inventory, ask for one.

The deposit is a sum of money, usually the same as a month's rent, you pay to the landlord as security. If you break anything, cause damage to the property that's more than a reasonable amount of wear and tear, or leave the place in a dirty state, the landlord can keep all or part of the money to cover repairs and cleaning. You should be given a receipt for the deposit that is signed and dated, with the sum of money clearly marked on it. Keep it for your records.

WHEN YOU MOVE IN . . .

Allocate rooms as fairly as you can. Flip coins, draw straws or pull names out of a hat if you can't decide who's going to get which room. If there's one tiny bedroom and the rest of the rooms are a decent size, perhaps the person in it could pay a smaller proportion of the rent. Make sure you know where the water stopcock and electrical fusebox are, and the tap to turn off the gas supply, in case of emergencies. Also find out where the electricity and gas meters are situated, so you can take your own readings later if you need to. Keep a torch handy for emergencies, and give everyone the contact number for the landlord in case something goes wrong with the house.

Plan something fun to do with your new flatmates to help you settle in together, like an expedition to find the nearest pub, or making and sharing a blowout home-cooked meal. Decide what level of home entertainment you all want for those long evenings in, like a shared TV and DVD player, or extra television channels.

COMMON FLASHPOINTS

Most of the time housemates rub along together fine and have a good time. But there are a few things about communal living that cause rows, so take steps right from the beginning to reduce the risk of an in-house slanging match.

DIRT AND MESS

Other people's mess pisses you off, but you don't notice your own quite so much. Somebody else's skanky trainers in the living room or their pubes in the shower tray make you retch, but your own aren't nearly as bad. Weird, huh? Try to keep your own mess to yourself, and clean up as you go with dropped food and spills. Think of it as a random act of kindness. Get your washing-up out of the way before you go to bed in the evening, before it starts to pile up and get in everyone's way. If your flatmate leaves dirty dishes everywhere for weeks in spite of a few polite reminders, and it's attracting flies, it's perfectly acceptable to transfer it into a bucket and put it in the shed or their bedroom. Nobody truly likes cleaning unless they're a bit odd, so spread the nasty tasks around equally using a cleaning rota. Make sure everyone gets a turn at emptying the bin, cleaning the loo, vacuuming and mopping floors. There's some simple advice about household cleaning in the appendix at the back of this book.

HOGGING

Some people use up more than their fair share, and tend to be oblivious of how annoying it is to everyone else. Get everyone to agree to time limits for using the shower in the morning, or the phone in the evening. If internet use is making it hard to use the phone, think about having another line put in or switch to a broadband provider where you can surf while someone else chats. If there's only one TV, you have to be prepared to negotiate for the programmes you want to watch. It can go either to a majority vote, or to a barter system – I'll trade you today's *Bargain Hunt* for tomorrow's *Countdown* or whatever.

NOISE

Sleep deprivation can drive anyone crazy, so try not to wake people up wherever this is feasible. Avoid clattering around if you're the first one up in the morning, try not to talk loudly or bump into the furniture if you come home late and pissed up, and never ever vacuum before 3 p.m. on a Saturday (hungover flatmates are mean when you rile them). If the walls are thin and the house is full of people studying or revising, don't play the stereo too loud. Still want to wage war on your own eardrums? Use headphones late at night, or the neighbours might do something nasty to you.

DECORATING

What you do in your room is your own private business, but don't take it upon yourself to make big design statements in communal areas without agreeing it with everyone else first. You might think it looks cool, but the rest of the world might think your mural, tie-dyed wall hanging and clashing sofa cover, life-sized skeleton, fairy lights or lava lamp look totally shit. And even the old student clichés of traffic cones and road signs stop being quite so hilarious after you've tripped over them a few times.

LOVERS AND MATES

Naturally you think they're amazing and wonderful, which can make you blind to the fact that they may be less than perfect, or your flatmates hate them. Avoid overkill by agreeing partners and pals only come over on certain nights of the week, up to a maximum of maybe three nights. Otherwise the place can feel overcrowded and you may be accused of using up more than your share of hot water, tea and coffee, bog roll etc. If you're a couple and want to live together, remember that if you live in a shared house with single people, it might get awkward. They could get paranoid that the pair of you will gang up on them during household arguments. You might be better off living as just the pair of you, or sharing with another couple. Having old friends over to stay for more than a few days can be cool for you, but may cause resentment with everyone else if they're bedding down in the living room and eating the entire contents of the fridge. Check with other flatmates first that it's OK, and think of ways to minimise disruption to other people in the house.

MONEY

There's always one person who's late with the rent, forgets to pay their share of the bills and doesn't see why they should chip in a few quid for the kitty. The best way to get the money is by politely reminding them every single day until they pay up. Rent and bill non-payment can lead to the rest of you being seriously inconvenienced, with extra charges being levied or utilities getting cut off, so don't let the situation drag on for too long. If they genuinely can't pay for the basics, harsh though it may sound, you might have to start looking for a new flatmate. You're probably broke too and you can't afford to carry someone indefinitely, even if they are a mate.

THE BILLS, BILLS, BILLS

You may have to pay a connection fee if your house doesn't already have a telephone landline. If the previous tenants were dodgy and got their power or water disconnected, check your contract because the landlord might be liable for the reconnection fee, rather than you. Think about whose names are going onto the bills, and make sure that it doesn't all end up in one person's name. Share them out if you can or get all the names on each bill. Some bills are charged monthly, like rental fees, or they can arrive quarterly (i.e. every three months), so plan your budgeting accordingly and you won't be in for a nasty surprise when your winter heating bill arrives. When another scary bill plops onto the doormat, open it up and try to pay it reasonably promptly or you could be in for red bills, disconnections and more unpleasant stuff.

If you find you're struggling to pay any bill, it's important to contact the supplier as soon as possible to let them know you are experiencing difficulty. Most companies will try to help work out an affordable repayment plan, and may also suggest other measures to help you with budgeting for future bills. If a flatmate has done a runner and left you with their portion of the bills unpaid, contact the landlord and the supplier at the same time and as quickly as possible. In theory, the landlord could give you money out of their deposit to cover the shortfall, or the company may sometimes let you off part of the bill.

ELECTRICITY AND GAS

Shop around for the best deal, and don't be in a hurry to sign up with salespeople who come door-to-door offering you price cuts on your energy bill (sometimes they're less than honest). If you have any consumer questions about energy-providing companies, contact the independent organisation Energywatch. They can help you to find the cheapest deal from the companies in your area or recommend ways to cut energy consumption and lower your bills. Try their website at: www.energywatch.org.uk/consumer, or their helpline: 08459 060708.

WATER

Find out if you're responsible for paying your water rates or not. If you are, double-check that you're not paying too much for the property you're in. Some areas have metered water, so watch out for high charges and learn how to conserve water. Get any dripping taps and leaking pipes fixed as quickly as you can by the landlord, even if they're in the garden.

COUNCIL TAX

If it's a house full of students, you're not liable to pay any council tax on the property. You may need to send your local council an exemption certificate from the university as proof of your status. When you're sharing with others who aren't students, it may get a little tricky as the property is likely to be charged.

TELEPHONE

This is the single biggest culprit for money-based arguments in shared houses. Some houses keep a log book by the phone to say what numbers they called and when, so it's clear who made expensive calls. Make sure it's an itemised bill, and get one organised person to be in charge of overseeing the sums. It's an equal share of the standing charge, line rental and discounts, plus the individual person's call charges, then the whole number is multiplied by 1.175 (to add on their VAT at 17.5 per cent) to give the person's final share of the bill. If there are a few unclaimed calls that nobody remembers making, split the cost evenly between you and avoid a witch-hunt. Or you could sign up with a telephone provider that gives each person in the household their own personal identification code – that way you always pay for your own calls.

INTERNET

If you're studying with a computer at home, it can help to have internet access in addition to your phone line. You can sign up for cheap deals where they charge very low rates for a connection, but you pay the phone company for the call time, so it's only good if you're all disciplined and don't stay online for long periods. You can also get flat-rate deals for standard-speed access that cost a bit more, but mean you don't run up a phone bill at all. Some areas have broadband, which tends to cost twice as much as the other deals, but it's much faster and you don't pay call charges.

RENTALS

You may decide that renting a washing machine is cheaper than going to the laundrette, and that buying one is unfeasible. Or perhaps you'd like a big communal TV for the living room, if nobody has one of their own or you don't want to buy one together. Compare high street prices, and make sure all the flatmates agree on the final decision.

TV LICENCE

A licence for your telly costs £116 per year, but if you don't get one you could be looking at a £1,000 fine. The detector vans are increasingly sophisticated and the licence people have a pretty good idea of where the student houses are in town, so your chances of getting caught are high. You can pay all in one go, or in instalments. If you're only in town for nine months of the year, you can apply for a refund on the remaining time. Telephone 0870 241 6468 for payments and rebates or use the website: www.tv-l.co.uk.

COMMUNAL ITEMS

It's probably easier to put money for toilet rolls, bin bags, cleaning products and shared food like milk or margarine in a kitty. The other option is to take turns in buying them, which can lead to 'it's not my turn' arguments. Don't leave the kitty jar lying around to be 'borrowed' from, put it away somewhere or leave it in the custody of an honest soul who won't buy chocolate bars or porn mags with it. They can also go around every week or month to make sure all the flatmates have chipped in their fair share.

TROUBLE SHOOTING

Student houses tend to have a special set of problems associated with them, partly because they're often old and run-down and partly because they are filled to the rafters with too many scruffy studes who wander around drunk and stoned, or leave leftover food lying around too. Security advice is covered in Chapter 9, but read on for the rest of the problem-busters.

Landlords are obliged to keep the following in proper working order: exterior structure of the house, water, gas, electricity, sewerage, space heating and hot water. This also includes basins, sinks, baths and toilets. If there's anything wrong with your property, notify the landlord in writing as well as telephoning. Set out exactly what is wrong in your letter and give the landlord a reasonable period of time to carry out repairs, then keep a copy of your letter. As a general rule, allow 48 hours for emergency works and one or two weeks for other works. If the landlord doesn't sort things out, go to your students' union or accommodation service for more advice, or speak to an organisation like a Citizens' Advice Bureau or the housing charity Shelter (contact details at the end of this chapter).

If the place is dangerous or uninhabitable, and the landlord won't fix things, you should consider giving up the accommodation. If it's just about bearable you may wish to get repairs done yourself and get the money back from the landlord, take legal action, or call in your local council's environmental health officer. Get advice first before trying any of these options.

BRRR, CHILLY BREEZES

For starters, most of these houses and flats are cold. Make sure the landlord fixes boilers, central heating, broken windows or damaged window frames, and ask for draught excluders to be fitted under doors and around the letterbox. You can buy cheap clear plastic seals in big DIY stores to cover whole windows and keep the heat in. If you haven't got gas central heating or gas fires, you have the choice of more expensive heating options such as electric central heating, storage or convection heaters, or plug-in radiators. Be very careful when using portable gas heaters, and make sure they have safety certificates, as they can give off poisonous fumes or cause house fires.

To save money, most students don't heat their houses for long periods every day, but it can work out cheaper to have the heating on longer but at a lower temperature. Turning the thermostat down by one degree can save 10 per cent on your normal energy bill, for example. When you're only feeling slightly chilly, put on an extra jumper, make a hot drink, or fill up a hot-water bottle. If it's very cold outside or even snowing, put the heating on at least once every day and stop showing off about how hardy you are; you don't want the water pipes to freeze. Wearing woolly hats and jumpers in bed is equally pointless if you have the option of being relatively warm. Unless that's what turns you on.

EVERYTHING'S GONE GREEN AND FURRY

Damp and mould are close friends. Wherever the water goes, the mouldiness tends to follow, and it's bad news for general health and personal belongings. If it's simple condensation, make sure your air bricks aren't blocked, and use extractor fans or open the windows when needed to let out steam. Wipe mouldy areas down with an anti-mildew product, then keep them as dry as you can. On the other hand, dodgy landlords who know full well that the roof is leaking or there's no damp course in the walls *always* lie and tell you that it's condensation. Don't let them fob you off, keep complaining.

WHAT'S THAT SCUTTLING NOISE?

You may find you have a few new pets, such as free-range mice or rats, or perhaps cockroaches. Let the landlord know straight away if there's any kind of infestation, and keep food firmly shut away in cupboards, jars and nibble-proof boxes. Clean up at night to get rid of leftovers and crumbs too. If it's mice or rats, you may find droppings and gnawed food, hear them running about in walls or under floorboards, or see them dancing merrily in the kitchen. Try putting down a humane trap to catch them alive, they cost about a fiver from hardware stores and they don't splatter Mr Mousey all over the floor. Cockroaches and other bugs are hard to get rid of, and the chemicals needed can be so strong that you have to move out of your place temporarily. If your landlord is unhelpful when you complain about the vermin, try the environmental health office at your local council for more advice.

FIRE SAFETY – SAVE YOUR OWN LIFE

Good landlords put in smoke detectors and perhaps fire extinguishers, but they're not forced to do so by law. If your house doesn't have smoke detectors, get some as soon as you can because smoke and fumes can kill quickly and silently. They only cost a few pounds and they're worth every penny. If possible fit one on every floor and test them once a month.

Common causes of fires in student houses:

- **Candles: never leave them unattended, make sure they're not easily knocked over, use a heatproof candle holder, and don't place on surfaces like televisions, bookshelves or wooden windowsills.**

- **Cigarettes and joints: don't smoke in bed (however fast you go), or while dozing off on the sofa, and make sure ciggy butts are firmly stubbed out in an ashtray.**

- **Kitchen fires: avoid using chip pans if you can. If one catches fire *never* throw water on it (this creates a massive fireball that fills the room). Put pan fires out by covering them with a damp wrung-out tea towel and turning the cooker off if possible. Leave the pan where it is, damp towel in place, until it has cooled.**

- **Heaters: don't cover them or knock them over while they're on, and don't hang clothes on them to dry unless they're standard radiators (no bar or flame).**

- **Electrical: report loose or cracked sockets to the landlord urgently, and don't overload a socket with too many plugs and extensions.**

Have a good think about how you'd get out of your house if there was a fire. Make sure fire exits are kept free from bags and boxes of rubbish, or stacked-up bicycles. Keep keys near to doors and windows to allow a speedy exit, but don't have them in view of passing burglars. Check your furniture: ask the landlord to replace old sofas and armchairs etc. Anything made before 1988 is unlikely to comply with government safety regulations. Get into the habit of going around the house, checking ashtrays and closing doors, before you go to bed at night.

If you discover a fire:

- **Raise the alarm by shouting loudly.**

- **Get everyone out of the house without putting yourself at risk.**

- **Shut the doors behind you and call 999. Stay outside until you get the all clear from the fire brigade.**

- **If you're trapped upstairs, shut doors and stay low to avoid rising smoke, and throw cushions or bedding onto the ground to soften your landing. Lower yourself out of the window and hang by the full length of your arms for a second before letting go, don't jump straight out.**

- **If the window is jammed, break it with furniture or the heel of a shoe, and line the jagged edges with a blanket or coat so you don't get cut while climbing out.**

- **If you can't jump, keep your head out of the window to breathe fresh air, and continue calling for help.**

- **If your clothes catch fire, roll on the floor to put the flames out.**

Find out more about fire safety at www.firekills.gov.uk.

GAS AND CARBON MONOXIDE

Carbon monoxide is a silent killer, responsible for around thirty deaths every year. This poisonous gas can seep out of old or unserviced gas appliances, and be made worse by blocked chimneys and flues. It is colourless and odourless. Landlords are legally obliged to have every gas appliance checked yearly by a CORGI-registered engineer, and should show you the safety certificate within one month. To check on any engineer, call CORGI on 01256 372300. Never block the ventilation that the appliances need, such as flues and air bricks. Although there may be no danger signs, make sure your appliances do not show any of the following: staining or discolouration, burning with a lazy orange or yellow flame, or a strange smell when in use. To be on the safe side, you or your landlord could install a carbon monoxide detector. Make sure it's one that meets British Safety Standards, and has a kite mark logo on it. For more information, call the British Standards Institute on 020 8996 7000.

Carbon monoxide poisoning is hard to spot, and the symptoms can mimic flu, food poisoning or depression. Be on the look out for headaches, dizziness, muscle weakness, tiredness, vomiting or nausea, diarrhoea, stomach pain or chest pain. It can come on slowly, or be sudden. If you think there's a chance you have carbon monoxide poisoning, speak to your GP or go to Accident and Emergency at your local hospital.

Gas leaks are relatively rare, but if you smell gas in your home then do the following:

- **Immediately put out any cigarettes.**

- **Open the doors and windows.**

- **Turn off your gas supply (the tap is usually by the meter).**

- **Don't switch anything electrical off or on, not even a light switch. They can cause a spark that ignites the gas.**

- **Get everyone out of the house and call Transco on 0800 111 999. The call is free, and you will get a free visit from an engineer.**

For more information about gas leaks or carbon monoxide, call the gas safety advice line on: 0800 300 363, or look at the consumer advice on www.corgi-gas-safety.com.

WATER AND PLUMBING
Dripping taps and leaky baths or shower trays are the landlord's responsibility, and it's probably better not to take things into your own hands unless it's the last resort. If there are large leaks that threaten to flood floors, turn off the water using the stopcock, put buckets under drips and ask for it to be fixed urgently. Blocked sinks are your responsibility if you've let hair or grease build up. See the appendix at the end of the book for how to keep them clear.

MEET THE NEIGHBOURS
Wherever possible, try to get on with your neighbours. Pop round and introduce yourself when you move in, and make a general effort not to piss them off with loud noise and late-night parties. Friendly neighbours will keep an eye on your property if you go away, so keep them sweet, and be extra considerate with the noise if they are shift workers or have young kids. If you're having problems with your neighbours, such as arguments about noise or harassment, speak to someone at the students' union about it. They may have a mediation service available, or can help you report incidents to the police.

If your neighbours are excessively noisy, you may have to make a complaint. If asking them politely doesn't work, ring up the council. Under the Noise Act 1996, the council should respond to complaints about noise being made between 11 p.m. and 7 a.m. by sending someone round to measure how loud it is. If the noise is excessive then the council can issue an abatement notice or a warning notice. In extreme conditions, the police can come round and confiscate stereos or other sound systems. This could also happen to you if you have a riotous party and are rude and unhelpful when the police are called.

LANDLORDS, WONDERFUL AND WANKY
Don't assume that your landlord is an evil money-grabbing person who forces students to live in slum dwellings. Some of them are very professional and reasonable, and they get repairs done on time. If you have a good landlord, treat them with respect and recommend them to other people when you leave. When your landlord is dodgy, don't resort to being abusive or withholding your rent without warning, seek advice and go through the proper legal channels instead. This applies to anything to do with harassment, illegal eviction and unsafe premises.

HARASSMENT AND ILLEGAL EVICTION

Tenants have the right to 'quietly enjoy' the property they're renting. Your landlord (or their agent) is not allowed to do any of the following things:

- **Turn up unannounced while you're out and let themselves into the property, unless it's an emergency**

- **Tamper with the locks or electricity, gas or water supply**

- **Interfere with your possessions**

- **Threaten you with violence**

- **Evict you without going through the correct legal process (giving you written notice to quit, a court order and their grounds for repossession of the property)**

- **Use physical force to remove you from the property**

- **Show sexual or racial discrimination**

If any of these happen, seek immediate help from the students' union and your council's tenancy relations officer.

IF SOMEONE MOVES OUT EARLY

Anyone who wants to move out before the end of their contract should give at least one month's notice to the landlord. Depending on the contract, they may still be liable to pay rent until the end of the agreement. In such circumstances, the best thing to do tends to be finding a reasonable replacement tenant, and the person who's moving out should make an effort to help.

If you're looking for a new flatmate, decide what kind of person you want to move in with you, then start advertising as soon as you can. Put ads in shop windows, on union notice boards or in the accommodation office. You can also place them in the *Loot* newspaper, which goes out in print and online (www.loot.com). For safety:

- **Don't put the address in any of your ads, just the area.**

- **Chat to them for a while when they ring up to get a good idea of what they're like. If you don't like the sound of them, you can always ring back later and say you're sorry but the room has already gone.**

- **Don't meet anyone on your own at home, get a friend or neighbour to be there too if the other flatmates can't make it.**

When you've narrowed your search down to one or two potential new flatmates, get them to meet everyone who lives in the house, before making a decision. You could all go out for a pint or a coffee to see how you get along as a group.

GETTING YOUR DEPOSIT BACK

British landlords hold almost £800 million in deposit money, and at least one in five tenants have problems in getting their money back. Students are particularly vulnerable to unscrupulous practices in this area, and need to be careful when leaving premises at the end of their tenancy.

- **When you move out, clean the place thoroughly, and check that everything on the inventory is present and in good working order.**

- **'Clean' means sparkling clean. Wipe down walls, wash stained carpets, wash net curtains and scrub tiled floors. Clean the hob and inside the oven thoroughly. Make sure there's no rubbish piled up outside the house.**

- **Pay all the bills and have proof of payment ready to show the landlord.**

- **Just before you move out, ask the landlord to come round and inspect. Have a friend or neighbour there as an independent witness.**

- **Get independent witnesses to check that the place is clean and otherwise in good condition on the day you move out. If necessary take photographs using a borrowed camera that prints dates and times onto the pictures, or get the witness to sign and date the back of them.**

- **Hand back all the keys and get a receipt for them.**

- **Agree a timeframe for the return of your deposit.**

Should your deposit fail to turn up, write to your landlord and ask for it back, and contact your nearest advice centre, such as the students' union. Students who have a bad relationship with their landlord, and suspect the deposit may be wrongly withheld, sometimes withhold their last month's rent. Doing this may put you on dodgy legal ground as you are breaking the terms of your contract, but you may decide it's the best way. In which case you must follow the moving-out checklist above carefully and keep evidence.

If your deposit is being held unfairly, the only way to stand a chance of getting it back is by taking the landlord to your local small claims court. Bringing most proceedings costs £60–£80, and if the landlord disputes the claim a hearing is called, which can take up to six months to get a judgement. If you lose your case there are no other fees to pay, but if you win it may still be difficult to recover your money. Don't let them get away with it! If you complain through the correct channels at least you will have alerted the authorities to their illegal behaviour.

BUYING

A few students are able buy their own houses, often with parental help, and then live there with their partner or let rooms out to flatmates. Sometimes the parents buy the house themselves and let their offspring manage the property.

Pros	Cons
A well-chosen property can be a financial investment and a source of rental income	You could have trouble with your tenants
It can be cheaper than renting	It can be a huge financial strain
You get to be your own landlord	It's a big responsibility
	Missed payments could lead to repossession

Anyone who wants to get their own place should think carefully about the financial side of things, as finding a mortgage suitable for a student-owner may be complicated. There are additional costs such as buildings insurance and solicitors. House-buying can be a long drawn-out process, and buyers need to:

- **raise the finance**

- **engage solicitors**

- **search for suitable properties**

- **have surveys to make sure the property is sound**

- **make offers and have them accepted**

- **exchange contracts with the buyer**

The Council of Mortgage Lenders produces a guide called 'How to Buy a House'. Write to them at 3 Savile Row, London, W1S 3PB, telephone: 020 7437 0075, website: www.cml.co.uk. Many of the high street banks and building societies produce their own homebuying guides too.

USEFUL HOUSING RESOURCES

SHELTER

The leading independent housing advice organisation in the UK.

For urgent housing advice, telephone Shelterline on: 0808 800 4444. Calls are free, and service includes minicom (textphone) and translators.

Shelter, 88 Old Street, London EC1V 9HU.

Shelter Scotland, 4th Floor, Scotiabank House, 6 South Charlotte Street, Edinburgh, EH2 4AW

Shelter Cymru, 25 Walter Road, Swansea, SA1 5NN

Main website: www.shelter.org.uk, consumer advice: www.shelternet.co.uk

CITIZENS' ADVICE BUREAUX

An organisation that provides a wide range of free advice and help on many matters, including housing.

Your nearest bureau will be listed in your local phone book, or you can look it up online at: www.nacab.org.uk. They also have an advice website at: www.adviceguide.org.uk.

THE HOME SAFETY NETWORK

A government website covering everything from general home safety to DIY accidents. Has an extensive list of useful links and contacts.

Website: www.dti.gov.uk/homesafetynetwork/

FREAKY FLATMATES

Domestic bliss with the students at www.virginstudent.com

'In my second year I lived with *Star Trek*-obsessed loons who were messy beyond belief. They left cake uncovered in the living room for three weeks – that's three weeks people!! When I asked them about it and said it was unhygienic they said, "No, it won't have things crawling on it for at least another few months!" Funny now, but NOT at the time.'

'Down our street there were loads of students, all-male houses unlike our all-female house, so we got lots of attention, good and bad (the good I'm sure you can imagine). The bad involved stealing items from our house, using our bath and leaving the water running so it came through the ceiling, ordering unwanted cabs/pizza etc. And – how cheeky is this – ordering takeaway for themselves AND SENDING THE DELIVERY PEOPLE UP TO US TO MAKE US PAY!! The buggers!'

'I lived with about eight people in a flat and we hated each other. One day we were very drunk and watching wrestling on telly and we ended up fighting just like on WWF. It was crazy. After that we just laughed and became friends again.'

'I had a flatmate who was totally mental. One night she brought this band back (on a night when we had all told her not to – we all had assignments and exams the next day). There were about thirty of them and they proceeded to trash the house. The next morning she hurled abuse at us and told us we were jealous cause she had brought some unknown freaky band back. Needless to say she moved out after none of spoke to her for about two months.'

'There's a couple of people who bollock me for not doing any washing up, despite me doing more than anyone else, which is a lil' unfair. But other than that all is good, cos we all help each other out, we all muck in, so it's cool.'

'We have just had the fun of bills. I am sure the lass that is controlling them is trying to skank us out of money. I may have to investigate!'

'Turns out two of my flatmates "christened" the kitchen table last year in our halls. Not too bothered though – me and my bloke christened it again soon after.'

'My previous flatmates from last semester were like the ugly sisters. One was tall and skinny and the other was short and dumpy. Apart from their physical attributes they also acted like them. One of them even asked me to clean the bathroom cause their friend was coming over. Yeah right, that was really going to happen. They complained about me having my boyfriend over, they were simply jealous as in eight months neither of them ever had a man stay over, and God they tried. They were horrendous yet they were so comical and whingy.'

'I was the only person who bought toilet paper and kept it in the bathroom. The others would buy their own loo paper and keep it in their rooms.'

6. MONEY

Money can't buy you love, but it's pretty handy for keeping a roof over your head and buying the occasional shandy. It's never been more important for students to get to grips with sensible budgeting, or to learn ways to get the most money coming in each term. Debt is the norm rather than the exception, and is a massive cause of stress among undergraduates, most of whom end up owing between £7,000 and £15,000 by the end of their courses. It's not all doom and gloom though, at least most of your friends are in the same boat, and the skills you pick up can last a lifetime.

This chapter covers:

- **Student banking and how to choose the best account**

- **Sources of money such as student loans, access funds and bursaries**

- **Expenses and simple ways to budget for them**

- **Money saving tips to keep your household and other bills down**

- **Coping with debt stress and how to control your borrowing**

STUDENT BANKING
Finding the right student account can save a lot of bother later on, and doing some research can also save you some money. Student accounts are similar to most current accounts, but they tend to have extras such as overdrafts where you aren't charged interest.

WHICH ACCOUNT IS RIGHT FOR ME?
As every academic year is about to start, most of the main high street banks and building societies start a charm offensive to get prospective undergraduates to open a student account with them. There's a reason why they're being so nice to all the skint students. After all, you'll probably end up owing them money on extended overdrafts, taking out a graduate loan after you leave uni, or even sticking with them permanently. Some of the offers are pretty good, but make sure you look up and down the high street at everything else that's available, or compare their terms online. When you're looking for a student account, the main things to consider are:

- **The amount of interest-free overdraft. Think about how much they'll let you have in the first year, and how much it goes up to in the final year.**

- **What an arranged overdraft costs, after you've used up your interest-free allowance. Find out what the rate of interest is, and whether there's an arrangement fee.**

- **What an unarranged overdraft costs (when you go over your arranged limit without agreeing it first with the bank). There may be a high rate of interest and a fee for sending you a letter.**

- **Where their nearest cash machines (ATMs) are, or whether you can use their card in the ATM of the nearest bank without paying a fee. You don't want to be wandering around for miles at night trying to get hold of some cash.**

- **Where their nearest branch with a student adviser is. Specialist advice comes in handy. You could have to go in and beg for yet more overdraft, so it might as well be conveniently close.**

- **How easy it is to pay in cheques and cash to the account.**

- **Interest paid on a positive balance (savings). Is there an incentive to stay out of the overdraft zone?**

- **What their arrangements for graduates are. Is there a period of grace after you graduate where you have low-interest on your debts? Can you convert expensive debts such as credit cards into a low-interest graduate loan? How long do you have to pay it off?**

Think about whether you'd like an account you can run using telephone banking. If you have your own computer, perhaps you'd like to have an account that offers internet banking, to help you keep control of your finances. You may also be interested in ethical banking, or human rights records of the institutions you're considering. Once you've narrowed it down to the best two or three deals, only then should you be swayed by the offers of freebies that they try to tempt you with. These range from money-saving rail or coach cards to shopping discounts and free mini hi-fi systems. There may also be incentives for signing up using the internet or joining the bank that your parents use. One or two banks offer no freebies at all, but you may decide that they offer the most convenient service or competitive rates overall.

Once you've opened your account, compare banks every year or so to see if the rates are still competitive. If your student account is not living up to your expectations, it's relatively easy to switch it to another bank. Shop around for the best deal, and then it's simply a matter of producing your ID and filling a form in. If your student loan or other funding is paid into your account regularly, don't forget to notify the sources of this funding about your new bank details.

For an up-to-date view of what the big banks are offering, and general advice about student finance, look at www.studentmoney.org. This website is provided free by UCAS and Hotcourses.

CREDIT CARDS

Unless you're skilled at money management it's better not to get a credit card. They are the most expensive way to borrow, and should only be used if you are capable of paying the amount off in full each month. The greatest danger is that students end up using them as an overdraft extension and carry the debt for years, just paying off the minimum amount each month. This can be financially crippling and it's hard to get back on top of it when the charges keep piling up. Credit cards are useful for when you're travelling, and also sometimes provide extra insurance on large purchases, but always read the small print. If you travel a lot, it might be worth considering one.

SAVINGS

Before you leave for university, it's good to have some savings in an easy-access account as an emergency fund, just in case your loan doesn't come through on time, or you have unexpected course costs. Savings may feel like a security blanket you don't want to give up, but remember the amount of interest you earn on your savings is always much less than you get charged on debts such as arranged overdrafts or credit cards. You save money in the long run by using your savings to pay off debts like these. If you're one of the lucky students who is in credit most or all of the time, look for a bank account that pays a good rate of interest on your balance.

OVER THE YEARS

Your first student loan is likely to be the biggest chunk of money you've had to deal with in your life, if you've just left home and haven't been completely responsible for your finances before. Don't go mad with it in the first week, no matter how tempting it may be. Learning how to budget and plan ahead with your money can take a while, so most banks allow you a fair amount of leeway in your first year. After this, they don't give you much extra in the way of free overdrafts and so on. You have to do a better job with your personal finances as time goes by.

KEEPING THE BANK MANAGER SWEET

This is as much a social skill as it is a financial one. If you think you're about to go over the edge of your agreed overdraft limit, phone in and tell them quickly. Explain how you're going to pay it off and when. This may prevent you from being slapped with £20 fees for stroppy letters or high interest charges. Be as polite as you can, even if they don't always let you get your own way. Banks like students who show that they are aware of the state of their bank accounts, and who think ahead. If you're having problems, they also like you to ask for help long before you get in too deep.

INCOMING MONEY

For most undergraduates, their main sources of money are student loans, financial help from their parents and wages from part-time jobs. Students may also be able to apply for additional bursaries, grants and benefits, and it's nearly always a case of 'if you don't ask, you don't get', so never be scared to ask for more.

STUDENT LOANS

Student loans are part of the government's financial support package for students embarking on a course of higher education, to help students meet their living costs while studying.

APPLYING

They are the cheapest way to borrow money at the moment, so it makes sense to claim for the full amount. After you've applied for your university course, your local award authority handles the first stage of your loan application. If you're from England and Wales it's done through your Local Education Authority, in Scotland you apply to the Student Awards Agency for Scotland, and if you are from Northern Ireland your loan application should be made to your Education and Library Board.

Since 1 September 1998, the type of Student Loan on offer has been the newer-style Student Support Scheme (also known as SSS or student support loans). Interest on the loan is linked to the rate of inflation, so in real terms the total amount that borrowers repay is equivalent to the amount they have borrowed. Part of all student support loans is means-tested, and you can choose whether you wish to apply for this extra means-tested 25 per cent. The maximum loan amount for 2003/2004 is £4,000 for someone studying outside London, and £4,930 for students in London.

Award authorities take various factors into account when they assess the total amount of money you are entitled to, such as where you're going to be studying, whether you will be living at home, and your parents' income. Extra help may be available from your award authority if you are disabled, have dependent children, have been in care or have extra travel costs to meet.

If you are a non-United Kingdom (UK) European Union student, you may be able to apply for help with tuition fees. Non-UK EU students are not eligible for a UK student loan, supplementary grants, hardship loans or Access Funds. There's more information available from the Department for Education and Skills (DfES), which is listed on their website: www.dfes.gov.uk/studentsupport/eustudents/index.shtml.

When your Award Authority sends you your Support Notification or Eligibility Notice, you should complete the Loan Request Form (which is on the reverse) and return it to the Student Loans Company as soon as you can. From this point onwards, The Student Loans Company (SLC) becomes responsible for the administration of your loan. The SLC sends you a loan acknowledgement letter after they've processed your loan application, followed by a payment schedule letter approximately 14 days before the start of your term. These will give you details of your payment dates and amounts, which should be split into three payments, one for each term. If your application is received within 21 days of the start of term you will only be sent a payment schedule letter.

PICKING UP THE MONEY

In theory, so long as the SLC have received authorisation in enough time, you can receive your first 'BACS' electronic money transfer payments direct into your bank or building society account in time for the start of your course. You will need a bank account that accepts direct credits to do this.

HARDSHIP LOANS

If you're in extreme financial difficulties, you may be eligible to apply for an extra hardship loan from the Student Loans Company. Before you can do this, you need to have applied for the full student loan that you're eligible for, and you must also have received the first instalment of your loan. Contact the student loans officer at your college or university, then your college can assess your circumstances and decide whether it's appropriate to allow a one-off additional loan amount, somewhere between £100 and £500.

REPAYING

After you've finished your course of study, from the April after you graduate it's time to start repaying your loans. Repayments for the student support-style loans, which started on or after 1 September 1998, are as follows. As soon as you graduate and start earning more than a set yearly wage (currently £10,000 but due to rise to £15,000 by 2006), repayments begin, unless you apply to defer your payments for 12 months. Repayments are set at 9 per cent of your monthly income, which means that if interest rates rise, the whole repayment period will be extended. The money is normally collected by the Inland Revenue via the employer. If you want to make additional payments, they can be sent directly to the SLC, but this will not reduce the size of your regular repayments. For mortgage-style loans (from before September 1998), repayments are set over a fixed five-year period, meaning that if interest rates rise, there will be an increase in each individual monthly repayment.

For information about any aspect of the student loans process, contact the Student Loans Company at 100 Bothwell Street, Glasgow G2 7JD, telephone: 0800 40 50 10, minicom: 0800 085 3950, or look at their website, www.slc.co.uk.

PARENTS

This is where keeping the old folks sweet can come in handy. Most parents are proud of their offspring for going off and getting a degree, and will be keen to help out in some way. If they have all or part of the funds available, it can help for you all to sit down and work out how much money you'll need for your living expenses. Set a realistic budget, and try not to go back begging for handouts simply because you can't handle your own cashflow. However, most parents will allow you a second chance or two if you do mess up with your money, even if you do get a telling-off to go with it.

If you don't get on so well with your relatives, it may be helpful to sweet-talk them a little when you need money, even if it does stick in your throat.

Whatever they're like, remember to make loud grateful noises if they do sign any cheques. Should you have a parent that you're estranged from, you may have to go to great lengths to make this clear when you're being means-tested by your local education authority. You may be able to get special consideration when applying for loans.

If your parents aren't willing to give you the money, they may be prepared to loan it to you instead. This isn't such a bad deal if they're giving it to you interest-free, as you'll end up paying less in real terms when it comes to giving them their money back. Also be prepared to blag as much cash as you can from your grandparents and kindly aunts and uncles on occasions such as Christmas and birthdays.

JOBS

A part-time job is a regular source of cash when you're broke, and it could be the difference between having a manageable debt and one that's growing out of control. Holiday employment is another useful source of income, and if you're lucky it can double up as relevant work experience for your CV. Your student union may have a job shop, with a range of paid employment to choose from, although many student jobs are badly paid, with anti-social hours that can leave you tired out. Choose your type of employment carefully, and try not to work too many hours each week, otherwise your coursework will suffer badly. Make sure you're not paying too much tax on your earnings by filling in the right forms when you start work. See Chapter 7 for more about the ins and outs of student jobs.

ACCESS FUNDS AND OTHER FUNDS

Your university will have access funds from the government, and possibly a number of its own hardship funds, to help out any undergraduates who are having a hard time financially. Ask for the application forms at the union building. Should you qualify after filling in the forms, you'll get a sum of money, which can be anything from a few quid up to a few hundred pounds, as a one-off gift that you don't have to repay. If in doubt, apply for everything. The Students' Union may also be able to make small loans to help tide you over in an emergency.

GRANTS AND BURSARIES FROM CHARITIES AND TRUSTS

There are large and small charities and trusts all over the UK that give money to students. The catch is that they're sometimes hard to find or contact, quick decisions are unheard of, the sums of money involved may be small, and they may have unusual conditions attached. Some of these trusts have been around for centuries, and may only be open to 'maids of the parish who need to buy art equipment for the first year of their degree, both of whose parents are deceased one-legged tailors' and so on. It still might be profitable to ask at your local library, church or town hall about grants and bursaries.

While you're in the library, check out *The Directory of Grant Making Trusts 2003–04*, published by the Charities Aid Foundation. At £80.00 it's a bit pricey for most students. You may be able to stretch to a purchase of *University Scholarships and Awards 2003* by Brian Heap, published by Trotman, £14.99, or *The Educational Grants Directory* by Alan French, Dave Griffiths, Tom Traynor and Sarah Wiggins, published by the Directory of Social Change, price £20.95. Failing that, your university may have a copy of one of these books in the careers library.

You can also contact The Educational Grants Advisory Service (EGAS) for more information about all kinds of student funding, including loans, grants, benefits, access funds, hardship funds, bursaries and charitable trusts. Write to: EGAS, 501–505 Kingsland Road, London, E8 4AU, look at their website: www.egas-online.org.uk, or telephone for an application form: 020 7254 6251, 10 a.m. to 12 noon, and 2 p.m. to 4 p.m., on Monday, Wednesday and Friday.

Your university department should have information about scholarships, bursaries and other funding or gifts-in-kind from various educational foundations. You may need to enter an essay-writing competition, for example, to be in with a chance of getting the money. Sometimes gifts or prizes are made in the form of book tokens, but at least that would be good for studying and solve a few Christmas and birthday present traumas.

GOVERNMENT GRANTS

Students from poorer backgrounds may qualify for means-tested grants. Welsh students can receive an Assembly Living Grant of up to £1,500. Scottish students with parents who earn less than £27,000 per year could receive a bursary of up to £2,100. From 2004, the British Government plans to make grants of up to £1,000 available to students with a parental income below £21,185.

SPONSORSHIP

Certain degrees attract sponsorship from industrial companies, the army and so on. The students they sponsor are given extra money for their living expenses, and the opportunity to do paid work during vacations. After graduation, the sponsored students are normally expected to work for their backers for a certain number of years. The small print is important: students can find themselves working for a pittance during their holiday periods, or having to pay back large sums of money if they decide upon a different career. *The Sponsorship and Funding Directory 2003* is published by Hobsons, costs £8.99, and could be worth a look.

EXTRA EDUCATIONAL LOANS

Many of the high street banks and building societies offer different educational loans, some of which run in conjunction with government schemes. There are Career Development Loans, Professional Studies Loans (mainly aimed at law, veterinary, dentistry, medicine and architecture students) and the Business School Loan Scheme, for people studying Master of Business Administration (MBA) degrees. Drop into a few of your local bank branches to see who's offering what.

OFFICER TRAINING CORPS

The Officer Training Corps is a special part of the Territorial Army, consisting of 19 contingents of University Officer Training Corps (UOTC) based at universities across the country. You do not need previous military experience, just British citizenship and a good general standard of fitness. Attendance at training weekends and camps will net you a sum of money known as a 'bounty'. For more information, apply in person to the branch of the Corps that's based at your uni, or look at the website: www.army.mod.uk/uotc/about.html.

COMPETITIONS

At the start of every academic year, large retailers such as bookshops and supermarkets run competitions and free prize draws that promise to pay your rent or grocery bills for a year if you win. They are creating a feelgood factor for their company, and possibly grabbing your name for their mailing lists. So long as it's free to enter and claim the prize, and it's a reasonably decent company who won't send you unwanted mailshots for the rest of your natural life, then go for it. You never know.

OUTGOING MONEY

Once you've sorted out a decent student bank account and maximised your income, you need to know where the money all goes, and how to control your cashflow. If you mess up your budget don't give up completely, get a grip on your spending and start again.

TUITION FEES

Some students will have to pay university tuition fees. The maximum amount to pay for 2003/2004 is £1,125. If you're living at home this is means-tested according to your parental income, and if it's below £20,970 no fees are due. It's tested on a sliding scale, and if parents earn more than £31,230 then the full fees are due, but most students pay none or only part of the charge. If you're financially independent of your parents and you have fairly high income, you may be liable for some or all of your tuition fees. Means-testing is done through your local educational award authority, and you should contact them to apply for reduced fees. If you are liable to pay for tuition fees, these are paid directly to the university. Arrangements are different from place to place, but most universities are flexible and let you pay by instalments. In 2003 the government announced plans to abolish up-front tuition fees in favour of 'top-up' fees. This means that from 2006 universities will be able to charge up to £3,000 a year for courses. The fees will only be paid back once students have graduated, started work and are earning more than £15,000 a year. If you're starting uni in 2004 or 2005, don't panic – you'll be exempt throughout the duration of your course (it's only for new students from 2006).

LIVING EXPENSES

In order to be able to make a budget, you need to have an accurate idea of what your living expenses will be. If you've never lived away from home before or you're moving to a big city, speak to the student adviser at your bank or your student union. They should be able to give you an idea of average rents, bills and so on. The NUS estimates that in 2003/2004, the yearly term-time expenditure of an average student living outside London is £7,317 (£8,400 inside London). Previous students can give you tips about regular outgoings too.

You need to think about:

- **Rent, the single largest student expense (average yearly cost £2,003 outside London, £2,814 inside London)**

- **Insurance**

- **Main bills: electricity, gas, water rates, telephone, mobile phone**

- **Other bills: TV licence, washing machine rental or launderette fees**

- **One offs: books, household items, deposits and so on**

- **Groceries and toiletries (£1,043 per year on average)**

- **Stationery**

- **Clothes (£394 per year on average)**

- **Entertainment**

- **Transport**

- **Birthdays, Christmas presents**

- **Having the occasional treat**

BUDGETING

Here are a few basic budgeting skills, plus a wide range of tricks and tips for saving money on all kinds of expenses.

BASIC BUDGETING SKILLS

It helps to know what kind of a spender you are, so that you know your weak spots and can plan around them. Fritterers spend small amounts of money several times a day, on magazines, muffins, posh coffees, cans of drink, small treats and so on. Splurgers do OK with their budgets most of the time, but then slip up with a massive blowout on something like a DVD player or a holiday in the sun that they can't quite afford. Miserly types keep their money under such tight control that much of their energy gets tied up with not spending anything, and it drives everyone around them crazy. Go for a balanced approach, and you won't need to worry too much.

Once you have a good idea of your basic living costs, you can start making a budget. You may want to work it out on a termly, monthly or weekly basis. For example, you could subtract termly costs such as hall rent and tuition fees from your incoming money for the term, then divide up the remaining amount into monthly or weekly sections. Write your budgets down and try your hardest to stick to them. You may have underestimated some of your costs at the beginning, so be prepared to be flexible and start to make more realistic plans as you go along. Between terms you may be living with your parents (cheaper costs) or doing holiday work (greater income), so your budgets need to be different.

Most students are going to be living on a very tiny amount of money, so it's useful to keep a track of everything you spend, and review it regularly to see if there are any expenses that can be trimmed back. Some people just write down the times they visit the cash machine, or write cheques or pay bills over the phone, but others prefer to keep track of every penny using a notebook. Having online banking can be a convenient way of seeing where the money's going as well. Try to get your spending to fit your incoming money if you can, although this isn't always possible even if you're brilliant at handling your own finances.

One way to cope with a tight budget is by working in cash for weekly spending. Work out your weekly budget after things like rent and bills have been paid, then take out the rest of what you need as cash. Put the cash card away somewhere safe. This leaves your money for groceries, toiletries, the launderette, travel, going out, photocopying and so on. Once it's gone, it's gone, don't go back to the bank for more. This method can stop you going completely overboard in the pub, where a few drinks can famously lower your resistance to temptation.

For more help with your budgeting skills, try reading *Money for Life* by Alvin Hall, published by Coronet, £5.99, or looking at websites such as The Motley Fool, www.fool.co.uk.

MONEY SAVING TIPS
General tips:

- **Make sure you're getting all your benefits for prescription charges, dental care and so on. If you don't have the right paperwork and have to pay out, you can fill in forms for a rebate later.**

- **Make sure the local council knows that you have student status and you're exempt from paying council tax.**

- **Beware of anything that says '50% off!' unless it's something you already use lots of. It isn't a bargain if you don't need it, no matter how cheap it is.**

Utilities bills:

- **Shop around for gas, electricity, telephone, and internet connection deals. Make sure that you really are getting a better deal by comparing their standing charge and price per unit, using the units you've used on your current bill. Try online price comparison information from www.uSwitch.com, www.buy.co.uk or www.saveonyourbills.com.**

- You may be able to save more by combining bills with one supplier, such as dual fuel (gas and electricity) or packages like electricity plus telephone.

- If you are sent an estimate for a bill, read the meter yourself or ask them to send someone round to read it. Estimates are invariably too high, and why pay for units you haven't used?

- Turn off lights, TVs and radios when you're not using them to save electricity. Don't leave the TV or stereo on standby, turn it right off.

- Set your boiler timer so that it isn't making hot water for longer than it needs to be each day.

- Switch your thermostat down half a degree to save pounds during the winter.

- Don't boil a kettle full of water if you're only making one cup of tea.

- Put the lids on pans and turn the flame down during cooking to save gas.

- Keep an egg timer near the telephone or keep an eye on your watch during calls, so you don't chat for too long.

- Find out what times your telephone provider designates as 'off peak' calls. Stick to these times whenever possible. If most of your calls are local, think about using a phone company that lets you make local calls very cheaply or for free.

- Find out about telephone discount cards for calling long-distance. Some are a bit of a rip-off but others save you a small fortune, especially if you have family or partners overseas.

- If you're on a water meter, don't leave taps running when you're washing up, cleaning your teeth and so on. Take quick showers or have shallow baths, but for the sake of the rest of us, please keep washing regularly.

Mobile phone bills:

- Although the cost per unit is higher, a pay-as-you-go mobile is the easiest way to keep your total bill manageable. It's also less stress if your phone is nicked.

- If you're very disciplined with your phone use, you may find a good line rental deal works out cheaper. Shop around before you sign up, and regularly check back to see if you're still getting a good deal. Go for one that lets you have enough free minutes and texts, and preferably doesn't charge extra for calls to other networks.

- Compare different mobile tariffs using www.switchwithwhich.co.uk, advice from the Consumers' Association.

- If your mate is a chatterbox, send them a text message rather than getting sucked into an expensive ten-minute call about absolutely nothing.

- Try to remember to say things to your friends while you're face to face!

- Use free university email and messenger software to keep in touch.

- Some websites let you send free texts to your mates. Remember to put your name at the end of the message or they won't know who it's from.

Food bills:

- Buy in bulk with friends, or get a relative to pick things up wholesale.

- Go to fruit and veg markets just before they're about to close. You can pick up bargains from stallholders who don't want to lug everything home.

- Buy from bargain supermarkets such as Aldi, Lidl or Netto. Or stick to the bargain ranges at the more expensive shops.

- Treat yourself to a cheap student cookbook and make meals at home rather than eating out or buying pricey supermarket ready meals.

- Base most of your evening meals on cheap filling foods like pasta, rice, potatoes, beans or bread.

- Buy seasonal local fruit, vegetables, fish or meat. It's cheaper, it's fresher, and it's better for the environment.

- Plan your weekly recipes and food shopping, and write a shopping list, but be flexible enough to grab yourself a bargain if one turns up.

- Go to the posher supermarkets last thing on a Sunday afternoon and buy a few of the still-edible reduced goodies on offer.

- Pick up bargain cast-iron pots and pans, and other equipment and crockery at car-boot sales or charity shops.

Clothes and toiletries:

- Ask for expensive clothes, trainers and toiletries as gifts from well-off family members, or ask people who are going abroad to get them cheaply for you.

- Avoid using designer cosmetics and toiletries for everyday occasions.

- Buy cheaper toiletries such as razors, shaving gel, shampoo and skincare from high street shops, or try the bargain supermarket own-brand ranges.

- Go for BOGOFs (buy one get one free) if they're products you like and use regularly.

- Use cheap makeup ranges such as Collection 2000 or Kolor from Superdrug, Barry M, Miss Sporty, or Maybelline if you're going for a high-fashion look that only lasts one season.

- Don't even think about dressing yourself head to toe with brand-new designer clothes. Buy designer labels in the sales or second-hand,

and mix them with high street and junk shop finds. Or buy similar high street versions from TopShop, H&M, Zara, Mango and New Look.

- **Purchase items like socks and pants in bulk. They don't have to be too posh if they're hidden away.**

- **Buy shoes that will last more than one season, and look after them. Get them mended if they start to show signs of wear and tear.**

- **For an individual look, customise second-hand clothes or make your own.**

- **Cheap accessories such as belts or jewellery can bring an old outfit up to date.**

- **If you love fashion, read the magazines in the local library rather than buying them all, or buy one and share other magazines with friends.**

Other bills:

- **Hiring a washing machine between five people can work out much cheaper than using the launderette.**

- **Don't do half loads at the launderette. Share a wash with a mate, save it up for another week, or hand wash it.**

- **Pay for your TV licence. You're not covered by your parents' licence and there's a hefty fine when they catch you.**

- **When renting TVs and videos, go for the cheaper student packages.**

- **Do you really need cable or satellite TV? If so, shop around for the best package and look out for seasonal deals.**

- **Some bills are cheaper if you pay by direct debit, but this is only feasible if you have one person who can cope with it coming out of their bank account all in one go, and everybody is willing and able to pay up on time. Otherwise avoid.**

- **Cut down on transport costs by cycling, or using student discount cards, or student bus fares.**

PEER PRESSURE

Dealing with peer pressure can be difficult, especially if you're the generous, giving sort. You may feel obliged to go out when you're broke, buy gifts you can't really afford, or always keep up with affluent mates. Learn to say no to spending sometimes, even if it doesn't come naturally to you. Make sure that you're not buying endless rounds or cooking for spongers who never get you anything in return, and remember that real mates understand when you can't afford stuff.

THE END OF THE OVERDRAFT

A common scenario: it's a while before the next loan cheque comes in, the bank won't let you borrow any more money, and you can't scrape the funds together from anywhere else. You're nearly broke for the next week or two, and you have to get by on very little money. How do you avoid starvation?

- Get money back from everyone who owes you.

- Tot up how much cash you have. Count the contents of the penny jar if necessary.

- Make a strict budget with the cash you do have.

- Put your bank cards away and work on a cash-only basis for the next few days. Don't buy anything unless it's essential.

- You could try keeping your money in separate jam jars or envelopes as a budgeting aid. One for travel, one for food and so on.

- Go back to the essentials – pay the rent if you haven't already. You can put off most utilities bills for a couple of weeks, but not too much longer. If your electricity is on a meter, buy this week's card upfront and be careful how much electricity you burn up. Put money aside for essential travel.

- Minimise mobile phone usage. Stick rigidly to free minutes allowances, or use only text messages. Don't make texts unless they're important, use free university emails instead if you can.

- Avoid going out for coffees, sandwiches, meals, or to pubs and clubs. If you have to go to the pub, get the people who owe you beer to get the drinks in. Otherwise, nurse half a pint for as long as you can. Visit nearby mates at home and you might get free coffee or food as well as their company, and there's nothing to shell out for.

- Cheer yourself up with the totally skint entertainment tips in Chapter 4.

- Sort out your food so you aren't hungry – keeping your belly filled now takes priority over eating healthily. Use up whatever you already have in the store cupboard, then buy enough budget food to eat for breakfast, lunch, dinner and snacks. Take packed lunches to college, or a cheap snack for staving off library or computer lab hunger pangs, to stop you buying expensive prepared food. Use an empty mineral water bottle to carry tap water for drinks. Try the flat broke recipes in the appendix that use the cheapest ingredients and fill you up, even if they're not gourmet fare.

- Make toiletries last a bit longer by watering down shampoo and shower gel.

- If you have a partner, tell them that the best things in life are free. You might even get a shag out of it if you're charming enough.

- Tell yourself the money situation isn't going to be like this forever.

DEBT

Student debt is a fact of life for most undergraduates, to a greater or lesser extent. If you live on a reasonable budget, take out your maximum loan amount, borrow a bit from parents and other relatives, and maybe get some extra cash from jobs and so on, your debts should remain manageable. However, if you spend heavily while you have a small income, or find your income is unexpectedly reduced, the amount you owe can spiral out of control. Being deeply in debt causes severe stress, damages your credit rating, can leave you with County Court Judgements against your name, and in extreme cases may make you bankrupt or land you in prison. It would be a great shame if you had to drop out of your course because of financial problems, so keep a handle on those debts.

MANAGING YOUR DEBTS

Borrowed money isn't your money – you have to pay it back eventually, plus interest (unless it's a private loan from the Bank of Mum and Dad). Don't fall into the common trap of thinking 'Well, I'm ten grand in debt now, so I might as well be twenty grand in debt.' Twenty thousand pounds will take more than twice as long to pay off, because of compound interest. Any graduate who has a crippling debt will tell you that it isn't worth it. You find yourself 'running to stand still', and all your spare cash from that plum job ends up going to pay your debts off. Too many people end up living back with their parents when they really don't want to, or missing out on holidays and gap years, or getting their foot on the housing ladder.

If you think you're sliding too deep into debt, have a close look at your budget again and make a few sacrifices. Then make sure you're getting as much money coming in as you can. Claim the full amount of your student loan, check you're getting all your benefits, claim back any travel expenses you can and see what the bank is prepared to do overdraft-wise. Seriously think about getting part-time or holiday work. Then go to your students' union and ask about hardship funds, or charities that may be able to help you.

ARE YOU IN SERIOUS DEBT?

There are several signs that suggest you're building up an unmanageable debt:

- **You're too scared to work out how much you owe in total.**

- **You avoid opening your bank statements and bills, you throw them away, or you hide them and they're starting to pile up.**

- **You have a debt on your credit card that's so big you can only just cover each monthly repayment.**

- **You're charging everyday items such as food and other groceries to your credit card because there's no money to be had anywhere else.**

- **You let unauthorised overdrafts build up, gaining additional charges, because you can't talk to the bank manager about it.**

- **You're borrowing money from friends, and deep down you know you won't be able to pay it back.**

- **You're taking out loans or other credit agreements to pay off other debts, in effect 'robbing Peter to pay Paul'.**

- **You get angry letters from companies you owe money to, or visits from bailiffs.**

- **You owe so much money to your university for rent arrears or tuition fees that they've threatened to withhold awarding you your degree, or to prevent you going on to the next year of your course.**

- **You go on a spending spree to cheer yourself up because you're so broke, and end up feeling worse afterwards.**

If you can't say yes to any of the points above, there's a possibility that your debts are relatively small or average compared to most students, but you're excessively worried about them. Does that sound plausible? Has anyone ever described you as a 'born worrier'? Talk to other students or NUS representatives about how much debt other people are in, and try to put it into perspective.

HOW TO SORT BAD DEBTS OUT

If your debts are out of control, the first thing to do is admit to yourself that you have a serious problem. Of course it would be lovely to stick your head in the sand and hope it all goes away, but while you're doing that, something nasty is likely to come along and bite you on the bum. Own up. It's frightening, but it has to be done if you want to stop the situation from getting worse.

After that, you need to work out exactly how much you do owe, and to whom. Make a list of everything, including overdraft, student loans, other unsecured loans, credit cards, money you owe to mates and family, hire-purchase agreements and so on. Then you can prioritise these debts while you get a handle on your spending. Your main aim is to keep a roof over your head, and to avoid getting your utilities cut off, so always make sure your rent and bills are covered first. In the meantime, make a strict budget for your everyday outgoings, and stick to it, even if that means unpleasant cutbacks and sacrifices. Get rid of your mobile phone, or switch to pay-as-you-go and severely limit your monthly voucher usage.

It's best to target anything that's being charged at a very high rate of interest, such as credit cards, and start sorting that out as a priority. Wherever possible, switch the balance onto cards with lower APRs so you're paying as little interest as possible, and cut up your credit cards if you're tempted to spend any more on them. Then tackle the remaining debts that have the highest interest charges, and start paying them off first. Write down a debt repayment plan, preferably with help from one of the non-profit organisations listed in the box at the end of this chapter, and include the amounts you're able to pay everyone each month. Money owed to the Student Loans Company, to people you know, and on interest-free overdrafts should be the last debts you repay – they're not going to grow bigger too quickly. As you are not earning anything, or you're earning only a little from part-time jobs, you may be able to defer some of your debts until after you graduate and get a job.

If there's anything you've missed a payment on, you need to write to the companies involved, and explain your financial situation. Offer to make reduced payments and pay the debt off over a longer period of time. Surprisingly, most companies are likely to go for this option. It's much cheaper for them to get their money back in this way because it costs so much to take legal action against you or send in bailiffs. If you have borrowed money from someone who has suckered you into an unfair credit agreement, i.e. they're a loan shark, you should seek free legal advice immediately. You may be able to get the payments drastically reduced or even have the agreement cancelled. If anyone you owe money to is threatening you with court proceedings, or has already started them, you urgently need to get advice from an organisation such as a Citizens' Advice Bureau, or the National Debtline. Harassment from your creditors, such as making nuisance visits and phone calls, or using threatening and abusive language, is illegal. If you are suffering from the actions of an unscrupulous creditor, get in touch with your student advice service, the local Citizens' Advice Bureau or the police, immediately.

Although it may seem tempting, avoid commercial companies that offer to consolidate your debts. They exist because they make a profit from you, and although your monthly payments may seem smaller, you will be paying them off for many more years. It's possible to end up paying out two or three times more than you borrowed in the first place. In the long run, you will be thousands of pounds worse off. There are several free advice services that can help you to manage your debts much more effectively, so use them instead. Maximise your income: make sure you're getting all the benefits you're entitled to, you're not paying too much tax, and you have a part-time job that hopefully doesn't interfere with your studies. If you have any savings then use them to pay off your debts, because although it's hard to wave goodbye to your emergency fund, it's the most cost-effective option.

If your debts have been aggravated by addictions to alcohol, drugs or gambling, you need to get to the root of these problems to avoid yet more trouble in the future. For advice on out-of-control gambling, try the GamCare helpline on 0845 6000 133, open daily from 10 a.m. to 10 p.m. For free and confidential information about drugs, call the Talk to Frank helpline on 0800 77 66 00 (open 24 hours). If you are having problems with alcohol, try speaking to someone from Drinkline by telephoning 0345 320202.

Paying debts off can take years, but if it's done according to a sensible plan you don't need to suffer from terrible hardship. Some people choose to be declared bankrupt to avoid their creditors, but think very carefully about this option, as it's not as simple as it first appears. Any assets you have may still be used to pay off your debts, you'll have to close your bank or building society account, and it can make it difficult to get credit even for household utility bills. It takes one to three years before you can be discharged from bankruptcy, your credit rating will be damaged for six years, and you'll still have to pay back everything you owe to the Student Loans Company as this particular debt will not be wiped out.

COPING WITH DEBT STRESS

Large, out-of-control debts are highly stressful. If you take steps to make your debts more manageable, you should find the emotional strain lessens, but it could still weigh heavily on your mind. Try not to keep it bottled up, it's better to talk to someone about it instead of suffering on your own. You can talk to a mate, a partner or family members, or you may prefer to speak to someone confidentially. In that case, try your student union, the university counselling service or a non-profit debt service that can give you specialist support and advice.

RELIABLE SOURCES OF DEBT HELP

CITIZENS' ADVICE BUREAUX

The largest providers of free and impartial money and debt help in the UK. Your nearest bureau will be listed in your local phone book, or you can look it up online at: www.nacab.org.uk. They also have an advice website at: www.adviceguide.org.uk.

NATIONAL DEBTLINE

Provide free telephone advice for anyone having problems with their personal finances in England, Wales or Scotland.

Telephone: 0808 808 400, or website: www.nationaldebtline.co.uk.

THE CONSUMER CREDIT COUNSELLING SERVICE

A charity that specialises in helping people to put together debt management plans to sort out their finances.

Telephone: 0800 138 1111 or visit www.cccs.co.uk.

THE STUDENT DEBTLINE

Staffed by counsellors who are trained to understand student loans and other benefits to which students are entitled.

Telephone: 0800 328 1813, open 8 a.m. to 8 p.m., Monday to Friday.

MONEY SAVING TIPS

Bright ideas from the students on www.virginstudent.com

'Believe it or not, doing a bit of study costs nothing. There are students who are reeeealy bored and go out to spend money, but they have an assignment in next week. Hmm, something wrong there. I'm the same. Isn't hindsight a wonderful thing?'

'GET A JOB! Students who sit on their arses moaning that they are bored and have no money but refuse to work get on my nerves! It doesn't have to be anything drastic, just weekends, that extra 50 quid a week is well worth it. And you also gain a circle of friends separate to your uni ones which is always good. If you are sensible it won't eat too much into your assignment time, despite what some people say.'

'If you're in your own house, check around for the best deals on gas, electric and combo deals from companies. We saved a bloomin fortune! Just make sure if the cost per unit is low that there isn't a whopping standing charge.'

'NUS – use it! Abuse it! "Do you take NUS/ give NUS discount?" should be voiced at every opportunity. If you can't be arsed to say it . . . wear a badge with it on or sumthin.'

'Bite the bullet. Buy the cheap food. Choose the Savers over the Finest range or whatever. It all comes out the same in the end. But don't buy the white label vodka *shudders*'

'If you're the "live for the moment" kind of person then you won't think twice about getting a Hardship Loan, which is £500, or a Hardship Fund (which you don't have to pay back). But do be wary, only go for it if you really need it. They will scrutinise your past bank statements so that XBox you just bought on your card won't do you any favours!'

'Instead of spending loads of money on nights out in town, just gather your mates and get to the student union. You're guaranteed not to spend even half what you would in town.'

7. WORK AND CAREERS

Whether it's just a bit of spare cash to pay for your social life or the start of your brilliant career, you need to have a good idea of what you want and how to get it. It's also good to know how the tax system works, so that you're not paying too much out each month. After graduation the majority of students are not quite sure about the career they'd like to have, but it can be useful to find a focus of interest and some ways to narrow down these choices, and to make a jobhunting plan.

This chapter includes information on:

- **Common part-time jobs for students**
- **Holiday work at home and abroad**
- **Work experience, placements and projects**
- **Tax for students and workers' rights**
- **Jobhunting and the maze of career choices**

PART-TIME JOBS

Over 40 per cent of students take on part-time jobs during term time, working for an average of 13 hours per week. According to the Student Living Report 2003, the main reasons given for working include wanting a bit of extra cash, paying for basic essentials, or paying for social life, new clothes and music, or mobile phones. An increasing number of students say they have to work just to survive.

Many think that having to work and study at the same time is one of the worst aspects of university life, and more than a third of students who are currently working say that it adversely affects their university studies. Students from working-class backgrounds are the most likely to say that their paid work is interfering with their academic performance, probably because they work longer hours on average, and their parents are less able to lend them money. The National Union of Students recommends that students do not work more than ten hours per week.

If you're going to get a part-time job, think about what you want before you set out on your search. Decide on the ideal hours you'd like to work, how far you're willing to travel and the types of work you're prepared to do.

Pros	Cons
A source of extra money	Can interfere with study
Good to put on your CV	Employment tends to be poorly paid
A way to make new friends and contacts	Work can be menial and boring
Helps develop transferable skills	

WHERE TO FIND WORK

The best place to start looking for jobs is around the university. There may be term-time work available on campus in the bars and shops. Local employers may place ads on jobs notice boards in the student union, with the careers service or at the job shop. If your university has a job shop, pay them a visit as they can give you specialist advice about the local employment market and jobs most suitable for your circumstances. The National Association of Student Employment Services (NASES) covers all student job shops in the UK, and has a website listing all their contact details at: www.nases.org.uk.

You can also try:

- **Asking around. Friends who work in bars and restaurants with a high turnover of staff could put a good word in for you. Try relatives and neighbours too.**

- **Commercial websites. Many of them have part-time or temporary work, sometimes in special student sections, such as the one on www.hotrecruit.com.**

- **Your local job centre**

- **Local papers and magazines**

- **Recruitment agencies**

- **Front windows of shops, bars and restaurants**

If there's nothing suitable on offer, take the initiative. Make a CV (see later in this chapter for how to write one), print off a few copies and hit the high street. Drop in on anyone you like the look of who might be hiring, and ask to see the manager or personnel officer, making sure that you look the part. Bigger companies prefer you to look smart and not too individual, so think about what your clothes, piercings and hairstyle are saying about you. The opposite tends to be true of fashion shops and many bars and clubs. Even if there's nothing currently on offer, if you make a good impression with an employer, they'll call you back eventually.

You might like to work part time in different jobs throughout your degree, to broaden your experience. This can go in your favour if you decide to work your way around the world, or suddenly find yourself unemployed at a later date and need something to fall back on.

WHAT TO EXPECT

The most frequent sources of part-time work for students tend to be found in retail, bars, clerical or office work, catering, and call centres. They tend to fit in around lectures, and working hours are often quite flexible.

- **Retail jobs are relatively easy to find, and high street stores, DIY warehouses, smaller shops and supermarkets all need extra staff at weekends or during the evenings. May involve sore feet, unflattering polyester uniforms or temperamental tills, or benefits such as free meals or staff discounts.**

- **Bar work can start quickly once you've got the job, and there's the possibility of tips and socialising after the shifts. Usually finish late – insist on a free taxi. Can be tiring and messy, or involve dealing with aggressive or lecherous customers.**

- **Office jobs can be anything from reception work to mind-numbing filing tasks, but can pay OK and don't get your hands too dirty. May have a regular employer or move from place to place with a temping agency.**

- **Catering covers everything from fast food to cafés, staff canteens to high-class restaurants. You could be flipping burgers, washing up, making smoothies in a health food café or doing silver service at weekend events for an agency. You may go home exhausted and reeking of chip fat, and tips are variable.**

- **Call centres can be a high-pressure environment, and you need an excellent phone manner for telesales or customer care lines. If you're working in sales, be wary of employers offering low wages and high commission unless you know the market and can sell well.**

OTHER PART-TIME INCOME

Door staff: Security people, stewards and ushers are needed for clubs, football matches, racing events, concerts, cinemas and theatres.

Your own business: Run regular or occasional club nights, a market stall or a baby-sitting or dog-walking service.

Teaching: Offer English conversation lessons to overseas students, or pass on your expertise in dance, rock climbing, life saving, guitar playing or surfing. Certified instructors are in demand.

Brand manager: Help companies market products to your fellow students, and feed back on what the students think of the brands.

Modelling: Hard to break into, but can pay very well if you have the right look. Target the big agencies first, take someone along with you to meetings for safety, and never part with any money for them to put your portfolio together.

Extra work: Being in the background in films pays about £80 per day, and can involve much waiting around. Avoid dodgy agencies by checking with www.hiddenextra.com first.

Guinea pig: Be experimented on by drug companies, university departments or surgeons. Make sure the experiment has been approved by an independent ethics committee, and be aware you may be taking a serious risk.

Sperm donor: Guys can get £15 plus reasonable expenses for each donation, but there are health checks to attend and other requirements. Only do this if you are completely comfortable with the idea of mini-yous running around that you'll probably never see.

Courier work: If you have a bicycle, motorbike or can drive a delivery van, you're in with a chance. Don't get duped into carrying anything illegal.

SAFETY

Be careful when replying to advertisements or signing up with agencies, and remember that anything that sounds too good to be true often is. The wages may be lower than advertised, or the work could be in a legal grey area. Jobs such as lap dancing and escort work may sound glamorous and the money may be tempting, but there is a high risk of assault and there are often links to organised crime. If an employer wants to interview you away from the workplace or employment agency, be very wary. Check employment agencies out to see if they have a good reputation and treat their workers fairly. During an interview, find out as much as you can about the job and whether or not it's suitable or safe. Trust your instincts and if you get a bad feeling about the company or the interviewer then make up an excuse and leave quickly.

GETTING PAID

Students do have to pay income tax and national insurance contributions, sorry! Tax is usually deducted from your earnings by your employer, and the amount deducted should appear on your payslip. You are not taxed on all of your earnings; everyone has a personal tax-free allowance and currently you can earn up to £4,615 per tax year, which runs from 6 April to 5 April the following year, without anything being deducted. This allowance includes taxable income such as wages and tips, or interest from savings, and non-taxable income such as loans, parental contributions and any academic funding. Fill in a P46 form if you're working part time during term to make sure you don't end up paying too much tax.

Most students don't earn enough to pay National Insurance (NI) contributions, which are only charged on income of more than £89 per week. You still need an NI number to work in the UK though; it looks something like this: JX 34 25 16 B, and if you don't have one you should contact your local tax office. For more information about tax issues, contact your local tax office and ask for leaflet IR60 'Students and the Inland Revenue', or look online at: www.inlandrevenue.gov.uk. If you think you've been overcharged, you can claim the tax back (see www.inlandrevenue.gov.uk/taxback for details).

European Economic Area students are all able to work in the UK and pay the same rate of tax as any British citizen. Non-European Economic Area students are restricted to working 20 hours per week or less during term time if their passport has a 'restricted' stamp, and those with 'prohibited' stamps cannot work. The DfES produce a work leaflet aimed at international students, and it can also be seen online at: www.dfes.gov.uk/international-students/workleaflet.pdf.

Students who have children and work for 16 hours a week or more, or have a partner who works, may be eligible for Working Families' Tax Credit. Call helpline: 0845 609 5000, textphone: 0845 606 6668, or see leaflet WFTC/BK1 'Your guide to Working Families' Tax Credit'. If you are disabled you could get Disabled Person's Tax Credit if you work for 16 hours a week or more. Call helpline: 0845 605 5858, textphone: 0845 608 8844, or see leaflet DPTC/BK1 'Your guide to Disabled Person's Tax Credit'.

Everyone should make sure that they're getting at least the national minimum wage. The 'development rate' for workers aged 18–21 increased to £3.80 per hour in October 2003, and is £4.50 for workers aged 22 and over. Call the National Minimum Wage helpline on 0845 6000 678 for more details or to make complaints, or look at www.tiger.gov.uk or www.dti.gov.uk/er/nmw to see if you're being paid fairly.

YOUR RIGHTS

Part-time workers are often confused about their rights. For example, if you're working longer than six hours at a time, you're entitled to a break of at least 20 minutes. The relationship between you and your employer is determined by your employment contract, so read it carefully. A spoken contract is legally binding too. Everyone has the right to work in a place which is safe, and your employer is responsible for providing adequate insurance cover and training you in health and safety issues. For more safety information, contact The Health and Safety Executive's infoline on: 0541 545500, or see their website: www.hse.gov.uk.

You also have statutory rights: all workers must be treated fairly and you should not be discriminated against because of your sex, race, disability or trade union membership. The Trade Union Congress have a 'Know Your Rights' helpline, call 0870 600 4 882, and a student help section on their website: www.tuc.org.uk/tuc/students_main.cfm. Contact The Advisory, Conciliation and Arbitration Service (Acas) for information and advice on a range of employment law matters, by phoning 08457 47 47 47. There's also an excellent website called www.troubleatwork.org.uk run by UNISON which has comprehensive content aimed at student workers.

HOLIDAY WORK

You can stay in Britain or combine work and travel to go just about anywhere in the world. Students who stay in this country often end up doing:

- **Clerical work and other office temping. The worker drones are in the sun for two weeks, replace them.**

- **Factory work on production lines or in packing rooms**
- **The usual suspects: bars, restaurants, fast-food outlets**
- **Shop work, such as extra cover for the Christmas rush**
- **Call centre cover, because the industry has such a rapid turnover of staff**
- **Work in the tourism and leisure industry: tour guides, lifeguards, deckchair attendants, souvenir sales, arts and music festival work**
- **Outdoor work: labouring, decorating, agricultural work such as planting or harvesting**

This kind of work is mostly done to pay off some of the debts that build up during term time, but if you have a career path forming in your head then you can create relevant experience for your CV. This doesn't have to be exactly what you want to do when you graduate, it could simply be in the general subject area. For example, if you wanted to work in media, you could get employed helping out with some aspect of the Edinburgh Arts Festival, or work in your local theatre.

If you're going to work in the UK during vacations, and don't expect to exceed your personal tax allowance, you should ask your employer to obtain form P38(S). This allows them to pay you your wages without deducting any tax.

Holiday work will be advertised in your university job shop, local temp agencies, your nearest job centre and on websites such as www.totaljobs.com, www.hotrecruit.co.uk and www.summerjobs.co.uk. There's also *Summer Jobs in Britain 2004* by Andrew James and David Woodworth, Vacation Work Publications, £10.99, which lists details of over 30,000 vacancies in the UK.

Working holidays abroad can be backbreaking or badly paid, but there's the added advantage of doing some independent travelling before or after the employment period. You might like the look of some of the following:

- **Teaching English as a foreign language (more about this in Chapter 10)**
- **Fruit or vegetable harvesting**
- **Chalet work or ski instruction**
- **Archaeological or conservation work**
- **Crewing on cruise ships or yachts**
- **Working with kids in holiday camps**

BUNAC offer non-profit overseas work/travel programmes that mostly fit into a long summer abroad, including Summer Camp USA. Write to BUNAC, 16 Bowling Green Lane, London, EC1R 0QH, telephone: 020 7251 3472, fax: 020 7251 0215, website: www.bunac.org.uk.

Have a look through *Summer Jobs Abroad 2004* by Andrew James and David Woodworth, Vacation Work Publications, £10.99. This guidebook gives details of summer jobs in Europe, Australasia, USA and beyond. Or you could try *Work Your Way Around the World* by Susan Griffith, Vacation Work Publications, £12.95.

WORK PLACEMENTS

Relevant work experience can give you a competitive edge over other graduates when you enter the job market. If you're not scoring top points academically, you could still beat a 'straight-A' student hands down by arranging the right practical experience. After all, companies want to see you've used your initiative to find a placement, show enthusiasm about their industry and have at least some idea of what the job entails. If you're with an employer for a long period you should get a reasonable wage, which will be taxed subject to the normal allowances.

WHY DO WORK EXPERIENCE?

- **Placements improve employment prospects**

- **There are some things you just can't get out of a textbook**

- **It's a chance to 'audition' the industry to see if it's right for you**

- **Gives you self-confidence**

- **You earn while you learn**

- **Great way to build up contacts and get inside information**

- **It stops you going on holiday and blowing all your cash instead**

It's not necessarily about being stuck in an office. There are opportunities in all kinds of organisations, from charities and small businesses to government departments and major blue-chip companies. You could be out doing fieldwork or working with the public and so on. Speak to staff in your department to find out what kind of work experience they recommend, and whether they have contacts in particular industries who might be able to take you on. Make use of your careers service who should have an alarming array of magazines and factsheets, lists of local vacancies and details of work experience fairs. If there are particular companies that you'd like to work for, try calling their human resources departments or checking their websites for details of placement schemes.

WHAT'S AVAILABLE?

- **Part of your degree: sandwich courses, projects, professional practice**

- **Holiday and part-time employment**

- **Structured internships with large organisations**

- **Voluntary work**

- **Mentoring and tutoring**
- **Work shadowing**
- **Overseas placements and exchanges**

A good placement is set up with the aim of benefiting the student, rather than the people they're working for, so if you're sweeping the floor and getting paid peanuts, something has gone horribly wrong. You should have training, objectives, supervision and opportunities to ask questions and give feedback. Supervisors should protect your working rights, teach you and provide a detailed assessment at the end of the programme, preferably using the guidelines set out by your university department. Keep in touch with your tutors during longer placements, to make sure things are still on track and meeting the right standards. At the end of the placement, you should be able to tell a potential employer about everything you gained from doing it.

Start looking for work experience early, preferably doing more than one placement during your degree, and avoid the rush that happens in the final year. The Higher Education Careers Services Unit (CSU) runs the National Centre for Work Experience (NCWE), which is one of the best places to start an independent search. They have hundreds of vacancies, and recommendations for students and employers. They produce a yearly free magazine called *Focus on Work Experience* which is available from your university careers centre or can be ordered from their website. Write to NCWE, Prospects House, Booth Street East, Manchester, M13 9EP, telephone/fax: 0845 6015510, website: www.work-experience.org. Students in Wales also have Cymru Prosper Wales (CPW), telephone: 0800 917 7403, website: www.cpw.org.uk.

Careers Research and Advisory Centre (CRAC) run Insight Plus, an initiative that was established to provide a national award for undergraduate key skills development. See www.insightplus.co.uk for more information about their UK work experience schemes. If you're interested in working abroad try AIESEC (www.aisec.org) or AIPT (www.aipt.org) for exchanges and internships.

Rolls-Royce run a research project with the University of Bristol Aerospace department each year. It involved four of us doing two paid ten-week summer placements and working two days per week at Rolls during the academic year. This project was the equivalent of a final year project, but done in my third year. My normal third year design project then got done in the fourth year. To get a place we had to have a technical and psychological interview, but as this happened late in the second year, not many people applied – maybe a dozen.

The Rolls project was well handled by Rolls, but the university kept changing the goal posts and the marking requirements as they weren't quite sure what to do with it. Rolls were very happy, however. To get a place on the graduate training scheme we still had to pass the Rolls-Royce Assessment day. Whether we all passed or not is very doubtful, but Rolls had seen the work we were capable of and offered three of us a job anyway. This happened early in my fourth year which happily meant I could concentrate on my finals instead of job interviews like most of my peers – a good thing as I was working about 20 hours a week at a shop to live.

The job is pretty good fun on the whole, I feel pretty secure – just coming up to the end of my graduate training in a couple of months. There are a lot of opportunities so you can really make a go of it. There's a very big culture of continual development and training there.

Alec Groom – a recent graduate in Aeronautical Engineering at the University of Bristol

VOLUNTEERING

About 30 per cent of students undertake some volunteer work before they graduate, according to the UNITE and MORI Student Living Report 2003. It offers the chance to give something back to the local (or worldwide) community, to meet new friends and make work contacts, and it looks great on a CV. You can volunteer through your local volunteer bureau, or through your university's branch of the national network of Student Community Action Groups (SCA). There are 180 groups around the UK, and 25,000 students get involved every year. To find out more about SCA, contact Student Volunteering UK by writing to Oxford House, Derbyshire Street, London, E2 6HG. Telephone: 0845 4500219, website: www.studentvol.org.uk.

You can also contact the National Centre for Volunteering at Regents Wharf, 8 All Saints Street, London, N1 9RL, telephone: 020 7520 8900, fax: 020 7520 8910, website: www.volunteering.org.uk. If you're interested in volunteering abroad, you could start by looking at the Youth for Britain website: www.worldwidevolunteering.org.uk, which maintains a database of 250,000 volunteer opportunities for 16–25-year-olds, both in the UK and abroad.

JOBHUNTING TOOLS AND SKILLS

A CV, or curriculum vitae, is a summary of your skills and experience. If you write a fantastic CV that's easy to read, set out well, and contains just the right amount of information, you have a much better chance of getting an interview. This is doubly true if it's accompanied by a covering letter that entices the employer to read more. The sad fact is that most recruiters are frantically busy, and may have to look at 300 applicants per post. If a CV or application form is scrappy and hard to understand, or full of spelling mistakes, it'll be in the bin in seconds. If you get as far as the interview then it's a great achievement, you might be on a shortlist of six chosen out of 300 applicants. Be ready to build on that achievement; make the most of the interview and be well prepared for it.

WRITE THE KILLER CV

- Do your CV on a computer and always keep a backup copy. This will make it easier to update or tailor to specific jobs. You shouldn't keep sending the same one out again and again.

- Think about the format. Most employers will take your CV in an electronic format, usually a Word document. If you're sending a printed copy, use decent quality white paper and black ink.

- Write in a simple font such as Helvetica or Times New Roman. Lay the text out in a simple, easy to read style. Allow enough white space between the sections of text so the pages don't look too cramped.

- Most CVs should be kept to two pages in length.

- Write your name at the top of the page, not 'CV' or 'curriculum vitae'. It's bleedin' obvious that it's a CV, the employer can work that out for themselves.

- Divide text into sections for contact details, education, work experience and references. You may also wish to include sections for related activities, prizes and awards, computer literacy skills, personal career aims, or hobbies and interests.

- Don't waffle or use flowery language to try to fill up space because the reader will get bored. For example, include the predicted class of your degree if you can, but don't clutter the pages up with unnecessary detail such as a full breakdown of your GCSE results.

- If your work experience is minimal or doesn't look very interesting, try to think about skills it helped you gain. Time management, dealing with difficult people, working under pressure, supervising or training others, being trustworthy with cash or being a first-aider can all go in your favour.

- Use dynamic language such as 'designed', 'attended', 'devised', 'organised'.

- Say what you've learned from various experiences, especially if it might be useful in the job you're applying for.

- Strike a balance between being bland and quirky. Try to make yourself sound interesting without making the employer think you're so individual that you won't fit in with the rest of the organisation.

- **Show your CV to tutors, friends or the careers service. Ask people who know you whether the document presents you as positively as it should. Get it checked thoroughly for typing errors and grammatical mistakes.**

- **However tempting it may be, never put an outright lie on your CV. An increasing number of employers use fact-checking services to find out if you're telling the truth or not. Something you've added to make yourself sound more interesting may drop you right in it at a crucial point during an interview.**

- **If you're putting your CV in the post, send it out with a good covering letter, which should be addressed to a specific person, and use an A4 envelope so they arrive unfolded and easy to read. Use a first-class stamp.**

BEEF IT UP

If you think your CV looks a little 'thin' and you have some time on your hands, why not try a few activities to pep it up. Think about what personal qualities, experience or skills employers might be looking for. Perhaps these examples might help:

IT training: complete courses in the most up-to-date versions of software, especially if there's an industry standard you need to learn for a particular line of work.

People skills: work for the university's entertainments committee, be the chair of a club or society, join a team or band, or volunteer to be a course representative.

Initiative: do some independent travel, or set up an interest group or fundraising scheme.

Interest in the field of work: arrange work experience, or join relevant occupational bodies as a student member. Attend conferences or extra curricular lectures. Ask lecturers if you can help out with their research, even if it's only something simple such as data entry.

Dedication: try enrolling in a challenging activity such as the Millennium Volunteers scheme, or the Prince's Trust.

Responsibility: take on jobs where you're mentoring kids, handling money or supervising other people.

Communication: learn another language if you're thinking about working abroad or with international organisations, or perhaps write for the university newspaper.

Driving: make sure you have a full clean driving licence. Many jobs require you to drive.

For more CV tips, try *How to Write a Winning CV* by Alan Jones, Random House, £6.99.

THE COVERING LETTER

Many job advertisements ask you to send your CV in with a covering letter. Keep this letter to around one page in length, and make it lively and interesting if possible. Make sure it has your contact details and address on it, and mention where and when you saw the advertisement. Use the covering letter to explain why you're interested in the job, what experience you could bring to it, why you'd fit in well with the organisation, and any qualities you have that would give the edge over the competition. Refer to part of your CV in a way that will make them want to look through it. If you're asked to provide a handwritten covering letter, decide in advance exactly what you're going to put in it, and then write it out in your best handwriting. If you make a mistake don't use correction fluid, write it out again and make sure it's well spaced and easy to read. To keep the lines straight, place a sheet of lined paper under your plain paper and use it to keep everything roughly horizontal. If you're sending your CV in as an email attachment, treat your email as the covering letter and send in an introductory paragraph or two.

APPLICATION FORMS

Some organisations prefer you to fill in an application form rather than send in the traditional CV and covering letter. If you receive one, start by photocopying it a couple of times. Read the instructions very carefully to make sure you're filling it in properly. Practice filling in one of your photocopies before you go anywhere near the real thing. Find out as much as you can about the company and think hard about the type of graduates they want to recruit, then use your answers to highlight everything about you that makes you the ideal candidate. Stick to making important points, sound as dynamic as you can, don't write more text than the boxes allow and keep your writing neat and legible and not too small. Some forms say you can continue onto a spare sheet of paper with some of your answers, but avoid this unless it's absolutely necessary. Get someone to help check your answers, then fill the real form in and take your time. Make sure the form stays clean and uncreased, and don't get tea stains on it. It's best not to drink or smoke when filling it in, just in case. Take a photocopy of the final document for your own records, then return it by first-class post well before the deadline. If you are sent an application form as an email attachment, you can fill it in on your computer, and you don't have to worry about handwriting, but you still need to think hard about your answers and use the spell-checking facility.

TESTS AND ASSESSMENTS

Some companies ask applicants to attend testing centres before they will invite them in for a formal interview, as a way of picking out the ideal candidates and narrowing down numbers. The tests may vary and can include intelligence (IQ) tests, personality and values questionnaires, teamwork exercises, interviews, problem-solving challenges, creativity tests, presentations and many more. Don't be too intimidated by them, it's not as bad as an end of year exam. Find out well in advance what format the tests will take, and think of ways you can show the assessors that you have the right characteristics for the job. Turn up smartly dressed, be polite and pleasant, and if you're reasonably intelligent and have a smattering of social skills, you should get through the assessments just fine. There's usually time to prepare beforehand, and you can improve your reasoning skills by trying a few puzzle books or tests to sharpen your wits, or invest in a book such as *How to Succeed at an Assessment Centre* by Harry Tolley and Bob Wood, Kogan Page, £7.99. Your university careers service will also have information to help you prepare, and may be able to tell you which types of testing particular employers use.

INTERVIEWS

If you're offered an interview then you're in with a serious chance of getting the job. Prepare for it as well as you can by:

- **Looking back at their advertisement**

- **Reviewing the copy of the CV and covering letter that you sent to them**

- **Finding out as much as you can about the company if you haven't already done so**

- **Checking with the employer to see if you need to prepare anything such as a presentation or a portfolio of work, and finding out what format the interview will take**

- **Thinking about questions you might be asked in the interview**

- **Doing practice interviews or brushing up your interview technique with help from a careers adviser, or answering questions in front of a mirror**

- **Working out exactly where their offices are, and how you're going to arrive there in plenty of time for the interview**

- **Putting together one or two questions of your own for the interviewers**

- **Sorting out your appearance**

- **Keeping in touch with the news in case you're asked topical questions**

First impressions are very important at an interview, and your words only make up about 7 per cent of that impression. Make sure you are dressed correctly, and use good non-verbal communication. Find out in advance what most people who work in the organisation wear, and go for something similar, but if in doubt choose something smart. If it's a formal environment such as a legal firm, wear a suit. Get your hair cut, clean your shoes, and make sure your clothes are spotless and in good condition. You don't need designer clothing, just something that fits you well and suits you. Try wearing new shoes around the house to break them in before the interview or you'll end up limping and blistered. The night before, pack your bag with the interview letter, your CV, the employer's contact details and a map of their location. Lay out your clothes so they're ready for the morning. Make sure you've eaten a proper breakfast before leaving the house and go easy on the coffee or you'll end up feeling jittery.

Arrive ten minutes early for your interview and check your appearance in a mirror before going in to meet people. If you have sweaty palms, wipe them on a tissue. When you're introduced to your interviewers, make eye contact, smile, shake hands firmly and say 'hello'. You'll be invited to take a seat, and may be offered a drink. If you get clumsy when you're nervous, it's best to turn the drink down unless you have a very dry throat, in case you spill it. Sit up straight in your chair and try not to fidget.

The format of the interview can vary. You may have one interviewer, a series of different interviewers or a panel interview. In panel interviews you have several people interviewing you at the same time, including someone who is a specialist in the area, and someone from the human resources department. Make eye contact with the person who is talking to you, but try not to stare at them. Don't look down at the table when you're talking, and try to look interested and confident. If you're in a panel interview, look mainly at whoever asked the most recent question, but glance at the other interviewers from time to time.

Check your body language throughout the interview. Avoid crossing your arms as this is a defensive gesture. If your hands get shaky when you're nervous, or you have a tendency to wave them around too much, you can try folding them loosely on your lap. Sit up straight or lean slightly forwards to look confident and motivated. Consciously try to relax your body, but don't create the impression that you're so relaxed you could fall asleep, it will make you seem either dopey or cocky.

Think about your voice. If possible, match it to the speed of the interviewer's delivery, and perhaps their tone (although if one of you is a squeaky female and the other is a bass baritone male this one's a complete no-no). Sound enthusiastic. Avoid talking in a boring monotone, and try not to rabbit on at high speed, both of which can happen when you're under pressure. Make sure you don't swear, or use too much slang or jargon.

The interviewers will probably tell you a few things about the company, ask you some questions about your CV or application form and then ask you some other general questions. You may also be asked to give a short presentation, talk through some of the items in your portfolio or take an aptitude test.

COMMON QUESTIONS:
- **Why should I give you this job?**
- **Tell me about something you've achieved that you're proud of.**
- **Tell me about something that didn't go so well.**
- **How would your friends or colleagues describe you?**
- **Describe a situation where you had to overcome an obstacle.**
- **What is your career goal, and where would you like to be five years from now?**
- **What have you gained from your work experience, travels or degree?**

You may also be given a hypothetical situation, such as: 'Your boss comes in at 5.25 p.m. and asks you to work late on something urgent. You have a prior arrangement to meet someone at 5.40 p.m. What do you do?' In this case, err on the side of being professional or showing personal integrity.

ANSWERING QUESTIONS:

- **Take your time and don't rush. Take a slow quiet breath in and out before answering.**

- **If you don't understand the question, ask the interviewer to clarify what they're asking you about.**

- **Always sound positive and never speak badly of anyone even if you think they're a total arsehole. Talk about their admirable qualities, and less admirable qualities in a dispassionate way, and try not to choke.**

- **If you're asked to talk about negative things such as your weaknesses, don't list too many of them, and go for 'weaknesses' that can be positive. For, example, you could say you have very high standards for your work and yourself. Or mention something that is not essential to the job.**

- **If you're asked about something that didn't go so well, be honest about it, then explain what you've learned from the experience and how you would handle things differently next time.**

- **Avoid giving one-word, or abrupt, answers, at least stretch it out to a sentence or two. Always back up your comments with examples of your personal experience.**

- **Try not to say 'um' or 'er'.**

- **Don't lie or act fake, the truth will eventually come out.**

At the end of the interview, you should be given the chance to ask some questions of your own. Pick two or three good ones that suggest you already know something about the company and would like to know more, and that you're ambitious and enthusiastic about working for them. For example, asking about how the company rewards good work is better than asking how much paid leave you get every year. When it's all over, shake hands again and say 'thank you' before you leave. If you don't hear from them within the agreed time, follow it up with a polite phone call.

Increase your interview repertoire further with *Perfect Interview* by Max Eggert, Random House £6.99, or *Successful Interview Skills* by Rebecca Corfield, Kogan Page, £7.99.

YOUR BRILLIANT CAREER

If you want a career, as opposed to a job where you work from nine to five and watch the clock all day, you need to know what kind of person you are and what motivates you. This should provide some suggestions for the type of work you might be best suited for. You then need to know how to find these jobs, and how to apply for them successfully.

SO, WHO THE HELL ARE YOU?

People who are successful in their careers all have one thing in common: a sense of purpose. Perhaps you have this already, but don't despair if your ideas are still fuzzy at this stage. To find your sense of purpose you have to dig deep to work out what makes you tick, then begin to select the types of work that suit your personal style and values. This navel-gazing at the start of your search helps to bring all your best qualities to the fore, and actually saves time even though you are reflecting on things and rolling ideas around in your head. Job-hunting is an intensive, time-consuming business and it's best not to take too many wrong turnings. Once you know what you want, you can make a better plan for how you're going to go out and get it. There are many elements to cover, including the following.

INTERESTS

When you're doing a job that holds your interest there are moments when it feels like you're being paid to do a hobby. Could you honestly stomach the thought of doing a job that bores you senseless for the next 40 weeks, let alone 40 years? Probably not. Pay some serious thought to what inspires you for the next few days. You could also try writing down a list of 15 things you enjoy doing: underneath the usual 'sex, booze and eating pizza' entries you might find something to work with. Perhaps there are things you love but don't do very often – could they be a key to a career?

PERSONALITY

Off the top of your head, try picking six words to describe your personality. You could be: confident, shy, talkative, analytical, creative, reliable, easy-going, determined, calm, idealistic, cautious, friendly, ambitious or any of a hundred other qualities. The university careers centre should have a number of personality tests that you can take to get a better overview of your temperament, and there are a few quality ones available for free on the internet. These questionnaires perform best if you are as honest as possible when filling them in, and put what you truly think and feel, rather than what you think you should be saying. Well-known resources used in industry include the Myers-Brigg Type Indicator and the Keirsey Temperament Sorter.

STRENGTHS

Everyone has their own special set of strengths and weaknesses, but may not be completely aware of them. One big eye-opener is to ask several people who know you to write down what they think your greatest strengths are. Pick people from all walks of life, some who have known you for many years and others who have known you for a few months or so. You may find they value many things about you that you were previously unaware of, or that you tend to place a lesser importance on. If you have ten of these lists in front of you, a strong pattern may emerge. If you're feeling brave, make a list of your weaknesses too. You can work on them to reduce their impact, or pick a career where they're not going to matter too much.

SKILLS

Ability in particular areas can be divided into 'hard' skills and 'soft' skills. Hard skills include IT training, being able to drive a car and so on, and if you don't have either of these already then you need to take steps to learn them. Employers are also looking for graduates who can demonstrate well-developed soft skills, such as effective communication, teamwork, negotiation, time management, problem-solving and commercial awareness. Employers sometimes talk about 'transferable' skills. These are simply skills that remain useful when you go from one job to the next, and maybe you already use them every day without even thinking about it. They include a mixture of hard and soft skills, such as the ability to use email or managing to get out of bed before lunchtime.

VALUES

These are the things you hold dear to your heart, and the right job for you has to match up closely with your top values. Values include how your job relates to society in general, plus external factors that can be measured such as salary, perks or the building you're based in. So, what floats your boat? Is it being independent, having authority, being accepted, doing good deeds for others, being important or being treated with consideration? Organisations have their own values and it's important to look for places where these have enough in common with your own. There are several helpful tests to get you thinking about your values; you can take them online or at your careers centre.

Particular outcomes for questionnaires suggest you may be suited to certain types of jobs, although they are not set in stone and should be treated as an approximate guide. It can be helpful to talk these suggestions through with an adviser, who can give you more information on these career paths and the range of jobs that lie within them.

GO GET THAT JOB!

Make friends with your university careers service early on in your course. Get a thorough understanding of your personality and values, and use this to find broad career paths that you might be interested in, as well as researching anything else that catches your imagination. The centre can offer:

- **Testing and interviews to help you find out what type of work might suit you best**
- **A CV service**
- **Books, booklets and leaflets about certain jobs**
- **Lists of vacancies**
- **Detailed advice about local employers**

- **Information about grants, work experience and post-graduate funding**

- **Seminars about subjects such as interview technique**

GATHERING IDEAS

Use careers advice from the university, job websites or handbooks to find out the range of jobs in these areas, and begin to narrow it down to a smaller range of job titles. Tip: do bear in mind that some of the more unusual or cutting-edge forms of employment may not always be suggested to you, or that the perfect job might not even exist yet and is waiting to be invented.

Research each of these jobs thoroughly. Find out about the qualifications and skills needed, the major employers, starting salary and speed of career progression. Read magazines, newspapers and journals to get a feel for the industry. Attend careers fairs, which may be advertised in the student press, higher education sections of newspapers or on notice boards around campus. If you know anyone who works in any of these jobs already, ask them what the scope is for employment, which employer has the best reputation, what the corporate culture is like and what they look for in graduates. While you are doing your research, keep building on your core skills. If you're lacking any that would be useful for your targeted lines of work, start thinking of ways that you could build them up. Do you need lessons, work experience or general life experience?

MOVE INTO ACTION

Prepare a killer CV as you start looking for suitable jobs (look at some of the tips in the Jobhunting Tools section p. 139). Be prepared to tailor each CV to match each type of job. You don't have to lie, it just means that you place the emphasis on different aspects of your work experience, qualifications, skills or personal aims. You can find advertised vacancies:

- **On careers centre lists**

- **At your university job shop**

- **In the local job centre**

- **In the graduate section of newspapers**

- **At employment agencies**

- **On graduate employment websites and email listings**

Start applying for jobs that catch your eye. Write or email in for application forms, or send in a CV and covering letter if requested. If a job looks fantastic but asks for a large portfolio of your work, or requires you to complete a report or project, make the effort and send them what they want. Many potential applicants are put off by time-consuming application processes, so at least that's less competition for you from the start. Although many undergraduates start applying for paid employment in their final academic year, you may be able to apply for some jobs long before this, and it could beat the rush. It can also be quite a strain if you're frantically looking for work in the spring at the same time as you're preparing for your final exams.

INCREASE YOUR CHANCES

Milk rounds are days or evenings when employers come to the university to look for the brightest graduates. Keep an eye out for these, and attend any that sound interesting. Take your CV along with you, and make a point of chatting with the recruiters to find out as much as you can about the company. Also go along to any nearby recruitment fairs, and treat them as though they were mini-interviews. Wear something smart, and turn up early in the day to beat the queues. Get a floor plan of all the exhibitors and target a handful of the ones that look most suitable, then later in the day you can go up and chat to the other recruiters to see if there's anything interesting that you'd missed.

Make the jobs come to you. Research individual organisations thoroughly with help from the careers centre, and get in touch with their human resources department, or check their website regularly for opportunities. Ring them up, ask them a few prepared questions and try to find out whether or not they'll be hiring new staff in the next few months. Even if they aren't currently recruiting, ask them if you can send your details in – if they like the sound of you they'll put your CV on file and may contact you at a later date.

Attend interviews, or preliminary testing sessions, bearing in mind all the tips and pointers in the section below. After the interview, if you haven't heard back about the job in the timeframe they gave you, it's OK to give them a quick phone call or drop them a line to see what's happening. If you are rejected don't be too disheartened, successful people tend to be the ones who don't give up after a few knock-backs. Write to the organisation and ask for some feedback, and try to learn from it.

THE FINAL PHASE

If the interview goes well you will be offered the position and a starting salary. The employer might expect you to ask for more money at this point, and you can negotiate for a little extra if you know the wage is less than the industry standard. You may decide to accept less money if the work is for a prestigious firm offering a low starting salary that rises quickly, or if there are many perks such as an excellent pension or a company car, or top quality training for fast-track graduates.

If you have more than one job offer on the table, you may be able to play employers off against one another, but don't be too greedy. Go for the job that's going to meet your needs and give you good long-term prospects, and talk it through with a careers adviser if necessary. Once you've decided to accept a particular offer, put it in writing that you're accepting the job, making sure you mention the specific title and salary. You may have to meet certain conditions before getting the job, such as passing a medical or getting a certain class of degree. The organisation will then send you an employment contract to sign, which you should check through thoroughly. Then all you have to do is start working. See Chapter 10 for tips on how to settle into your new job. If you decide to decline an offer, write to them as soon as you've made your mind up and be very polite, remembering to say thanks and that you regret you will not be able to take the job.

PAID WORK

CV fillers from the students at www.virginstudent.com

'For the summer in France I was in charge of the Go-Karts which was great. I got to ride around for free everyday, just to teach the juniors to drive.'

'Supermarkets suck! They won't arrange shifts to vaguely suit a student and they are just boring. I can't listen to 80s music anymore because it reminds me of working in one.'

'Proofreading is ideal for those students who have lots of time on their hands. The work is kinda casual so you can do it on the train, during the day, at night if you wish, or at those times when you are just bored.'

'Waiting on is good, as long as you're working with people your own age you can have a real laugh. Most places will shift hours around to suit you.'

'Office junior, got treated like a total dogsbody.'

'Don't write off all bar work as rubbish, you just have to work in a good bar that's all. I love my job, because the people, customers and music are fantastic so I always have a great time when I work. And I basically work whatever shifts I want.'

'No such thing as a good part-time job, just be grateful you are earning. Working is just about earning so you can live and survive.'

'Done telesales and fruit packing, also I was one of the people (mugs) that stuck the pens on the front of quiz magazines.'

'I used to work in one of the busiest night clubs in my town and I loved it! Sure people will bitch that you're taking too long with their order but let's be honest if they've ordered 6 pints it's not like you can just pull them out of the fridge is it?'

'I was an ice-cream man a couple of summers ago. Ah, the sweet sound of those chimes . . .'

8. HEALTH AND STRESS

Student health services are there to be used, which is just as well because they're often snowed under. The commonest reasons for students consulting their doctor are mental and emotional distress, contraception, sexually transmitted infections and sports injuries. Sexual health, contraception, alcohol poisoning and drug-related emergencies are all covered in Chapter 4, and this chapter covers the remaining information, including:

- **What practical and financial help is available**
- **A few tricks for keeping yourself healthy**
- **How to spot meningitis and what to do**
- **Common germs you'd prefer to avoid**
- **Mental and emotional health problems**
- **Other common student ailments and injuries**

HEALTH SERVICES
If you're attending a large university there will usually be a designated student health centre on campus. Staffing varies from college to college, but there will normally be at least one or two GPs and a nurse available most weekdays. Many have specialist training in treating problems that commonly affect young people, such as sports injuries, sexual health or mental health. Seeing a doctor or nurse is mainly done by appointment only, but there may also be drop-in sessions where you can just turn up and try your luck. If it's something urgent, they will also see you as an emergency appointment. All visits to a doctor are completely confidential.

You may also have a dentist and counsellors or psychologists at the Student Health Centre. Counselling is sometimes arranged through student welfare services, or may have its own building. The reception area or waiting room of a student health centre will have leaflets or other information about various health problems, what services are available and the hours that they operate. Write down the phone number for student health and keep it somewhere safe in case of emergencies.

Join up in your first week of uni, when you aren't too busy, and save loads of hassle later. Yes, it's tempting to put it off when you feel perfectly well and the union bar is beckoning, but let's face it, we all get ill sometimes and it always happens when you least expect it. There's nothing worse than having to fill in loads of forms when you're stuck in a packed waiting room and feeling unwell. Although you're advised to sign up with student health as soon as you can when you first arrive, that doesn't mean it's compulsory to use it. You might decide that you're not keen on the particular doctor or dentist that you first meet, for whatever reason. If that's the case, it's relatively easy to go to another practitioner at the same centre, or sign up with a different non-university practice.

Smaller colleges don't tend to have their own health centre, but when you arrive you will be offered information about recommended local GPs whose lists are open (i.e. practices which still have places for new patients). Again, it's better to sign up with a doctor when you arrive. Many local GPs will see unregistered or new patients as emergency cases, but you will probably be asked for identification, and may face a long wait if the surgery is busy.

HEALTH BENEFITS

In England and Scotland, if you are a full-time student under the age of 19 you should get NHS prescriptions, dental treatment and sight tests free. Other students on a low income, or who have chronic medical conditions, should fill in Form HC1 to apply for free or reduced-cost prescriptions and other fees. You can pick one up from any Social Security Office and most health centres. Young people living in Wales get free NHS prescriptions, and free courses of dental treatment before their 25th birthday.

WHEN TO CALL AN AMBULANCE

It's safer to err on the side of caution rather than hope for the best, so don't be scared to call 999 and ask for an ambulance. It's obvious that you'd contact the emergency services if someone was bleeding heavily or having a severe asthma attack, for example, but here are some common examples of situations where someone needs urgent medical attention, but people might think twice about calling for help:

- **Someone has been knocked unconscious, even for a few seconds, after an accident or attack.**

- **Anyone might be having, or have had, a fit (seizure).**

- **Someone is showing possible signs of meningitis (see below for more details).**

- **Drug-related collapses, fits, violence or extreme paranoia. The hospital staff will not land the person in trouble with the police just for taking drugs, so make their health your first concern.**

- **Severe alcohol poisoning (see Chapter 4 for more details).**

It's also OK to walk in to the casualty department if you:

- **Need the 'morning-after' pill at the weekend or over a bank holiday and can't get hold of your GP or a pharmacy that sells it without prescription.**

- **Need emergency dental help at the weekend for broken teeth or bad toothache.**

- **Have been sexually assaulted or think you may have had your drink spiked.**

If you're still unsure, call the NHS Direct Helpline (0845 46 47, open 24 hours daily), and speak to a trained nurse for further information and directions.

STAYING HEALTHY

A FEW USEFUL 'FIRST-AID' ITEMS

It's good to have a mini-kit at hand for minor accidents and illnesses, or just the occasional aftermath of a big night out. Keep some mild painkillers at home such as paracetamol or ibuprofen, some plasters for cuts and grazes, and a tube of antiseptic cream. Many halls of residence and university houses will have a full first-aid kit. You might also want to attend a first-aid course with an organisation such as the Red Cross or St John Ambulance to learn skills that would make you more confident in an emergency. Even if you never need to use them, they'll look great to a potential employer when you include them on your CV.

SCREENING

Checking yourself out regularly can pick up illnesses before they become serious or even life-threatening. For example, everyone should keep an eye out for moles that spread, change colour, itch or bleed. Young men should be particularly aware of testicular cancer, which is relatively easy to cure if it's caught early enough. Get to know the shape and feel of your testicles, and check them out for any new lumps, bumps and tenderness. Most student health centres have leaflets readily available on how to check yourself. If you do find something, don't let those understandable feelings of fear or embarrassment make you delay visiting the doctor. They are professionals who have seen it all several times before, and are there to help you.

On a similar note, young women need to know about breast checks and cervical smear tests. Check your breasts every month, about a week after the end of your period. Look out for tender areas, lumps, tissue thickening, changes in the shape of the breast or the nipples, and for discharge or bleeding from the nipple. Although breast cancer is rare in young women, it is still possible to get it, so make an appointment to see your GP if you do find anything that worries you.

Depending on your local health authority, you'll be invited for a smear test every three years, either as soon as you reach a certain age (around 20) or when you tell your GP you're sexually active. It's a very simple procedure that looks for abnormal changes in cells at the neck of the womb (the cervix). A sterile instrument called a speculum is inserted into the vagina and the doctor or nurse takes a tiny scraping of cells from the cervix, which are then sent off to a lab for testing. It can be slightly uncomfortable, but is over in a few minutes, and gives peace of mind.

EATING OK

Yes, it's true, it really is hard to eat properly if you're rushing between lectures, part-time jobs and social events. The odd burger or skipped meal isn't going to kill you, but if you're eating junk food regularly you'll feel the effects sooner or later in your wallet, your general health, your skin and your waistline. Aim to eat balanced meals most of the time, and drink enough water to keep yourself hydrated, about six to eight glasses per day. Taking vitamin and mineral supplements can help to prevent major dietary deficiencies, but they can be expensive and are not necessary if you're eating well. Having said that, if you rush around a lot and don't have time to eat regular meals, or take regular very strenuous exercise, you should think about taking a multivitamin and mineral supplement.

There's a lot of conflicting advice around about healthy eating, and a new fad diet seems to be promoted every few months or so. Stick to the basic advice that most professional dieticians and nutritionists give: try to eat five portions of fruit or veg every day, base your meals around complex carbohydrates (starchy foods) such as rice, pasta, bread or potatoes, and have protein in the form of lean meat, fish, eggs, lentils and pulses, or other vegetarian alternatives. Fat is not the enemy, but moderate your intake of saturated fats such as butter and other animal fats, and hardened vegetable oil. Don't eat processed, sugary or salty food too often, but don't feel that you have to cut it out of your diet completely either.

If you want to eat well on a low income, be prepared to shop around a little more and perhaps do extra preparation of your food. Buy fresh fruit and vegetables cheaply in season from the market, and make friends with your local butcher, fishmonger and baker. Supermarket 'value' ranges are good for basic things like bread, tinned beans and so on. Learn how to cook a few easy healthy dishes such as pasta with sauce, baked potatoes with toppings, stews, omelettes and so on.

SLEEPING JUST ENOUGH

Another simple way to keep yourself feeling healthy is getting the right amount of sleep. It's part of the deal to have a few late nights partying, or sitting up until the small hours doing last-minute work to get an essay in on time. Just remember to catch up on that missing kip at some point. One easy way to do this is by aiming to have an early night once or twice a week. Sleep deprivation can make you tired, clumsy, unable to concentrate and irritable, and is bad for your health in the longer term. On the other hand, fairly or unfairly, some students have a bad reputation for sleeping too much, which strangely can also leave you feeling tired and washed out.

Sleep problems such as insomnia and snoring can make life difficult for you and the people around you. Insomnia can rear its ugly head in more than one way, such as difficulty dozing off when you go to bed, waking up in the middle of the night, or waking up too early and not being able to get back to sleep. There are a few simple ways to get back to the land of nod, for example: keeping a regular bedtime to get your body back into the routine, taking exercise, avoiding caffeine, alcohol and other drugs in the evenings, having a warm milky drink before bed, and addressing anything that is making you feel stressed or anxious. Make your sleeping area as good as you can, with heavy curtains to stop light getting in, fresh air to avoid stuffiness, and if you can't keep the noise down wear some earplugs. Sleeping tablets are a last resort, and should only be used for short periods. Snoring can drive you, your partner, your roommate and your neighbours mad. You can wake yourself up several times in one night with those deeply unsexy warthog noises. If it's due to colds or hayfever then it's likely to be only temporary, but see a doctor if it carries on. Simple self-help includes sleeping on your side and not your back, avoiding drunkenness at bedtime and keeping to a healthy weight.

KEEPING FIT

Taking regular exercise is good for toning up, increasing stamina and decreasing stress levels. While you're at university there will be many opportunities to get fit for free, or for a few pounds each term, so there are no worries about swanky and expensive gym membership. Most colleges have football pitches, training fields, running tracks and gym facilities, plus various exercise classes. Some lucky students also have access to a swimming pool and a boathouse. If you're a sporty person, look out for societies for football, rugby, basketball, hockey, athletics, karate and so on. They're also good for your social life and put on various events off the field.

If you hated team games at school, or just don't think of yourself as a 'fitness' person, you still have many opportunities to keep in shape on your own terms. The trick to keeping up regular exercise is to find something you love doing, rather than something you force yourself to do. That could be anything from hillwalking, swimming, aerobics or yoga to self-defence, scuba-diving or tai chi. Speak to a member of the sports staff, or look at the message boards at the sports centre to find out what's available. The staff will also be able to give you training on how to use the equipment safely, and can show you how to plan an effective exercise regime that fits in with your lifestyle. And try not to worry: you won't turn into a gym bunny bimbo or a meathead jock. Not overnight, at least.

If you've never been even remotely fit before then don't worry, it isn't too complicated. Start gently, with about three exercise sessions per week, building up the intensity and length of the sessions over time. Warm up before exerting yourself, and warm down with plenty of stretching afterwards. Aim for exercise that makes you feel like you're working, and need to breathe deeper than usual, but stop if you feel wheezy or faint. If you have a medical condition, talk to your doctor before beginning an exercise programme.

SMOKING

Or more to the point, not smoking. In addition to costing hundreds of pounds over the course of a year, cigarettes and roll-ups are bad for your immediate and longer-term health. You know this already but there's no harm in repeating it. Smokers are more prone to chest infections, and over time it will give you premature wrinkles and dog breath, dull the skin and increase your risk of heart disease, leg amputations, lung disease and several forms of cancer. Being a light smoker is still risky, and smoking cigarettes that are labelled 'light' or 'low tar' is not a safety measure, so don't be fooled. If you want to give up, you have the choice of willpower, nicotine inhalers, nicotine gum, nicotine patches and, as a last resort, prescription drugs from your doctor. There are also support groups and organisations that are there to help you through the worst of the cravings and out onto the other side, such as Quitline: 0800 00 22 00. Your local chemist will also be a good source of advice.

BUGS AND GERMS

Viruses spread like wildfire during the first term. Get together thousands of young people with their own bugs from all over the country, cram them into crowded halls, bars and lecture theatres, and lower their immune systems with late nights, pills and booze and stress. What do you cook up? A massive dose of 'fresher flu'. Most people come down with something sooner or later, and not just the freshers. Older students, lecturers and various other staff members are similarly stricken down. Certain departments might as well have 'Plague' written on the entrance door. It's tempting to pretend that you have it when you're not ill, so that you can have a few days off or go home early for the holidays, but beware. You may succumb to it later, and then you'll have to explain how you somehow managed to catch it twice.

COLDS

Colds are caused by contagious viruses that infect the soft tissues that line the nose. There are over 100 different cold viruses, and most people catch them between two to four times each year, especially during winter. They are relatively mild and most people recover from them during one week. The main symptoms are sneezing and a runny nose. There may also be a sore throat, a bunged-up feeling in the nose and a slight temperature. Female students have occasionally been known to call the common cold 'boy flu', owing to the way their boyfriends behave when cold-ridden.

Just like a broken heart, there ain't no cure for the common cold, no siree. You have to let it run its course, rest and look after yourself. Hot drinks, over-the-counter remedies, sore-throat sweets, aspirin gargles and lashings of daytime TV watched from under a duvet on the sofa are all proven to help. To ease congestion, put a towel over your head and inhale steam from a bowl filled with hot water, and avoid smoking. It's caused by a virus, so unless there are complications such as ear or sinus infections, or tonsillitis, then antibiotics won't make the slightest difference.

COUGHS

A cough is a reflex mechanism that acts to clear the throat or lower airways. It can be caused by any irritant, such as mucus, dust, smoke or infection. Coughing is often caused by colds and flu and other viruses, but it may also be due to underlying problems such as allergies or undiagnosed asthma. Most coughs can be soothed by liquids from the chemist, whether they are dry and tickly or chesty coughs that bring up lots of phlegm. Any cough that lasts for more than two weeks needs checking out by a doctor.

INFLUENZA (FLU)

Flu, also known as influenza, is another contagious virus that's more common during winter months. It has a sudden onset, with aches and pains, headache, nausea and runny nose. Flu affects the upper airways and lungs, and causes a harsh dry cough. Unlike the common cold, there is a loss of appetite, and there can be vomiting or diarrhoea too. While men who catch a common cold tend to insist they have flu, men who really have flu either say they are dying or may even be ill enough to stop moaning. The illness peaks after two or three days, and the person tends to feel much better within a week. Coughing and tiredness can carry on for another fortnight after this.

If you catch real flu, the best thing to do is sleep or rest in bed, and drink lots of fluids like water, diluted fruit juice or weak tea. Paracetamol or aspirin help with the headache and muscle pains, and can bring the temperature down too. Steer clear of alcohol and ciggies. If symptoms last longer than a week, or you start coughing up blood or lots of green phlegm, consult a doctor. The aftermath of a serious dose of flu can include mild temporary feelings of depression, a lasting cough, bronchitis and pneumonia. If you have bad asthma or an underlying heart condition, think about getting a flu vaccination in the autumn each year.

GLANDULAR FEVER

This is sometimes called infectious mononucleosis, and is caused by the Epstein–Barr virus. It's caught from saliva, which is why it's nicknamed 'the kissing disease', and can be spread by people sneezing too. Glandular fever tends to start with one or two weeks of flu-like symptoms, followed by other signs. There is enlargement of the lymph nodes (sometimes called your 'glands') giving rise to small rubbery lumps in the neck, armpits and groin. A very sore throat can develop, often causing a white covering on the tonsils, and swallowing can be painful. There is usually extreme tiredness, muscle pain and sweating. In some people, there may be stomach pains and the spleen can become enlarged, or the liver may be affected, causing yellowing of the eyes and skin (jaundice). There may be a rash over the body, sometimes made worse by antibiotics.

Diagnosis is made by taking a blood sample and a throat swab. If glandular fever is confirmed, you need to drink lots of fluids and rest. It's a virus, so antibiotics won't help, but most people recover in less than a month. It is highly advisable to resume activities slowly, and to avoid strenuous activity for at least the first four weeks after you've started to feel better. Complications can, rarely, include long-lasting infection, pneumonia, infection of the nervous system and problems with the spleen or the blood. To avoid infecting other people, don't share food, cutlery or cups with anyone while you're sick. If it interferes with your exams, notify the university and resign yourself to doing resits, rather than trying to struggle in and do them.

MENINGITIS AND SEPTICAEMIA

Although it's fairly rare, all students should be aware of meningitis because it's such a serious illness. Meningitis is an inflammation of the brain and spinal cord, caused by bacteria or viruses. There may also be septicaemia, which is blood poisoning. The symptoms can come on in only a few hours, and can vary from person to person. If it's caught early enough then most people make a full recovery, but it can cause deafness, depression, coma or even death.

Look out for **any** of the following:

- **Severe headache**
- **Pain or stiffness in the neck**
- **Dislike of bright lights**
- **Fever and vomiting**
- **Drowsiness or unconsciousness**
- **Stomach cramps or diarrhoea**
- **Signs of septicaemia: a rash of tiny red pinpricks or purplish-red blotches, chills, cold hands and feet. If you press on the blotches with a clear glass tumbler, they do not fade or blanch.**

If you suspect meningitis, don't wait for all the symptoms to appear. Contact your doctor's surgery immediately for more advice, and demand to speak to someone urgently. If the person is unconscious or having fits, call 999 for an ambulance.

The Department of Health recommends that all first year students are immunised against meningitis. However, this vaccination does not protect against all forms of the illness, so it's important not to be complacent. For more information about meningitis call the National Meningitis Trust on 0845 6000 800 or the Meningitis Research Foundation, tel: 0808 800 3344, or look at www.meningitis.org.uk.

FOOD POISONING

Food poisoning can make you incredibly ill, and affects about 5.5 million people in the UK each year. It is usually caused by bacteria, but there are a few viruses that can cause it too, such as Hepatitis A, and one or two yummy parasites. If you're preparing food at home, one of the simplest ways to keep down germs is by washing your hands thoroughly before you start cooking. Store food at the correct temperature, especially if it's poultry, meat, eggs or fish, and don't use ingredients that are well past their sell-by date. The other handiest tip is to avoid wiping everything in your kitchen down with the same dirty dishcloth, especially an old one that hardly ever gets a thorough wash, or that your flatmate secretly uses to wipe the floor with. This may all sound somewhat anal-retentive, but if it means you can avoid the biggest puke-a-thon and diarrhoea-fest of your life, who cares?

Be careful when you're eating out, especially if it's late-night kebabs and burgers. Recent research has shown that around 10 per cent of fast food is highly contaminated with bacteria that can cause food poisoning, so pick your place carefully. When ordering seafood like mussels, only buy them from busy restaurants that have a fast turnover, and avoid ordering fish on Mondays because it's unlikely to be fresh. Rumours usually abound on campus about a nearby cheapo restaurant or curry house that seems to make lots of its customers sick. Surprise tip: don't eat there.

Signs of food poisoning vary according to the type of germs involved. There may be violent vomiting within half an hour of eating, fever, chest pain or full-on diarrhoea that starts a while later (hours or even days). Most cases are easy to fight off by taking mild painkillers and drinking lots of fluids, and symptoms are usually gone after three to five days or so. There are several over-the-counter treatments for diarrhoea, but they work by slowing down the bowel rather than killing the bugs, so don't be too quick to start using them. If you can't keep water down, are in severe pain, pass bloody diarrhoea or have violent diarrhoea persisting for more than 24 hours, call your GP.

MENTAL HEALTH

The late teens and early twenties are a common age for people to experience mental health problems for the first time, and they affect a significant proportion of students. Although times are changing for the better, there is still some social stigma attached to these problems, and people who experience them may find it difficult to ask for help. It's important to realise that there is a wide range of support out there, and that conditions such as depression are treatable illnesses.

DEPRESSION

Around one in nine people experience some form of depression, and students may be even more at risk for a number of reasons, such as life stresses like leaving home for the first time, relationship breakdowns or serious money problems. It isn't a sign of weakness or lack of character, it really can happen to anyone. Clinical depression is not something you can just 'cheer up from', and being told to 'pull yourself together and snap out of it' isn't much help.

SIGNS AND SYMPTOMS

Depression can have classic signs such as feeling miserable for long periods of time, but it can also present itself in other, less obvious ways. Most of us will feel bad every now and again, but with depression this is longer-lasting. The list below covers some of the various signs and symptoms, although if you're depressed you're unlikely to suffer from all of them at the same time:

- **Feeling down, miserable or tearful most days for more than two weeks.**
- **Difficulty sleeping, or waking up very early and being unable to get back to sleep, or having nightmares.**

- **Spending less time socialising or becoming withdrawn.**
- **Feeling hollow, empty, bored or unable to see a future.**
- **Lack of sex drive or general loss of energy.**
- **Not wanting to be alive, or having thoughts about suicide.**
- **Feeling guilty, ashamed or worthless.**
- **Loss of appetite and loss of weight, or excessive comfort eating.**
- **Feelings of anger, restlessness or frustration.**
- **Using drugs or alcohol to try to escape from bad feelings.**

WHAT HELP IS AVAILABLE?

There's a range of medical treatments for depression, and a number of positive self-help techniques to try. Even if you're suffering from one of the milder forms of depression, don't slip into thinking that's how it always has to be, or that it's somehow OK because other people out there are worse off than you. If you sort things out sooner rather than later you'll be able to get much more out of life.

If you think you might be depressed, the best place to start is by talking to your GP. They won't be shocked or look down on you in any way, and they probably already deal with several depressed patients on an average working day. If you find it hard to talk about the way you feel, try writing it down and showing it to your doctor, or get a friend to come along with you for moral support. Your doctor can then offer you a range of tests and treatments, or refer you for counselling or other specialist help.

You may be offered antidepressant tablets. They're not 'happy pills', they are not addictive, and their main function is to even out the levels of chemicals such as serotonin in your brain which become low when a person is depressed. They can take between two and four weeks to have a positive effect, although some tablets do not work for certain people, so it may be a case of trying different drugs until you find one that suits. Take them according to the instructions on the packet, don't stop taking them suddenly without talking to your doctor, and don't mix them with alcohol or street drugs. It's not 'weak' to take them, and their function is mainly to help you get back on your feet, so that you can deal with your problems in your own time. You won't need to be on them forever.

Counselling can be very effective, especially if you have unresolved issues from your past that you need to come to terms with, or have had painful recent events such as the death of a loved one or a bad relationship breakup. It should help you to learn more effective problem-solving skills, or ways to cope with difficult situations. Good counselling may also prevent you from becoming depressed again in the future. It can be arranged through your GP, or through student welfare services.

There are also some effective things that you can do to help yourself, such as taking regular exercise and getting back to the activities that you enjoy doing. Recent research from mental health charity MIND suggests that eating regular healthy meals and avoiding caffeine and refined sugar may all help to reduce mood swings, perhaps by regulating blood sugar levels. A number of support groups exist for people who have depression, or depressed friends or relatives. Some people take herbal remedies such as St John's wort, but this is not always effective, has possible side effects such as making the contraceptive pill less effective, and can't take the place of a medical assessment.

Thoughts of suicide should be taken seriously, especially if there is a specific plan of action involved. Go to a doctor as soon as you can, and if you need to talk to someone while you're waiting for the appointment, don't be scared to call the Samaritans. They're open day and night for anyone who is feeling down or has reached a crisis point. If you think a friend is seriously depressed or suicidal, be as supportive as you can, and help them to get medical attention.

ANXIETY AND STRESS

Some unrealistic folks still think that student life is all about having fun, skipping lectures, getting drunk at the taxpayer's expense and very little else. While that does still go on to some extent, student life can be much harder than people imagine. Financial pressures are worse than ever before, part-time work leaves you tired, and you're expected to adapt to a whole new way of living and studying. It's not surprising that students can end up feeling overwhelmed or stressed out.

SIGNS AND SYMPTOMS

- **A sense of not being on top of everything, or that things are out of control.**
- **Lying awake worrying, difficulty sleeping.**
- **Feeling that something bad is about to happen.**
- **Dry mouth, feeling shaky, sweaty palms.**
- **Increased need to pass urine, or having diarrhoea.**
- **Difficulty concentrating or getting things done.**
- **General feelings of being tense and miserable.**
- **Panic attacks: sweating, dizziness, racing heartbeat, difficulty breathing, or a sense of impending doom or death.**
- **Phobias: irrational fears of things or situations, such as crowded places, blood, spiders, birds or heights.**
- **Obsessions and compulsions: ritual behaviour that's usually carried out to cope with unpleasant thoughts. May include cleaning, hand washing or checking locked doors several times.**

WHAT HELP IS AVAILABLE?

A certain degree of stress is normal in everyday life and can improve performance, but specific measures are sometimes needed to reduce it to manageable levels. Talking to someone and getting it all off your chest can be one of the most helpful things to do, whether that's talking to a friend, relative or counsellor. Bottling worries up can make it much worse and lead to things getting out of perspective.

Stress or anxiety may be a sign that you need to make some alterations to your behaviour and lifestyle. Maybe you need to plan your time management better, or learn to say 'no' to people who keep asking you for favours when you're just too busy to help them. If your academic workload is out of control, speak to a tutor before things get any worse and sort out your priorities. If you have extra stress around exam time, it might be helped by more organised preparation, rather than rushing at the last minute, or you might just need to improve your exam technique.

Most universities run stress reduction courses and relaxation sessions where you can learn simple but effective techniques that will help you to be calmer in a variety of situations. These tend to be free of charge, and are worth checking out. The more you practice relaxation techniques, the more effective they will be. Many people also say that exercise such as yoga or swimming can be very relaxing, or that meditation helps. Avoiding caffeine can be a simple way to reduce feelings of jitteriness, so cut right back on coffees, colas and strong tea.

If you have strong feelings of anxiety, or think you're about to have a panic attack, try the following:

- **Try not to breathe too quickly as this makes you feel worse. Concentrate on your breathing and take long, slow breaths in and out.**

- **If possible, sit somewhere quiet while you calm yourself down.**

- **Tell yourself that your anxious thoughts are creating these feelings, and that you can get in control of these thoughts.**

- **Shift the focus of your attention away from how bad or panicky you are feeling, and on to something else. Some people like to look at their watch, others like to look more closely at their surroundings, for example.**

If anxieties, phobias or obsessions are affecting your daily life, it's best to get to the bottom of them. Your doctor will be able to provide you with explanations and reassurance, and give you a thorough checkup to rule out any other underlying illness. They can also teach you about relaxation techniques, or refer you to a specialist for further treatment such as counselling or psychological help. Drugs have a very limited role in treating anxiety and stress-related problems, and should only be used for very limited periods because many of them are addictive and don't help you to develop healthy coping mechanisms. Anxiety and stress are very common problems, and you might be surprised to learn that many successful and confident people have suffered badly from them at one time or another, but have overcome their difficulties.

MANIC DEPRESSION AND SCHIZOPHRENIA

Manic depression and schizophrenia each affect around 1 per cent of the adult population, and can show up for the first time in the teens or twenties. They are often confusing or frightening for the people concerned and those who know them. There may be a family history of these illnesses, and episodes of illness can be brought on by stress.

SIGNS AND SYMPTOMS: SCHIZOPHRENIA
- A feeling that thoughts are being controlled by someone or something else, or that other people can read or hear private thoughts.

- Hearing voices: being talked about, running commentaries being given during activities, or hearing one's own thoughts as if they were being echoed or spoken out loud.

- Giving extraordinary meanings to ordinary events (delusions).

- Feeling as though sensations or movements are being controlled by an outside force.

- Making conversation that lacks a logical flow or contains made up words.

- Hallucinations with things that may be seen, touched, tasted, smelt or heard.

- Becoming socially withdrawn, speaking very little and not coping with everyday living activities.

- Flat moods, where there is little up or down.

SIGNS AND SYMPTOMS: MANIC DEPRESSION
- Swinging between symptoms of depression and mania (see the symptoms below).

- Increased feelings of energy, self-esteem, self-confidence and restlessness.

- Embarking on reckless behaviour, such as grand business schemes that haven't been properly thought through, spending vast sums of money or having several sexual partners in a short period of time.

- Sleeping very little or not at all, and not feeling tired.

- Speaking and thinking in a very rushed manner, and not making much sense to others.

- Acting in a grandiose, self-important way, or becoming deluded and believing things that aren't true.

WHAT HELP IS AVAILABLE?

The main treatment for manic depression and schizophrenia is with drugs and good social support, such as regular visits from community psychiatric nurses. Anti-psychotic medications are used to reduce symptoms such as hallucinations and delusions. If someone is in the acute phase of either illness, they are usually admitted to a psychiatric inpatient unit at a hospital. In the depressive phase of manic depression, antidepressants are often prescribed, and they may also be given mood-stabilising drugs such as lithium. Many people only have one or two episodes of illness, and others find that their symptoms are controlled well by drugs. As with depression, it may be a case of trying different treatments until you find the one that suits you best. If you already know that you have tendencies to either of these illnesses it's very important to stay away from street drugs, including LSD and cannabis, as these can make symptoms much worse.

EATING DISORDERS

Eating disorders include anorexia nervosa, bulimia nervosa and compulsive eating. They all have a distorted attitude to food in common, where emotional needs drive eating behaviour, rather than hunger. Nine out of ten students with eating disorders are female, but males can be affected too and may use excessive exercise to control weight and body shape. It's not known why anyone develops an eating disorder, but it may be genetic, down to family pressures or caused by the body-obsessed society we live in.

ANOREXIA NERVOSA

It's thought that 1 per cent of teenage girls suffer from anorexia, and around 5 per cent of girls and young women show symptoms to a lesser degree. It's characterised by:

- **Deliberate weight loss, over 15 per cent below what's considered to be your healthy body weight.**

- **An intense fear of being fat, or a desperate wish to be thin.**

- **Loss of periods for three months or more in females.**

- **Feeling fat, even when the evidence suggests otherwise.**

- **Placing all your sense of self-worth on weight and appearance.**

- **In some cases, laxative abuse or excessive exercise.**

Dieting often brings a sense of control over the body or problems in life, and sufferers may have perfectionist tendencies or difficulty expressing their needs or feelings. Severe weight loss causes tiredness, faintness and dizziness, and an emaciated appearance. There may be constipation, stomach pains and hair loss. There can also be a growth of fine downy hair all over the body, and a constant feeling of coldness. Over time, anorexia may cause osteoporosis (thinning of the bones) and damage to the heart, and depression and anxiety are common. There's a high risk of death if help is not given.

BULIMIA NERVOSA

Bulimia is most common among women in their late teens and early twenties. It can be recognised by the following:

- **Recurrent episodes of binge-eating, where large quantities of rich or sugary food are consumed in a short period of time, usually in secret.**

- **Lack of control over the amount of food that's eaten during a binge.**

- **Weight is usually within normal limits.**

- **After a binge, attempts to lose weight again such as vomiting, purging with laxatives, fasting or strict dieting.**

Bulimics may feel that they are worthless or 'no good', despite being popular or high achievers, and sometimes have a history of dieting or being obese as a child. Regular vomiting can erode the enamel of teeth, and sometimes causes the glands on the side of the face to swell up, causing a puffy appearance. It can also cause bleeding in the throat and dangerous disturbances in the balance of the body's fluid and mineral levels. Long-term laxative abuse can cause the bowel to stop working properly, leading to constipation and bloating.

COMPULSIVE EATING

This is probably the commonest eating disorder, where the person consumes large amounts of food, either by bingeing or by 'grazing' or snacking throughout the day. It may be an extreme form of comfort eating. The act of bingeing tends to cause strong feelings of unhappiness or disgust, or of being unable to control the behaviour. Men are more likely to have problems with compulsive eating than with anorexia or bulimia.

RECOVERING FROM EATING DISORDERS

If you think you may have an eating disorder, the sooner you seek help, the more likely you are to recover completely. Start by speaking to a doctor or nurse, or one of the organisations listed in the box below. Treatment includes changing to a healthier eating pattern to get to a normal weight, and various types of therapy. Therapy could include cognitive behavioural therapy (CBT), interpersonal therapy, family therapy and support groups. Antidepressant drugs may also be prescribed.

SELF-HARM

This problem is a little-understood one. Sufferers deliberately harm themselves, most often secretly, as a temporary way of coping with unhappy or unpleasant feelings. This can take the form of cutting the skin, picking or bruising skin, pulling out hair, taking small overdoses and so on. It isn't normally carried out deliberately to seek attention, but may sometimes be a cry for help. Treatment is a course of counselling, designed to bring personal problems out into the open and provide healthier ways of coping with negative feelings and stress.

USEFUL CONTACTS AND RESOURCES FOR MENTAL HEALTH

MIND
Leading mental health charity with information, local support and campaigns.

Infoline: 0845 766 0163, website: www.mind.org.uk

DEPRESSION ALLIANCE
A charity dedicated to helping people understand and recover from depression.

Telephone: 020 7633 0557, website: www.depressionalliance.org

EATING DISORDERS ASSOCIATION
Information and help on all aspects of eating disorders, including anorexia, bulimia and binge-eating disorder.

Adult helpline: 0845 634 1414, open 8.30 a.m. to 8.30 p.m., Monday to Friday
Youthline: 0845 634 7650, open 4 p.m. to 6.30 p.m., Monday to Friday

Minicom: 01603 753322, open 8.30 a.m. to 8.30 p.m., Monday to Friday

NO PANIC
Confidential help and rehabilitation for anyone suffering from anxiety, phobias or obsessive compulsive disorder.

Helpline: 0808 808 0545, open 10 a.m. to 10 p.m. daily, website: www.nopanic.org.uk

CRUSE
Information and advice for people who are bereaved.

Helpline: 020 8940 4818, open 9.30 a.m. to 5 p.m., Monday to Friday

BRISTOL CRISIS CENTRE
Service dedicated to helping women who harm themselves, helpline covers the whole of the UK.

Helpline: 0117 925 1119, open 9 p.m. to 12.30 a.m., Friday and Saturday, and 6 p.m. to 9 p.m. Sunday.

SAMARITANS
Confidential service for anyone who is suicidal or despairing.

Telephone: 08457 90 90 90 (UK), 1850 60 90 90 (Republic of Ireland), email: jo@samaritans.org

OTHER COMMON HEALTH PROBLEMS

SKIN TROUBLE
It's a bummer walking around with a face that looks like a pizza or a pile of flaky pastry. There's plenty to do to get it back to normal, and it probably doesn't look nearly as bad as you think it does. No, honestly it doesn't.

ACNE

Hormone changes, increased oil production, stress, dead skin cells, inflammation and bacteria all gang up on your skin to give you acne, or zits. It tends to be worst on the face, chest and back. Wash the skin gently and regularly, and don't pick it or things will get much worse. For mild acne try products from the chemist that contain benzoyl peroxide, salicylic acid or tea tree oil, and expect improvement after around one month. For moderate acne, your GP can prescribe antibiotic tablets or lotions, or for women a certain brand of the contraceptive pill may work. If the acne is severe, you can be referred to a dermatologist for stronger medication, such as retinoids that decrease inflammation and oil production.

ECZEMA

Areas of skin affected by eczema become very dry, itchy and flaky. It can also be reddened, sore, inflamed or weepy. It tends to affect areas such as the elbows, wrists, hands, face and the backs of the knees. The itchiness can keep people awake and make them feel irritable, plus certain foods and stress can make it worse. There are several different types of eczema, including contact eczema and atopic eczema. Contact eczema, or contact dermatitis, is caused by the skin coming into contact with drying or irritating substances such as nickel, soap, perfume or glue. Atopic eczema tends to run in families and develop during childhood, and is linked to an increased chance of having hay fever or asthma. Although there is no 'cure' for eczema, there are many ways to keep it in check and prevent it from flaring up again. It's important to stop the skin from drying out, so using soapless cleansers and emollient (moisturising) creams and lotions helps. Corticosteroid creams and antihistamines may work too, so try talking to your local chemist.

PSORIASIS

Psoriasis sometimes starts during the teenage years after sore throats or chest infections, or stressful events such as exams or relationship problems. The exact cause of it is unknown, but it sometimes runs in families, and it definitely isn't contagious. Normal skin cells are renewed every 28 days, but in psoriasis they are replaced every four days, causing 'plaques' where the skin is thicker. Plaques tend to be itchy red or dark pink areas, with a silvery scaly surface, and are most common on the knees, ankles and scalp, or on areas that get bumped or injured. It can be kept at bay with treatments, taking care of general health and reducing stress levels. Keeping skin moisturised reduces itching. There are several products to get rid of the plaques, such as Vitamin D-like creams, steroids, coal tar and ultraviolet light treatment.

HAY FEVER

Sniff. Snuffle. Atchoo! Sore eyes, runny nose, sneezing and a general yucky feeling are the last things you need in the spring and summer. Especially if it clashes with your finals. It's an allergic reaction to grass, flower or tree pollens that affects up to one in five students. To combat the miserable symptoms, there are antihistamine tablets, nasal sprays, eye drops or immunotherapy. Reducing contact with the pollen can keep the symptoms down: try closing windows, wearing sunglasses to keep eyes clear, showering and washing hair after going out, or putting a little Vaseline inside nostrils to catch pollen. If the symptoms go on all year round, it's called allergic perennial rhinitis, and is probably caused by allergies to dust mites or pets.

ASTHMA

Asthma is a long-term condition that affects the breathing, and can range from very mild wheeziness to full-blown asthma attacks. The lining of the smallest airways in the lungs becomes inflamed, and the muscles in the walls of the airways may contract, causing the airways to become narrowed. Asthma can be made worse by cold, exercise, cigarette smoke, viruses or specific substances such as certain foods. There may be wheezy breathing and coughing, which is at its most extreme during an attack. Sometimes there is no wheezing at all, just a persistent cough at night. Using a device called a peak flow meter to monitor breathing can show whether the asthma is getting worse or improving.

Someone having a severe asthma attack needs urgent medical attention. The signs of an attack are: bluish skin or lips and gasping breath, restlessness, confusion or a drawn-in ribcage. Asthma can be kept under control in most people by regular use of inhalers. Salbutamol (also called Ventolin) and similar inhalers help to relax the airways and widen them, and steroid inhalers or tablets decrease inflammation in the lungs. There are several other drugs that can be used, and they work by relaxing muscles in the airways, drying up secretions or disrupting allergic reactions. Using inhalers regularly and keeping an eye on the state of the asthma tend to be the most effective ways to manage the condition. If you know you have asthma, make sure you're registered with a GP, and always have enough inhalers so that you don't run out. Some people find that avoiding certain foods reduces the number of attacks, or say that regular exercise such as swimming works for them.

SPORTS INJURIES

These are very common among super-active and slightly-less-active students. To reduce the risk of sports injuries it's important to warm up fully when exercising, use the right protective equipment and warm down gently afterwards. Injuries include bruising, sprained tendons, broken bones and the occasional love bite from an over-eager rugby opponent. There tends to be swelling, pain and loss of function of the affected limb if there are broken bones or bad sprains involved. If that happens to you, don't soldier on, get off the pitch before you make it worse for yourself. An ice pack or bag of frozen peas may help to bring the swelling down while you wait for the doctor or X-ray technician. If you undertake any contact sports, be aware of the possibility of facial, head, neck and back injuries. Never move someone with a suspected injury of this type until qualified help arrives, unless the person is choking and you have to clear their airway.

Treatment for most sport injuries includes rest, painkillers, strapping or other support, and possibly physiotherapy and anti-inflammatory drugs. Don't go back to playing your sport until you get the all clear, or you risk the injury flaring up all over again.

OBESITY

As a nation, the Brits are getting fatter and fatter. Carrying extra weight can worsen existing health conditions, and may make you at risk of certain health problems in later life such as high blood pressure and heart disease. If you think you're overweight, there's no need to weigh yourself every day and go on a crash diet. Get weighed properly by the nurse at your health centre, find out if you really do need to lose a few pounds, and ask for a healthy eating plan instead. Get down to your recommended weight slowly, and take regular exercise to make sure it doesn't go back on again.

RELIABLE SOURCES OF HEALTH INFORMATION

Asking your mates for health advice or doing random internet searches don't always get you the best information. Stick to well-known, reliable sources such as the ones below:

NHS DIRECT

Advice helpline staffed by trained nurses, plus a website containing comprehensive, easy-to-understand advice.

Telephone: 0845 46 47, open 24 hours daily, website: www.nhsdirect.nhs.uk

HEALTH INFORMATION SERVICE

Information on all health-related subjects including where to get treatment.

Telephone: 0800 665 544, open 9 a.m. to 5.50 p.m., Monday to Friday

NETDOCTOR.CO.UK

The UK's leading independent health website, with drug and illness encyclopaedias, message boards and an email query service.

STUDENTHEALTH.CO.UK

Extensive website aimed at students, containing advice on travel, sport and sexual health.

SICKLY STUDENTS

Tales of woe from the students on www.virginstudent.com

'We all got freshers' flu and I don't think it disappeared until Easter. We were in catered halls and we had ten rooms in our corridor. And yes, the doors were propped open so the germs could circulate freely. Weakness, red nose, coughing, croaky voice, all a nightmare for lectures.'

'Watch out for those pesky sexually transmitted diseases! Always be safe, never be sorry. An illness that hinders your sex life – now that's annoying!'

'I got shingles in my first year and the secondary pain lasted for months. At first I thought I had meningitis coz of the chickenpox rash, I was v scared! I just thought OAPs got it, but my doc said if you are run down (too much partying), don't take care of yourself or eat properly (daily beans on toast), drink excessively (mmmm, all day everyday practically), and are stressed (goddamn those essays!) then you can also get it.'

'A guy in the first year got hepatitis and was in pain, bedridden for two weeks. Not good.'

'The worst ailment can be feeling depressed. The best thing to do to avoid feeling lonely is to socialise. Even if pubs and clubs aren't your thing try to find something. Don't sit in your room every night feeling all alone, talk to people and you will eventually meet someone on your wavelength.'

'Alcohol poisoning is the worst thing that can happen to you, especially if you're a big drinker. Made me throw up for days. Soon as I got better I started drinking again though . . .'

9. CRIME AND SAFETY

One third of students have been the victims of crime in the last twelve months, a sobering statistic. The most common crimes are burglary and other robbery, and criminal damage. Thieves deliberately target students more than any other group in society, probably because students tend to own several expensive items that can be sold on quickly, such as bicycles and mobile phones. All students should be aware of the safety measures they need to take to safeguard themselves and their belongings, many of which are simple and easy things to do. Personal safety is an issue for men just as much as it is for women, especially when you realise that male students are twice as likely to be the victims of violent crime.

If you see a crime taking place, find someone who has been attacked or injured, or you think you're in danger, call 999 as soon as you can. To report petty theft or other similar crimes, it's better to contact your local police station directly. Your local police can also advise you on a number of ways to make your home safer, and it's useful to have their number to hand.

All students should be aware of:

- **Simple home safety measures to deter burglars**

- **Crime on the street or on campus**

- **Safety issues when going out at night and coming home**

- **Harassment and sexual assault**

- **Their rights if they're stopped by the police**

Everyone at university should get themselves some insurance for their possessions. Ask your parents if their home insurance also covers you while you're away from home during the term. You may have to pay a premium to cover expensive items such as bikes and computers, but it may still work out cheaper than taking out a separate policy of your own. Otherwise, ring around well-known and reputable insurance companies or big insurance brokers, or check out the insurance on offer from high street banks. Get several quotes, and check the small print to make sure you're covered properly. All insurance policies require you to take reasonable care of your own property, and some of them insist you fulfil certain conditions, such as fitting specific locks to your bedroom or front door. If you're careless, for example your unattended bag is stolen from a pub bench while you're at the bar, they simply won't pay out.

SAFETY AT HOME

Burglars tend to target student accommodation because they believe they'll be able to grab several small expensive items in one go. Many thefts are opportunistic, with the burglar gaining access via an open window or door in about a quarter of robberies. Being careful about who you let in, remembering to lock up regularly and taking a few extra security measures will reduce your chances of being burgled.

ACCESS

Be very careful about who you let in to your home. If you live in halls or shared flats and somebody turns up claiming to be visiting another student, don't just let them straight in, unless you're already expecting them. Find out exactly who they are looking for, then go and get the student in question to see if it's a wanted visitor. Some chancers may ring the buzzer and say they're looking for 'Dave' or 'Mike', but if you think they're dodgy, tell them to come back later. They can always leave a message. Wherever you live, think twice before you let anybody in who claims to be from a utilities company, or 'sent by the landlord'. Ask to see some proper identification, and call the company or landlord to check if necessary. A genuine operative will be used to customers carrying out this safety procedure, and should be patient. Get them to put their ID card through the letter box, or open the door with the door chain on.

HALL SAFETY

Leaving your hall room unattended while you shower or make a cup of tea could allow a sneak thief to grab your personal belongings, or give an attacker enough time to hide in your room to await your return. It might seem boring and restrictive, but security measures in halls are there for a reason. Look after any pass keys and swipe cards, and follow the rules for signing guests in and out. When letting yourself into entry halls, shut the door firmly behind you and don't let unfamiliar people in with you. Report anything suspicious to the person on duty.

LOCKING UP

Get into the automatic habit of locking up whenever you leave your room or house. It's a simple measure that's very effective. If you live in a shared house or flat, always check around before you go out or off to bed, making sure that doors are locked and windows closed. Get all your flatmates to agree to do the same thing, but don't automatically assume they will always remember. Think for each other. Keep your garden gate firmly locked, especially if there is an alleyway down the side of your house that could provide easy access for thieves. If you have a flatmate who frequently comes home inebriated and leaves the front door open, you have to talk to them about this urgently. It's an open invitation to anyone dodgy in the neighbourhood, and you won't be able to claim any stolen goods back from your insurers.

SECURITY MEASURES

- **If you're thinking about renting a place, try to pick one that has a sturdy door with strong locks and secure windows, preferably with a burglar alarm.**

- Students who are living in accommodation that isn't secure should nag their landlord to provide decent locks on the front door and bedroom doors, a door chain and window locks. Check your insurance for the type of locks they recommend you use.

- Having a visible burglar alarm can be a deterrent in itself, but make sure it's put into service on a regular basis.

- Try not to display valuable items such as computers and televisions near your windows, especially if it's on the ground floor.

- If, like most students, you are going to leave your house unattended during the holidays, do not leave your valuables inside the property. Put them in secure storage, take them with you or leave them with a trustworthy friend nearby. Ask a friendly neighbour to keep an eye on the place and leave a contact phone number with them.

- Mark expensive items with an invisible UV pen, using the postcode of your term-time address or your parent's postcode. If your goods are stolen, there's a chance the police will be able to find them and return them to you.

- Don't leave spare door keys outside, for example under the doormat or in a nearby plant pot or shed. It's the first place a burglar will look.

ON THE STREET OR ON CAMPUS

Try not to attract attention to yourself unnecessarily. Don't flash around cash, mobile phones or laptops in the street, it could make you a target for theft. Don't leave purses, wallets or bags unattended at college or when out shopping, even for a brief moment. Unattended coats are frequently stolen because of what they might have in their pockets, so look after your jacket when you're in the library or cafés and so on.

YOUR BAGS AND WALLET

Students are often loaded down with books and folders. Try to keep one hand free, walk confidently and be aware of your surroundings. Clear your bag out regularly and only take what you need out with you. If you aren't going to need your laptop computer or credit card that day, leave it at home. It's wise to get insurance for credit cards too, just in case. Don't keep your cheque card and cheque book in the same bag or jacket, to reduce the risk of fraud, and avoid keeping your keys in the same place as letters or bills with your home address on them, to prevent burglary. Don't put your wallet in the back pocket of your jeans, it's much safer in an inside or zipped pocket.

MOBILE PHONES

When you're out, keep your phone tucked away and be careful when you answer a call in the street. To protect your mobile phone, type the following five-digit sequence into the keypad: *#06#. This will make your phone display its unique SIM card serial number. Write the number down and keep it in a safe place at home. If your mobile phone is stolen this unique number can be used to block the phone, and stop the thief from making calls at your expense. Report the theft of your phone to your service provider and the police as soon as you can. If you don't have the service provider's emergency number, ring the Immobilise mobile phone crime line on 08701 123 123, which will tell you the right one to call.

CASHTILLS

Never write your secret cash card PIN down on anything, and don't tell other people the number. If you have the option of changing the number, avoid using dates to make up the digits, or repeating sequences such as 2222. Use cashpoints in daylight if you can, and look out for people standing too close to you or trying to distract you while you're taking money out. Make sure nobody can see you entering your PIN, and don't count your money in full view of people on the street.

OUT AT NIGHT

When you're going out make sure someone knows where you are going, who you're supposed to be meeting and when you'll be back. Always plan how you are going to get home – if possible book a taxi before you go out or arrange to stay over at a trusted mate's place. Try to share taxis with a friend who lives close by. Some student unions have a free night safety bus, or a taxi firm that they recommend. Think about getting a personal attack alarm, they are cheap or sometimes free for students. Know how to use it to shock and disorientate an assailant so that you can get away.

Know your limits if you're drinking, and remember that alcohol will relax you and could affect your judgement. When you are going out with a group of people then watch out for each other and make sure everyone stays safe. Don't let friends wander off on their own drunk or on drugs, and don't let anyone walk home alone. Watch your drinks and food to ensure that nothing is added to them, and be especially careful never to leave your drink unattended, even if you are going onto a dance floor or to the toilet.

If you do meet a problem, your primary aim should be to get away – forget looking tough or acting like a hero. Trust your instincts and start running for a place where you know there are people. Physical defence should only be a last resort. Report any incident as soon as possible even if you were unharmed, because you may save someone else.

GETTING HOME SAFELY

Avoid walking home alone late at night whenever you can. If you are out at night, try to walk with a group of people, preferably a mixed group of males and females. Avoid danger spots such as poorly lit areas and walk facing oncoming traffic. Walk quickly and confidently, and carry an attack alarm in your hand if you have one.

- **Only 'Black Cab' taxis can be hailed in the street. Other registered taxis and minicabs have to be booked in advance by phone or from an office.**

- Never get into an unlicensed or unmarked minicab that pulls up beside you – any car touting for business on the streets is illegal and could be dangerous.

- Carry the telephone number of a trusted, registered taxi or minicab company with you, and when you book, ask for the driver's name, as well as the make and colour of the car.

- Confirm the driver's details when they arrive and sit in the back of the car, not the front. Be careful not to give out any personal details when talking to the driver, for example that there's nobody else in at your house.

- When using public transport, make sure you check departure times, especially of last trains, tubes and buses.

- Try to have your ticket, pass or change ready in your hand so your purse or wallet stays out of sight, and wait for your bus, train or tube in a well-lit place, near other people if possible.

- Take note of where the emergency alarms are and try to sit near to them – there are alarms on every bus, tube and train and on every railway platform.

- If a bus is empty, stay on the lower deck and sit near the driver or conductor.

- On tubes or trains try to sit with other people and avoid empty carriages. Move to another seat or carriage if you feel worried or uneasy.

- Speak to the driver or other transport staff if someone is bothering you or scaring you, and make sure they can't follow you off the bus or train.

- Don't hitchhike.

VIOLENCE

The best way to defend yourself from an attack is by not being there. Avoid well-known rough areas at night if you can, and do your best to get away quickly if a situation looks like it might turn violent. In smaller towns there may be 'student bashing' where locals attack students, especially in socially deprived areas where better-off students stick out like a sore thumb. Stick to student-friendly pubs and bars, or ask older students about places to avoid in town. Report any incidents to the police and the university. Drunken fights and muggings are also common, with male students being targeted more often than females. Most muggings take place near pubs and clubs at night after victims have been drinking, so take care when leaving places. If somebody is trying to take your bag or mobile, it tends to be safer to let it go, rather than get into a fight.

HELPING OTHERS

If you see someone else in trouble, think for a second before going to their aid. If you're on your own, you could be outnumbered, or facing an armed attacker. You may help more by alerting the police or university security. If you see someone lying in the street who looks as though they've been attacked or injured, your priority is to make sure the attackers are no longer around before you offer help. Someone who has been robbed or attacked may be in shock, so speak gently to them and call for help if they look pale and shaky. Put a coat over their shoulders, and avoid giving them alcohol or cigarettes as this can make them worse. If you find someone who has been glassed or bottled, leave the glass in the wound and call 999. Glass cuts on the way out and the way in, and could be keeping severed blood vessels pressed shut. If someone has been stabbed, press the sides of the wound together while you're waiting for the ambulance. The knife may have been left in the wound, and if so don't try to remove it. Be careful not to get cut, and protect yourself from their blood. Try not to move anyone who looks like they've been badly beaten or hit by a car, unless they are not breathing or there's a danger of them choking. If someone is drunk and has been in a fight or mugged, sit them down to wait for medical attention even if they want to go home. They could have been hurt more badly than they realise.

CARS, MOTORBIKES AND BICYCLES
No matter how old your car or bike is, somebody will be tempted to steal it. Here are a few tips:

- **Park in well-lit, busy places, especially if you're on your own at night.**

- **If you want to park your car on campus, set off early. Parking spaces are limited and you could end up having to park down a quiet back street if you're late.**

- **Don't leave chequebooks, mobile phones, wallets or coats on display in your car. Put anything valuable in the boot and lock it securely, or take it with you.**

- **Remove the car stereo and take it with you.**

- **Lock the car up properly every time you leave it, even if it's only for a brief period.**

- **Get a steering wheel lock, an immobiliser or an electronic alarm system for your car.**

- **Think about what you leave in the glove compartment. Don't keep vehicle registration documents or cash or credit cards in there.**

- **Buy a D-lock for your bicycle, and attach your bike to something sturdy such as railings or a purpose-built stand. Remove easy-release wheels and put the lock through both wheels and the frame.**

- **Get a security number etched onto your bike frame such as your postcode, and fill out a recorded cycle form at your local cycle shop.**

CARD FRAUD
There's been a sharp increase in credit card fraud recently. If you have a credit card, take out some insurance for it to cover you against fraud, or you

could end up liable for all or part of an enormous bill. Keep a note of all your card numbers and bank emergency card-theft hotlines at home so you can report it if your wallet gets stolen, and think about leaving a copy of these details at your parents' house as well. Don't let cards out of your sight during transactions in shops or restaurants in case they get 'skimmed'. Skimming is where a thief or dishonest employee runs your card through a tiny reader to copy the details on it, then the number is used to obtain goods without your knowledge. Report stolen cards to the company that issued them as soon as you can, to get them cancelled. If you buy goods over the internet, only use reputable established websites that offer you a secure service, and never put your full card number into an email. Check your statement from the card company every month to make sure there are no unexpected purchases on it, and always phone them up quickly to query any strange items on the bill, no matter how small.

SAFETY FOR MEN

Men are twice as likely as women to be subjected to a violent attack, so although personal safety has traditionally been seen as a women's issue, it applies equally strongly to men, if not more so. Most attacks by strangers take place in the evening or at night, and are common around pubs, clubs or anywhere else that serves alcohol. Men are also likely to be attacked by people they already know.

You don't need to fit into the stereotype of being tough and strong, in fact this can make some situations worse. Try to be relaxed rather than aggressive, and think about how you may appear to others. Crossing your arms, leaning over people or wagging a finger in someone's face can be intimidating or attract the attention of a violent person who's spoiling for a fight. If you find yourself in a bad situation, you don't have to act the hero. Physical self-defence should only be used as a last resort. It limits your options and commits you to a fight you could lose. It is not weak to walk away from violence, and you don't have to prove anything to yourself or others.

Even if you're the soppiest bloke on the planet, remember that people who don't know you may be intimidated by you in certain circumstances. Avoid walking just behind a woman who is going home on her own late at night. It would be less threatening if you crossed over the road to walk on the other side instead.

RAPE AND SEXUAL ASSAULT

Both men and women can become the victims of rape or sexual assault. This includes date rape and drug-assisted rape.

AVOIDING DATE RAPE

A Home Office research study published in 2002 found that only 8 per cent of rapes were carried out by strangers. Women were most at risk from their current partners, former partners, men they were dating and their acquaintances. Here are some strategies to help reduce the risk:

- If you are meeting someone new, tell a friend where you're going, who you're meeting and when you expect to return. If your plans change, tell someone.

- Try to arrange your first meeting with someone in a busy public place, preferably in daylight hours. Avoid being completely alone with them.

- If it's a blind date, think about taking a friend along with you who can watch and wait nearby. Take a mobile phone with you.

- Trust your instincts; if someone makes you nervous or uneasy leave immediately. Make up an excuse and go.

- Don't drink too much alcohol, and watch drinks and food to ensure that nothing is added to them. If something tastes odd, do not eat or drink any more of it.

- If you feel ill or light-headed tell a member of staff straight away and ask for help.

DRUG-ASSISTED RAPE

Drug-assisted rape is not a new phenomenon, in spite of current media awareness. Both males and females have been drugged and robbed or raped, so look out for yourself and all your friends. Surprisingly, the most common date-rape drug is alcohol. Victims are often unaware that extra shots of alcohol have been added to their drinks making them far stronger. There are at least thirty other drugs that have been used in drug rape cases, and some of them are colourless, flavourless and odourless. Many of them interact dangerously with alcohol, and leave victims unconscious or unable to defend themselves, sometimes with no memory of the attack. They may be added to foods, soft drinks, alcoholic drinks or hot drinks. Exercise great caution when you're out drinking, and don't slip into complacency.

- If someone you do not know or trust offers to buy you a drink, it's best to decline politely.

- When at the bar, watch that nothing is added to your drink.

- Don't let your drink out of your sight, even for a moment. That includes turning round to chat to friends, going to the toilet or hitting the dance floor.

- Buy bottled drinks and keep your thumb over the top when you're not drinking out of them.

- If your drink has been left unattended, do not drink any more of it. It's not worth taking the chance.

- If something tastes or looks odd, do not eat/drink any more of it.

- If you feel ill or light-headed act quickly – you may not have long. Tell a trusted friend straight away and ask for a taxi to take you home, or ask a member of staff to call for medical help.

- Signs of having your drink spiked include suddenly feeling much drunker, more than you'd expect for the amount of alcohol you've consumed, or feeling sick or nauseous.

- Make sure that anyone who offers to look after you or take you home is someone you really trust. Many people are raped by people they know: friends, colleagues from work, fellow students.

- If you suspect your friend has had their drink spiked, ask nearby staff for help, and call an ambulance. Stay with them at all times and look after them until the effects of the drug have worn off.

- Report any suspicious incidents to the police.

- Vomit on someone's clothing can contain the drug that was used, even if the drug leaves their body quickly. If possible, keep the clothes for evidence.

AFTER AN ATTACK

If someone has been raped or sexually assaulted, or thinks they may have been drugged and attacked, be aware that they may be in shock and will need medical help. They also have the right to go to the police and report the attack, if they want the attacker to be prosecuted. If so they should go to the police as soon as they can, taking a friend or counsellor along for support if possible. Keeping on the clothes they were wearing and avoiding showering is necessary to preserve evidence, and it helps to take along a set of clean clothes. The trauma can affect people differently, and may bring up strong feelings of shame, guilt, disgust or anger. This may happen immediately or after a long or short delay. Support from an organisation such as Rape Crisis or Survivors can be extremely helpful, no matter how long ago or how recently the attack took place. Rape Crisis exists to help any woman who has been raped or sexually assaulted, telephone 0115 900 3560, 9 a.m. to 5.30 p.m. on weekdays to find out the details of the nearest Rape Crisis centre, or look in the local phone book.

MALE RAPE

Rape is one of the most misunderstood and damaging forms of attack on men by men. Research suggests that the primary motivation behind rape is not to release sexual frustration but to humiliate, hurt and destroy, and many victims feel too traumatised or ashamed to seek help. Male rape victims still need to seek medical attention, and have the right to report the attack to the police, get their attacker prosecuted and have counselling. Survivors is set up to help male rape victims and their helpline is 020 7833 3737.

HARASSMENT

It is illegal to threaten or pester another person, and this includes making nuisance phone calls, stalking and homophobic or racist behaviour. The police have special units to deal with all of these problems, and your local station should be your first port of call if you wish to complain or ask for protection.

MALICIOUS PHONE CALLS

If you get a malicious call, stay calm and don't make any response. Put the handset down and walk away. If calls persist, unplug your landline or switch off your mobile for a while. Then contact your phone provider for more advice. British Telecom offers an advice service and leaflet on how to deal with malicious callers. Call 0800 666 700, for a recorded message, or 0800 661 441 (free) for further advice 8 a.m. to 6 p.m., Monday to Saturday.

STALKING

Stalking is persistent unwanted attention from another person, and some studies suggest it happens to around 3 per cent of students. It may take the form of death threats or being followed everywhere, or it may seem to take a less threatening course where someone keeps asking for dates or sends unwanted notes, love letters or gifts. Stalking victims live in chronic fear, which takes its toll. Because there are no physical injuries, victims have a hard time being believed, or people tell them not to be so paranoid or to pull themselves together. If you think you are being stalked, go to the local police, and write down the crime number and the name of the officer in charge of the case.

Tell family, friends, neighbours and people at work what is going on and ask them to look out for you. Do not agree to meet with your stalker, and if you do see them, try to show as little emotion as possible. Make a note of any incidents that happen, and if anything arrives in the post try not to handle it, placing it in a plastic bag to preserve fingerprints or other evidence. Get a mobile phone and a personal alarm, and make sure your home security is up to scratch. You may also wish to engage a solicitor to take out a restraining order. There's more advice available by writing to Network for Surviving Stalking, PO Box 7836, Crowthorne, Berkshire, RG45 7YA enclosing a stamped self-addressed 'A4' envelope, or look at their website, www.nss.org.uk. Victim Support and the Suzy Lamplugh Trust are also able to provide information.

USEFUL NUMBERS

VICTIM SUPPORT

An organisation that exists to help all victims of crime. They can help by offering counselling, practical advice and support to witnesses in court. You can telephone their Victim Supportline on 0845 30 30 900. It's open 9 a.m. to 9 p.m. Monday to Friday, 9 a.m. to 7 p.m. weekends and 9 a.m. to 5 p.m. bank holidays. There's also a minicom (or text telephone) number on 020 7896 3776, and a website at www.victimsupport.com.

THE SUZY LAMPLUGH TRUST

This organisation has provided much of the information in the personal safety section of this chapter. They are the leading UK safety advice charity and can be contacted for more information by writing to them at: PO Box 17818, London, SW14 8WW, telephoning 020 8876 0305, or via their website: www.suzylamplugh.org.

YOU AND THE LAW

If you're stopped in the street by the police, you have to give them your name and address if they ask for them. You don't have to answer any other questions there and then if you don't want to, but failure to do so may mean you end up being arrested. You have a right to ask why the police have stopped you, and if they are plain clothes officers you have a right to see their warrant cards. Try to be courteous, and move along if they ask you to. If they want to search you in public they can only check through your outer clothing, and the search should be done by an officer of the same sex as you.

The police may ask you to accompany them down to the station. You can refuse to do so voluntarily, but they may then arrest you if they suspect you have been involved in a crime. Should you be arrested, you have the right to know exactly what for, and the police have to show you a written copy of your all your legal rights. You must also be given the chance to see a duty solicitor, which is a free service, or your own solicitor if you have one. Wait until the solicitor arrives before you answer any police questions. You can also have one other person notified that you've been arrested. Once you've been arrested, the police can search, fingerprint and photograph you. If you're not charged with an offence, these records must be destroyed afterwards.

Anyone who thinks they have been treated unfairly by the police can make a complaint. If you are at the police station ask to see the Duty Inspector, who will tell you how to make your complaint formal. You can also write a letter to the Chief Constable, complain to a civil liberties group such as Release or contact a solicitor about possible legal action. Contact the Release Legal Helpline on 020 7749 4034 10 a.m. to 6 p.m., Monday to Friday.

CRIME TIME

Experiences from the students on www.virginstudent.com

'I had my bag nicked from the computer labs at uni. I wasn't too worried about most of the contents and it was fortunate my folder was on the desk where I was working. The only thing that I did find that I missed was my calculator, I knew where all the scientific buttons were and everything. I had an exam the following day and I didn't do too well as the calculator I had managed to borrow had different ways of getting the same results. I got my bag back after two weeks and nothing was missing from it at all. Just the inconvenience of it all really.'

'We were burgled in our second year while there were five of us in the house. They forced open the kitchen window at the back of the house, stole the microwave from the kitchen and the telly from the living room, neither of which were worth very much money because they were pretty old and cheap to start off with. They let themselves out of the front door with the spare key we keep next to it. My flatmate's dad was lovely, he drove miles the next day to fit window locks on all our downstairs windows. At least we were insured, but it was so scary that people got into our house in the middle of the night and we didn't even hear them.'

'You think you'd be safe in your own uni library but no, some thieving little eejits (students themselves) took to organising a mini-crime wave. Their target was unattended bags to steal mobile phones. Pop off to get a book for a few mins and you'd be phoneless. The buggers! GRRR! You can't even trust fellow students, what is the world coming to? They were caught though I think – justice prevails!'

10. GRADUATION AND BEYOND

All good things must come to an end, but as graduation looms and your time as an undergraduate draws to a close, you might be able to line up something even better. As you wave goodbye to your undergraduate days, you have all kinds of choices and opportunities available to you.

This chapter looks at:

- **The graduation process and getting your certificates**
- **How to make the most of your new graduate job**
- **Other employment options and work searches**
- **The scope of graduate study and funding opportunities**
- **Taking a gap year after finishing university**

WHAT GRADUATING IS REALLY LIKE

You've taken your final year exams, and you've handed in your assignments. Now comes the agonising wait to see whether you've passed your degree or not, and what class degree you've been awarded. Depending on the timing of your exams and the processes in your department, this wait can be anything from a few days to a few weeks. Your department will tell you in advance what day and what time the results will be announced.

When you arrive in your department, or other announcement place, there will be a crowd of worried-looking students jostling each other to look at the results. Some people just like to find their own name, others are a bit more nosey and want to see how everyone else has done too. If you got the results you wanted then it's time to celebrate. If things didn't go so well, you might have to contact your course tutors to talk through what went wrong, and whether or not it's appropriate to take resits.

Your department may have laid on a few drinks, or something more formal. This is your chance to celebrate or commiserate, and to make sure you have the contact details of all the people you want to keep in touch with. Some of them will be going straight off on holiday, or out of town to do summer jobs or work experience, and you might not see them at the graduation ceremony. It's also a good time to make sure you have the correct names and addresses of any tutors who have agreed to act as your referees.

Once you're sure you know you're going to be graduating this summer, you can decide whether or not to attend the ceremony. Many students say going along to this event is more of a 'thank you' to their parents than anything else, and if they've helped to put you through university then it's a kind gesture to make towards them. They get to dress up smartly and be proud of their offspring for a morning or an afternoon, and for some reason most of them love doing this.

THE GRAND CEREMONY

Formal graduation ceremonies require you to dress in university robes and caps, preferably with something smart on underneath. You hire the robes in advance, with contact details supplied by your department. Some token details about gown and cap size are taken, but rest assured it's always a loose-fitting unflattering garment. At least everyone else is looking equally stupid as they struggle to do the things up, and put the mortarboard the right way round on their heads. It's fun to see most of your year flapping around like oversized owls, and it makes for some interesting photographs later.

The presentations take place in a large hall, overseen by the university's chancellor who will probably be wearing a ridiculous official gown-and-gold-chains outfit. You queue up alongside the stage, take your turn to shake the chancellor's hand and make a little small talk, get a touch of stage fright, and exit stage right with a degree certificate in your hand. Your time in the spotlight takes a few seconds, but the whole ceremony can take hours because of all the speeches and the sheer number of graduates who are lined up. Even if you're bored silly, your parents will probably be loving it and may insist on having your picture taken by a professional photographer afterwards. Some universities then lay on a garden party, or a formal lunch or dinner for the new graduates and their guests. If you can't make it to your graduation ceremony, or you don't fancy it, you can make arrangements to graduate 'in absentia'. This means that you sign a form to say you won't be there in person, and they send you your degree certificate in the post later.

COMMON CHOICES FOR NEW GRADUATES

At the moment, among students who have just graduated:

- **33 per cent go straight into a graduate job that they've already arranged**
- **29 per cent go on holiday, or take a gap year**
- **23 per cent are looking for a graduate job**
- **20 per cent go straight on to do further study**
- **17 per cent take temporary jobs**

(figures from the UNITE and MORI Student Living Report)

If you don't have anything lined up right away, or you're still not sure what you want to do for a living, don't despair. The majority of graduates aren't sure exactly what kind of career they're after, and you don't have to decide immediately, even if you feel under pressure to do so. It's better to get over the aftermath of finals and award ceremonies, clear your head, then take some time to think about what you want to do.

STARTING YOUR GRADUATE JOB

Before you go in for your first day, have a good look through all the literature that your new employer has provided for you. Although some of it might make you doze off, persevere and try to get a better idea of the organisation. Check your contract to see whether or not you have a probation period, and what targets you have to meet within it to be kept on. Then be on your best behaviour for as long as it takes, because they're expecting you to prove yourself now.

Sort yourself out a few outfits that look good and help you fit in with the people around you. Don't go overboard and buy a whole new wardrobe before you've even earned your first pay packet though. When you turn up looking smart on your first day, be sure you know where you're going and what time you're expected. You should then be given an induction into the heady world of graduate work.

Inductions can vary. If you're lucky you get a welcome pack, all kinds of training, a supervisor you can always contact if you're stuck, and orientation for the whole building. If you're not so lucky, you may find yourself dumped in a cubicle with no idea of what you're supposed to be doing, a computer you can't use because the password is a mystery, and a long trek to find the well-hidden toilets. Whatever happens in your first few days, make the best of it, and try to keep a note of everything important that's said such as names, departments, phone numbers and codes. In an unfamiliar, confusing, slightly stressful environment it's very easy to get distracted and forget important things, so taking notes helps.

Be polite and friendly to everyone, even if they seem a bit distant or grumpy. Say hello over the water cooler or in the tea room, and don't be scared to say that you're new and you don't know where anything is. Sooner or later someone will take pity on you and offer to help you out. Volunteer to do a few things such as make the coffee or take files up onto a different floor, and get your face seen. Beware of the office gossip and the office letch, and make a few friends you can go down the pub with after the end of the working day. Do your best to remember people's names, and if you're having trouble look out for boards in reception with employee names and photos on them, or look at the company website for similar information.

The first few weeks can be unsettling and tiring, whatever type of work you're doing. Stick it out unless you're convinced you've made a terrible mistake, or the position is nothing like the one that you signed up for. If you find you're mostly doing menial tasks such as filing or data inputting, don't worry too much at the beginning. Do your tasks well and on time, and try not to look bored or stroppy, then start asking for more responsibility or training. Use those brain-dead moments to chat to people to increase your social network and find out more about the company. If the work doesn't get any more interesting after the first few weeks, speak to your supervisor about your expectations for the job, to see if anything can be done.

Once you've settled into the job properly, think about how it matches up with your career aspirations. Is it worth staying and finding out how easy it is to rise through the ranks, or should you consider stepping up to a better position by moving to a different organisation? Every six months or so, make a mental check of what you have learned or otherwise gained from your current job, and set some modest targets for the next six months, so that you're always challenging yourself. Keep an eye on the employment market to see how your current work matches up, and what your other options are.

STILL LOOKING FOR A GRADUATE JOB?

Thousands of graduates leave university without a 'proper' job to go to. It's not the end of the world, and may turn out to be a highly varied and interesting start to your working life. If possible, stay in touch with the university careers centre over the summer and beyond, keeping an eye on their job lists and looking for employers who catch your eye. Make sure you have an idea of the type of work that would suit you best, and spend more time looking out for vacancies. In fact, it sometimes helps to treat your job search as if it were a type of employment itself. Get up on time and plan your week around finding something. Job centres often say that the best jobs are snapped up first thing in the morning by keen people.

Be careful not to slip into a lifestyle where you sleep in, give up on getting a good job, or spend hours hanging around doing nothing. The longer you carry on like this, the harder it is to motivate yourself to get into employment (or do anything at all), and the more trouble you will have adjusting to a working environment.

Go back and look through your search strategy and consider the following:

- **Broadening the subject areas or types of work you could try.**

- **Visiting careers centres and job centres more regularly.**

- **Reviewing your CV and interview technique, and adapting it accordingly.**

- **Reading through newspapers that have graduate sections, such as the Rise supplement in the Guardian every Saturday.**

- **Doing targeted voluntary work or work experience to make contacts.**

- **Checking local businesses, newspapers or shop windows for opportunities.**

- **Talking to everyone you know about your search, they may know someone who knows someone . . .**

- **Signing up with all job websites that have suitable vacancies, and using their full range of facilities: email alerts, the chance to regularly look at all their new vacancies (which aren't always included in the email alerts), job hunting advice, chat sessions with experts, message boards, and the chance to post your CV online (without your home address on display).**

- **Trying advice websites such as www.prospects.ac.uk, www.thebigchoice.com or www.doctorjob.com.**

- **Introducing yourself to graduate recruitment agencies.**

- **Continuing to hunt for suitable employers, and presenting yourself to them.**

- **Being more flexible about location or salary.**

- **Taking on a stop-gap job or part-time or temporary work to get some money coming in while you continue to look for something more suitable in the long term.**

- **Keeping your job searching records in a neat file, including ads and clippings, company research, copies of CVs and application forms, and rejection letters or other feedback.**

If you're unemployed when your course ends, get down to the nearest employment job centre with your national insurance number as soon as you can, have a new jobseeker interview and sign on for Jobseeker's Allowance (JSA). Apply for anything else you may be eligible for, such as housing benefit, getting independent advice from your local Citizens' Advice Bureau if necessary. JSA isn't much to live on, but if you're used to living on a tight student budget already, you should have some good coping skills. Most job centres ask you to turn up once a fortnight to sign on, and may ask you for proof that you've been actively seeking work. This is where keeping a file of your records comes in handy; if nothing else it will help to keep the benefits officers off your back. Find out more about benefits at www.dwp.gov.uk.

Anyone who is unemployed or in a low-paid job and has serious debts should take a long hard look at their finances. If you're earning less than £10,000 per year then you won't have to make any student loan repayments, so don't worry about them at all for the time being. However, if you owe money on credit cards, high-interest loans or overdrafts with a hefty fee, then you need to make a plan. If you can't borrow money from family to clear some or all of these debts then you'll have to write to your creditors to explain your financial situation, preferably before you start to miss your regular payments. Say that you're currently jobhunting and hopeful, and that you would like to discuss ways to repay the money more slowly. Once you do find work, throw as much money at your high-interest debts as you can to begin with. Have a look at the debt information in Chapter 6 for more details about paying your creditors off.

TAKING A STOP-GAP JOB OR TEMPING

If you've been unemployed for a while and the chance to break into your ideal vocation hasn't presented itself yet, you might have to think about taking a stop-gap job or working for a temp agency. A stop-gap job is anything that helps you pay the bills, from stacking shelves in Woolworth's to pulling pints down the local. Tell yourself that it isn't going to be forever, and get stuck in.

Temping has more potential than most stop-gap jobs because it can pay fairly well, gives you variety, and could allow you to work widely in your chosen field. If you are friendly and hard-working, the employer may even take you on as a permanent employee at the end of the contract. Sign up with every reputable temp agency who places workers in the area you're interested in, and ring them up daily sounding keen; you'll soon find out which agency gets you the best and most frequent placements. Keep building on your skills and soon you'll be able to command higher daily rates. Some agencies even offer you subsidised training, or free online courses to make you more marketable.

A major downside of agency work is that they are paid for placing you in any old temp job, rather than the type of work you'd prefer. Don't get pushed into doing stuff you know you'll hate, unless it's your first job with a new agency and you want to get your foot in the door. Keep an eye on the local employment market too, and be certain your agency is paying you the correct going rate for what you're doing. It helps if you can strike up a rapport with one of the recruitment staff at the temp agency, so they get to know you better, remember your name and help you find the best jobs.

BECOMING YOUR OWN BOSS

Perhaps you aren't cut out for working for other people, or you have a brilliant idea for a business. If that's the case, you might like to think about becoming self-employed. Many arts and media graduates work as freelancers, and graduates from other disciplines might want to try their hand at being an entrepreneur.

Benefits of being self-employed:

- **The freedom of running your own company**
- **The achievement of setting something up from scratch**
- **Potential earnings can be very high if you do well**

The downside of being self-employed:

- **Companies may delay paying you for the work you've already done**
- **You have to keep good records and sort out your tax**
- **Long hours and lots of responsibility can be a strain**
- **The majority of new businesses go under in the first two years**

To start your own business successfully you need a detailed plan and will have to carry out extensive research. First of all, you need to identify a market for your services or products, otherwise your business will fail quickly. You don't necessarily need a unique service or idea, you could start by looking at companies that are already doing well in the area you're interested in. Carry out some market research to work out whether there's sufficient demand for your skills or goods.

If you think your idea is likely to sell, you will probably need some start-up money to help you get going. You might need money for premises, equipment, stock, staff, training, insurance and so on. This can come from savings, bank loans, small business support networks, venture capital or grants. Think hard about how you're going to market your business, because you won't get any work if nobody's heard about you. You'll also have to register as self-employed with the Inland Revenue and pay your tax differently from people who are in full time employment.

ORGANISATIONS PROVIDING FREE HELP AND ADVICE
The National Federation of Enterprise Agencies is a non-profit independent network of agencies committed to helping small businesses start up and grow. To contact them, write to George Derbyshire, National Federation of Enterprise Agencies, Trinity Gardens, 9–11 Bromham Road, Bedford, MK40 2UQ, telephone: 01234 354055, or look at their websites: www.nfea.com and www.smallbusinessadvice.org.uk. The Startups website: www.startups.co.uk, is a comprehensive resource with news, advice and chat forums. The Prince's Trust provide people aged 18 to 30 with support from a business mentor and may be able to make small grants. Telephone: 0800 842 842, website: www.princes-trust.org.uk. Shell LiveWIRE helps young people aged 16 to 30 to start and develop their own business, and hosts a national competition for new start-ups. Telephone: 0845 757 3252, or see website: www.shell-livewire.org for details.

POSTGRADUATE STUDY
Around 400,000 students per year enrol to take further university study. It's intensive, requires hard work and dedication and can be an enormous financial strain. Postgraduate study can also be a way into a career in academia or a prerequisite for certain careers outside academia. Employers tend to see these qualifications as a sign of motivation and intelligence, and may pay salaries accordingly.

WHY DO POSTGRADUATE STUDY?
- **To learn more about a subject that interests you**

- **To improve your career prospects (make sure it's the right qualification for your industry, and the institution you study at is a recognised one)**

- **Because it's required for your chosen job (certain qualifications in social work, journalism, accountancy, law, teaching, clinical psychology and so on)**

- **To convert to another subject area (conversion courses in IT, for example)**

Don't do it simply because you can't think of anything else to do, or because you can't face the idea of leaving a safe university environment to go into the real world. You need to be motivated and dedicated or you will not be able to go the distance.

TYPES OF COURSE
Postgraduate courses are broadly split into research-based and taught courses.

Research-based courses:

- **Doctorates: PhD or DPhil. A PhD takes three to four years of full-time study, or around five to six years part time. You're expected to carry out original research, write a thesis of around 100,000 words, and complete a *viva voce* (spoken) presentation at the end of it.**

- **MPhil: similar structure to doctorates, but have a shorter course (two years or so full time) and a shorter thesis.**

- **Masters: MSc, MA, MRes. Research degrees that take 12 months or so to complete, and involve writing a short thesis. Many students who take Masters courses go on to do PhDs in similar subjects.**

Taught courses:

- **Masters: MSc, MA, MBA. These are in the sciences, the arts or business administration. They can last one or two whole years full time, or two to three years on a part-time basis. They include a mixture of lectures and tutorials, practical experience, research and a thesis, essays and exams.**

- **Postgraduate diplomas and certificates: last around nine months, and can be vocational training or conversion courses.**

- **PGCE: the most common type of teacher training. Includes classroom experience, lesson preparation and exams.**

- **Professional qualifications: may be taken at the same time as holding down a job, or doing other postgraduate courses such as diplomas.**

HOW TO FIND COURSES AND APPLY

If you're thinking about doing some postgraduate study, start by talking to staff in your department to see if they think you're suitable, and by looking at information websites such as www.prospects.ac.uk. Your university careers centre should also be a mine of useful information. Discuss your career goals and interests with an adviser, and they should be able to tell you all about the range of qualifications on offer. They can show you postgraduate directories, information booklets about postgraduate study and research, books that outline the current research programmes in Britain, and the postgrad prospectuses for all of the universities in the UK. Depending on your location and the time of year, you might be able to attend a postgraduate study fair too.

When you've narrowed it down to a type of course and a subject area, begin to gather detailed information about individual departments and courses. Use national newspapers and websites such as *The Times* Higher Education Supplement, the *Independent*, the *Guardian* (www.educationguardian.co.uk/courses) and www.prospects.ac.uk to find out course details. Specialist magazines and journals such as *Prospects Today*, *Hobsons Postgraduate Update* and *New Scientist* are other good sources. Look out for salaried academic posts, such as research assistantships, that offer you the chance to do research and gain a qualification while you're working.

Check for requirements, closing dates and contact details. Ring the course organisers up or arrange a visit, and make sure you ask them some tough questions. Consider the following when looking at specific universities:

- **Does this institution have a good reputation for research? How do they score in their official Research Assessment Exercise gradings?**

- **Is the qualification well regarded in the UK? Can it be used internationally?**
- **How are you going to fund your studies? (more about this later)**
- **What's the surrounding area like? Is it cheap and pleasant to live there?**
- **Will staying at the same university you did your undergrad degree at look bad to potential employers?**
- **What happens to graduates who complete this course? Do they go on to well-paid jobs and cutting-edge international research, or are they claiming benefits?**
- **Is there a thriving postgraduate community or will you be socially isolated?**
- **Do you think your proposed supervisor will be able to teach, support and inspire you brilliantly?**
- **Can you undertake online or distance learning?**

Ideally you should start looking at research degrees one or two years before you are due to finish your undergraduate studies. This will give you time to decide what's appropriate for your chosen career path, to discover the full details about the courses on offer, and apply and be interviewed. The best time to apply for places and funding is about a year to six months before courses are due to begin, but don't worry if you've left it later than this. Many courses have empty places left on them, or you can apply for entry in the following year. Most postgraduate degrees don't have a closing date for applications, unless they have a taught component to their timetable, such as some Masters and PGCEs etc.

Application methods vary between universities. Sometimes it involves sending in a CV and covering letter, and sometimes application forms are used. Include a mention of study areas you're particularly interested in, and make sure your academic references are as good as possible. If you're a suitable applicant, you'll be called in for an interview. Expect to be interviewed by more than one member of staff, usually the proposed supervisor and perhaps the head of department. Brush up on basic research techniques before you go, and read around the subject area, including topical items in the news or in the relevant subject journals. Use the interview as a chance to get to know the people in the department, and to see if you like the place and the supervisor.

Teacher training information can be obtained from the government's Teacher Training Agency, Portland House, Stag Place, London, SW1E 5TT, telephone: 0845 6000 991 (For English speakers) or 0845 6000 992 (For Welsh speakers), minicom: 01245 454 343, or websites: www.tta.gov.uk and www.useyourheadteach.gov.uk. If you've already decided to take a PGCE course, go through the Graduate Teacher Training Registry, Rosehill, New Barn Lane, Cheltenham, Gloucestershire, GL52 3LZ, telephone: 0870 1122205, website: www.gttr.ac.uk.

FUNDING IN THE UK

Postgraduate students need to find money for fees and living expenses. Your department of choice may be able to help you out with funding from a number of sources, but you also need to think about finding some money of your own from funding bodies such as:

- **Various research councils such as the EPSRC and MRC**

- **The Arts and Humanities Research Board**

- **The Student Awards Agency for Scotland**

- **Charities, foundations and trusts**

- **Employer sponsorship**

- **Local education authorities (teacher training courses only)**

To find out more about sources of funding, ask your careers service about databases such as Funderfinder and Moneysearch. They may also have the Postgraduate Funding Guide which is a booklet published yearly by Prospects, and directories of funding bodies, research councils and grant-making trusts.

Full-time students may be able to gain additional income from lecturing, tutoring or supervising practicals. Part-time courses may mean that you can take on paid employment at the same time. There are also Knowledge Transfer Partnership schemes, where the student works full time for an employer but also undertakes related research and has expert academic supervisors. Contact the organisers at KTP Central Office, Brunel House, Volunteer Way, Faringdon, Oxon, SN7 7YR, telephone: 01367 245200, or see their website: www.ktponline.org.uk.

STUDYING OVERSEAS

Going abroad for postgraduate education can be a fantastic opportunity to study in centres of excellence, experience another culture and see the world. It can take a long time to put this type of study into place, so it's best to allow at least 18 months to do your research and make your arrangements. Your undergraduate tutors may have international contacts or your department may run exchange schemes with other universities, so ask around and check notice boards regularly. The university careers centre should have a whole section devoted to working and studying abroad, including information about courses in Commonwealth countries, mainland Europe, the USA and Canada, Japan and many others. Individual universities have their own International Offices which can be contacted by telephone and email, and have information displayed on their websites.

You may be asked for letters of introduction, a research plan, certificates of education, medical examinations and aptitude tests. You'll probably need help from a careers adviser to track down funding, which comes from many sources, including: awards from the individual university, funding from organisations such as the Commonwealth and NATO, awards from overseas governments, charities and trusts, and sponsorship from industry or commerce.

> I'm doing a robotics research project. At the moment there are two of us working on it – I'm in charge of the motion planning and my friend is responsible for the control mechanisms. The study is government-sponsored and must be completed within 36 months. I'm not socialising very much at the moment because the work is more important to me, and there's pressure to achieve the targets and get it done within the time scale. I'm taking a PhD so that I can become a lecturer afterwards.
>
> Mohd M Mohamad is studying for a PhD in Electrical Engineering (Robotics) at Heriot-Watt University

TAKING A GAP YEAR

Gap years are becoming more popular before and after university, and there's even a growing trend for people to take them as career breaks in their late twenties and early thirties. Most people who use their gap year to travel, or to work on worthwhile projects at home or abroad, tend to go all misty-eyed when they talk about their exploits, or have a treasured collection of photographs or diaries from their journeys.

A well-planned gap year can bring all kinds of benefits, including:

- **An initiative test if you're planning it yourself**
- **Eye-opening travel experiences**
- **A break from academia**
- **The chance to learn new languages**
- **Some time to think about your future**
- **The chance to help others**
- **Experience of fundraising**
- **Increased self-confidence and maturity**

There may be a downside to a gap year too:

- **A whole year lying on a beach doesn't impress employers**
- **Your debts may get out of control**
- **It can be hard to readjust to normal life back home**
- **Your friends and family might change a bit while you're away**

WHAT DO YOU WANNA DO?

There's an enormous range of choice for your gap year, which can be spent in the UK or pretty much any country you'd like to imagine worldwide. For example, you could try any one or a combination of the following:

- **Independent travel**
- **Expeditions**

- **Voluntary work, such as conservation**

- **Paid work**

- **Learning languages or other skills**

- **Teaching English as a foreign language (TEFL)**

There are hundreds of organisations involved in arranging gap year activities, some of them commercial and some of them non-profit. You could end up helping to build a health centre in Peru, conserving a coral reef in Australia, teaching English in Ghana or Au Pairing in the USA. *Taking a Gap Year* by Susan Griffith, Vacation work, £11.95, lists the main players in the world of gap placement organisations, which would be useful if you're thinking about using one.

You can talk to your university careers service, who should have plenty of advice about international schemes, voluntary work at home and abroad, exchanges, work experience and more. Chat to other people who've already taken a gap year, but be careful: some of them may be so enthusiastic to talk about old times and adventures that it might be hard to get them to shut up. Another way to get ideas is by using message boards on websites like www.gapyear.com and www.yearoutgroup.org, to see if anyone else has done the same thing, and what their tips are for travelling in certain areas or working for specific organisations.

RIGHT, THAT'S IT, I'M OFF

Not so fast, mate. You need to find out if the placements you fancy have any spaces left on them, and it's essential to work out a budget for the year. Think about the total you'll end up paying for transport, hotels and hostels, visas, insurance, a backpack and its contents, fees to gap organisations if you're using them, and general living expenses. Once you have a sensible figure for these expenses, you need to raise the necessary funds.

Funding may be attached to certain programmes, or you may be able to get hold of grants and other money from charitable organisations. Perhaps you could raise some of the money by writing to local businesses or doing a stunt and asking people to sponsor you. Many gappers end up working frantically in crappy jobs in the UK to get some money together for the first few months of their gap year before going travelling, or do casual work when they're abroad to cover their living expenses.

You also need to sort out most or all of the following:

PLACEMENTS FOR WORK AND VOLUNTEERING

It can take a while to find a suitable placement and complete all the necessary paperwork. Think hard about the place you want to visit, what the accommodation arrangements are, whether you'll be with similar people your own age or on your own, and what backups exist in case something goes wrong. Don't be scared to ask the organisation some tough questions, or to ask around to see what last year's intake thought of their placements.

TICKETS FOR TRAVEL

If you're planning on visiting several places, you might save a fair amount of money with a round-the-world ticket. Compare prices from different operators, and find out what restrictions apply. If you're in Europe or the USA, think about getting one of the discount coachcards or railcards such as an InterRail Pass. Contact specialist travel organisations such as STA Travel (www.statravel.co.uk) and Trailfinders (www.trailfinders.co.uk), and ask them for their best quotes.

VISAS AND WORK PERMITS

These may be tricky to obtain for some countries, and there may be long delays or mountains of red tape to wade through. It can sometimes get expensive as well. If you're going to be travelling as part of an organised gap year programme, this is where being part of a larger organisation comes in most handy, because they can give you expert advice and backup when it comes to sorting the paperwork out.

COMPREHENSIVE INSURANCE

Never skimp on the insurance cover. Get good insurance for your health and belongings, and if you're planning to go white-water rafting or bungee jumping then make sure it's covered in the small print. Unplanned use of private healthcare and emergency rescue and repatriation can set you back hundreds of thousands of pounds. Think about it.

YOUR HEALTHCARE

If you're going to be away from home for a year, have a checkup with your doctor and your dentist before you leave. Take plenty of medication with you if you have any long-standing condition. Arrange any vaccinations well in advance; some of them have to be spread out in a course that lasts several weeks. Required vaccinations for certain areas seem to change every few weeks, so talk to your GP or nearest vaccination centre, and check health and safety website www.fco.gov.uk/knowbeforeyougo. You may need proof of vaccination before you can cross some borders.

LUGGAGE AND PACKING

Carrying an overloaded pack around slows you down and tires you out. Travel as light as you can, and pick things up on the way if you need them. Take comfortable clothes in breathable materials, a washbag and towel, a small day pack, a change of shoes, a body belt or other way of keeping your valuables hidden, a camera, a small first-aid kit and so on. Depending on where you're travelling, you may also want to take water purification tablets or equipment, insect repellent, sun block and a hat.

YOUR LOCAL KNOWLEDGE

Find out as much as you can about the culture you're visiting, and be respectful of local traditions. Don't cause unnecessary upset by flashing too much flesh or not covering your head and shoulders at certain religious sites. Learn enough of the language to get by, including please and thank you. Shouting very loudly and slowly in English doesn't work anywhere in the world, but any attempt to speak the local lingo tends to be received well.

QUALIFICATIONS

If you're hoping to teach English as a foreign language abroad, be careful which TEFL qualification you take before leaving because some of them are recognised internationally and others aren't. You can still teach on some schemes if you don't have a certificate, but a good qualification gives you a better range of choice.

ACCOMMODATION

If you're travelling independently, arrange somewhere half decent in advance to crash out at, for when you finally crawl off that cramped and sticky long-haul flight. It's difficult to find cheap and pleasant accommodation when you're wasted and jet-lagged, and it's dangerous to try this at night in a town you don't know. Pay the extra for the first night or two, and then you can start searching for a place that's more of a bargain.

YOUR CAREER

If you've been offered a graduate position by a good employer, but desperately want a gap year, you may be allowed to defer your place for one year. Speak to them as soon as you can once you've made your decision, to give them time to make any necessary arrangements.

WHEN I GRADUATE FROM UNI I'M GONNA . . .

Dreams and schemes from the students on www.virginstudent.com

. . . spend two months playing top tunes to smiley happy people and then bite the bullet and become a corporate lawyer. Now there's an antithesis for you.

. . . attempt to pay off the crippling and mind-consuming debt

I can't wait to join the rat race. I want to earn enough money to holiday four times a year and take out shares in Jimmy Choo and Chloe. Obviously, this is a tad dreamful for the near future but entering the business world, earning a decent wage and being able to look at clothes rails (which don't say sale above them) is definitely a thought that excites me!

. . . go to graduate school in America. Another five years in uni before I have to face the big bad real world

I'm a mature student and I have been working for twenty years of my life in secretarial-type jobs. I have just joined university to do an environmental science degree and hopefully I will graduate and go into the field of environmental management/consultancy.

. . . claim bankruptcy

When I graduate I'm going to get a job at Marks and Spencer where I mindlessly man the tills, counting the long months until I can afford my postgraduate in magazine journalism. Oh wait, that's the present.

. . . book in for two weeks of electro convulsive therapy. It might help me forget just how bad Exeter was.

I'll have to get a good job to get a bit of cash behind me, then I want to own my design business and do some travelling. I really want to go to Iceland, New Zealand and Austria.

Whatever you decide to do, enjoy yourself and good luck!

APPENDIX 1: THE BASICS

About 50 per cent of new students arrive at university unable to do at least one of the following tasks: change an electrical plug, budget their money, cook a meal for four people, use a washing machine or an iron, or do their own cleaning. So if you haven't got a handle on these yet, you're in good company! However, there's nothing quite like learning how to live like an independent adult, and nobody wants to look like a spoiled princess or a helpless mummy's boy. Here are the basics for your home, electricals, car and bike, plus a selection of different recipes to stop you from going hungry.

ELECTRICAL KNOW-HOW
Basic safety:

- **Never handle electrical equipment, switches or sockets with wet hands or anything metallic.**

- **Don't overload wall sockets with too many appliances. If you have to use an extension, use one with the sockets in a row, rather than a cube-shaped one.**

- **Never be tempted to do any re-wiring in a rented house – it's the landlord's responsibility.**

If the lights all go out:

- **It could be a general power cut, or an electrical circuit could have tripped out.**

- **Look to see if your neighbours have been affected – if not, it's probably a problem inside your house.**

- **Start by checking your electrical fuse box, which should be near to your electricity meter.**

- **If the trip switch is on the 'on' position, turn it off and then back on again. If power is not restored, press the 'test' button – if this trips the trip switch into the 'off' position there is a problem with your house wiring or an appliance. If it doesn't go into the 'off' position, contact your electricity provider because your supply has been lost.**

- **If, when you look at the fuse box for the first time, the trip switch has moved to the 'off' position, try switching it back on again – if it switches itself back off again straight away, this suggests that one of your electrical appliances is faulty.**

- **Turn off all your electrical appliances, and push the trip switch back into the 'on' position.**

- **Next, switch all your electrical appliances back on one at a time. If the trip switch goes off again when you get to a particular appliance, that's** the one that's probably faulty. Unplug it and get it checked by an electrician.

Change a lightbulb:

- If it's an overhead light or a wall light, turn off the switch. If it's a table or floor lamp, unplug it.

- Use an alternative source of light if it's dark.

- Remove the old bulb with a dry cloth, it may be hot enough to burn you.

- Bulbs have either a bayonet fitting or a screw fitting at the end. If it's a bayonet, push it gently into the socket as far as it will go before turning the bulb clockwise. If it's a screw, just screw it in.

- Use the right wattage bulb for the appliance. For example, soft table lighting usually takes a 40 watt bulb, bright overhead lighting takes a 100 watt bulb, and so on.

- Dispose of the old bulb safely, wrapped in old newspaper.

Wire a three-pin plug:

- Most modern appliances are sold with their own plugs already attached. Sometimes you may need to replace a plug, or undo one to sort out loose wiring.

- Unscrew the screw in the middle of the plastic cover, and take the cover off so you are looking inside the middle of the plug, with the metal pins facing downwards.

- The terminal (the top of the inside of the metal pin) at the top of the plug, sometimes marked 'E', is the earth terminal. The terminal at the bottom of the plug with the fuse attached and marked 'L' is the live terminal. The terminal at the bottom of the plug without a fuse attached and marked 'N' is the neutral terminal.

- Take the electrical cable, and carefully strip off the end of the outer plastic casing (which is usually white) to reveal 4 cm of coloured wires.

- Strip the coloured plastic coating off the last 1 cm of each wire to reveal strands of copper. Twist the strands together neatly.

- In new electrical cables, the green and yellow striped wire is Earth and goes to the terminal marked 'E', the brown wire is Live and goes to the terminal marked 'L', and the blue wire is Neutral and goes to the terminal marked 'N'. Some appliances do not have an earth wire in their cable.

- In older electrical cables, the green wire is Earth, the red wire is Live, and the black wire is Neutral. Do not wire this plug alone if you are colour blind, it's dangerous to get the colours mixed up.

- Fit the right coloured wire into the right terminal and turn the tiny screws at the top of each terminal until they tighten and hold the exposed copper part of the wire in place.

- Make sure there are no loose bits of copper wire, and that the plastic covering the wire goes right up as far as the outer edge of each terminal.
- Fit the flex into place by screwing down the cord grip (the flat piece of plastic at the bottom of the plug that has two small screws in it).
- Check the fuse is the right amp fuse for the appliance.
- Screw the plastic cover of the plug back into place.

Replace a fuse:

- Turn the plug over so the metal pins are facing upwards.
- Unscrew the screw in the middle of the plug and lift off the plastic cover.
- The fuse is the small whitish tube with metal ends that's clipped into a small holder inside the plug. Gently lift it out, and replace it with a new fuse.
- Make absolutely sure you've used the right kind of fuse. The plug should have whatever amp fuse it requires written on it somewhere.
- Replace plastic cover and screw back into place, then plug the appliance in and switch it on to see if it's working.
- If it's working OK, throw away the old fuse.

COMPUTER CARE

- Use an extension plug with a circuit breaker. This will protect your computer from damage due to power surges.
- Use the 'defragment' function and 'empty trash' function regularly to help the computer to work more efficiently.
- Pay the extra for an up-to-date version of a virus protection programme, and check for any available free updates online.
- If you have broadband internet access or spend a long time online, consider getting a firewall.

CAR BASICS

Buying a used car safely:

- Take along a mechanic friend or independent examiner and look at the car in broad daylight.
- Look for signs of rust, and check seat belts, tyres, door and window seals, worn tyres or oil and water leaks.
- Look for patchy paintwork or signs of welding in the boot, they could be signs that the car has been in a bad accident previously.
- Ask for registration documents, service record and MOT certificate, check that the address of the seller and the details of the car match up, and see if the mileage and condition of the car are right for its age.

- If you're buying privately, call the DVLA for free on 0870 241 1878 to see if the registration document is genuine.

- Have a test drive watching for rattles and clunks and smooth braking, and use a fault checklist from the Office of Fair Trading (08457 22 44 99). Beware of cars with shaky steering columns, pulling to one side when driving, or giving off a strong smell of petrol.

- Read the small print of any garage guarantee or warranty.

Before a journey:

- Look under the car to spot oil or water leaks.

- Make sure you've topped up the water supply for the windscreen washers.

- Have a quick look round the headlights, tail lights and brake lights to see if they're working.

- Check tyres for wear or damaged areas.

- Using your car manual for guidance, check levels of engine oil, engine coolant and brake fluid.

- As you pull away from your parking spot, and before you get onto a busy road, take a moment to gently test your brakes.

BICYCLE BASICS

Buying a second-hand bike:

- If you're buying a second-hand bike, a reputable bike dealer is a good option. Whoever sold it to the dealer will most likely have provided the dealer with identification and proof of address so there's a good chance that the bike hasn't been stolen.

- If you are concerned about being in receipt of potentially stolen and security tagged bikes, ask for references, get recommendations from friends and use your common sense.

- Bike sizing is important. If you prefer a mountain bike, allow for at least 4 inches of clearance between the top tube (the one running from the base of the headtube to the top of the seat tube) and your bits. When seated on the bike, your elbows should be bent to allow free movement to steer but not so bent that you can't steer. For Tour de France-style road bikes, allow 3 inches of clearance and use the same principle for the elbows.

- Always have a test ride because comfort and safety are the key things to look for. If the bike doesn't feel comfortable to ride, don't buy it. Saddles can be changed but if you don't feel comfortable in the riding position then, chances are you either have the wrong size bike or the bike type may not be suitable for you. Try another bike.

- There may be minute cracks in the tubes of the bike framework, which could snap under stress. Apply the front brake, grab the head tube (the part of the frame under the handlebars) and rock the bike back and forth. If there's any movement, creaking or clunks from within the head tube, the headset may be loose.

- Check the brake and gear cables, and make sure they're clean and unfrayed. Look for brake blocks to make sure they're unworn. Test the brakes during your test ride.

- Spin the wheels and look down at them between the brake blocks to see if they're bent.

- Check the gear mechanism. It should look clean and well lubricated.

Before a bike journey:

- If you're not used to cycling in an urban area, build up confidence on quieter streets.

- Always wear a helmet, front and rear lights, and high visibility clothing.

- Carry a spare inner tube, a pump, tyre levers and spare batteries for your lights.

- Check the tyres and chain are OK, and the brakes are working.

FIRST-AID BASICS

- Nosebleeds can be stopped by sitting still, tilting the head forwards slightly, and pinching the nostrils together. Hold this position for ten minutes, then gently release the nostrils to see if the bleeding has stopped. If not, pinch nostrils together for another ten minutes and check again. Call 999 if bleeding has been going on for 30 minutes or more.

- Small cuts and grazes can be wiped with antiseptic and gauze to remove grit and dirt, then covered with a sticking plaster. If you can't get the dirt out, or the cut's more than 1 cm deep, see your doctor.

- Burns and scalds should be run under cold water for ten minutes to get the heat out. Use lukewarm water on larger burns as it is less of a shock to the body. Never put butter or oily lotions on a burn, it's an old wives' tale and can make the burn worse. If it's fairly small but bigger than a 10p piece, cover with a loose breathable dressing and get it checked by a nurse. If it covers a large part of the body, call an ambulance.

- The swelling of bruises and sprains can be brought down with an ice pack or a bag of frozen peas wrapped in a clean tea towel. Bear in mind that if the injury is severe there may be a broken bone underneath the swelling, and medical attention will be needed.

Deep cuts:

- Expose the cut area. Push the edges of the wound together, using a clean dressing if possible.

- **Get the person to lie down, raise the affected limb to help stop the bleeding.**
- **Cover the wound with a sterile dressing if you have one, and call 999 for an ambulance.**

Asthma attack:

- **Be calm and reassuring and sit the person down on a chair.**
- **Help them to find their inhaler and use it.**
- **If there's no response to the inhaler, or you can't find the inhaler, call an ambulance.**

Major fits (seizures):

- **If the person is unconscious or semi-conscious and lying down, get them onto a carpet or put coats or cushions underneath them so they don't hit their head on a hard surface.**
- **Loosen collars, belts or other tight clothing. Remove any sharp objects nearby.**
- **Do not restrain the person, force anything into their mouth to keep it open, or pull on their tongue. These can make the situation worse.**
- **If possible, roll them into the recovery position (see p. 205) and keep a close eye on them.**
- **If the person is not fully conscious again within 10 minutes, or they have a second fit, call an ambulance.**

Collapse:

- **Check to see if they are breathing. If they're not breathing, call for help immediately. If you know how to do cardiopulmonary resuscitation (CPR or mouth to mouth), then turn them onto their back and administer it. If not, turn them onto their side and wait for help to arrive.**
- **If they are breathing, loosen any tight clothing or belts and put them into the recovery position, lying on their left side and with their right arm and right leg bent. See diagram below. Call 999 for an ambulance, and keep checking them from time to time to see if they're breathing OK or have regained consciousness.**

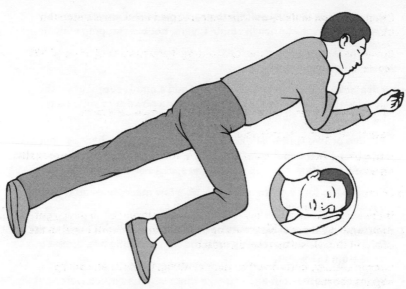

Copyright St John Ambulance 2003

RECOVERY POSITION

LAUNDRY
Using a machine:

- Sort your clothes out into two piles, light and dark colours, which should be washed separately. Check the washing care labels of every item, and remove anything which is labelled handwash only, or dry clean only.

- Take one of your piles of washing and place it inside the washing machine, but do not fill the machine so full that you're stuffing things in forcefully.

- Read the instructions on your laundry detergent packaging carefully. Put the powder, tablets or liquid into the drawer at the top of the machine OR inside the machine with your clothes, according to the instructions.

- Close the door and drawer of the machine, then choose a program.

- Pick the right program for your wash, only as hot as the labels on your clothes can take. For example, most mixed washes are able to take a standard wash at 40 degrees, but light cottons can take a standard wash at 60 degrees.

- After selecting the program, switch the machine on and leave it until it has finished the wash.

- If you have new bright- or dark-coloured clothes, like jeans, wash them separately from your other clothes for the first couple of washes, as the dye in them could get onto your other clothes and stain them.

- **Hang up your laundry quickly to dry, to prevent it smelling musty. Preferably hang clothes in single layers, not overlapping with other clothes.**

Handwashing:

- **Fill a bowl with lukewarm water and add a small cupful of washing powder to it. Check first that your washing powder is suitable for handwashing.**

- **Put one or two clothing items into the bowl and rub them against each other for a few minutes in the soapy water. Pay attention to areas that get heavy soiling, such as shirt collars, cuffs or underarm areas.**

- **Remove the first few items and scrub a few more, until all the items have been scrubbed.**

- **Throw away the washing water and re-fill the bowl with cool water. Rinse the clothes thoroughly until the soapy feeling has completely gone from the water.**

- **Wring the clothes out and squeeze them to get as much water out of them as possible.**

- **Hang the clothes up to dry, remembering that they might drip water onto the floor. If they drip badly, wring them out again or place a bowl underneath them to catch the drips.**

Tumble dryers:

- **Remove anything from your wash that has a washing instructions label saying 'do not tumble dry'. In general, this means synthetics or anything delicate.**

- **Wring out anything that's dripping wet before it goes into the dryer.**

- **Put the rest of your clothes into the tumble dryer, and switch on. The length of time it takes to dry the clothes/bedding will depend upon the fabric, the heat of the dryer and the amount of clothes/bedding.**

- **Check every 20 minutes to see if the contents are dry.**

- **If you plan to iron clothes afterwards, take them out of the dryer when they are still slightly damp, to make ironing easier.**

Ironing:

- **Check the labels of everything you're about to iron, to see what heat is needed. If in doubt, use the coolest setting.**

- **Set up the ironing board and check the base of the iron to make sure it's clean.**

- **Put water into the iron if you want to use the steam function.**

- **Lay clothing flat on the ironing board and run the iron smoothly over the surface of the fabric until all the creases are gone.**

- **When ironing a complicated garment like a shirt, iron the collar and the shoulders first, then the sleeves, then the front and back of the shirt.**

- **Hang clothing up immediately to prevent new creases from forming.**

STAIN REMOVAL

For general stains and spills, act quickly. Blot liquid spills up firmly from carpets and clothes using absorbent kitchen paper, until they become as dry as possible. Do not scrub anything at this stage, because it will grind the stains further into the fabric or the carpet pile. After blotting, use a cleaning agent that's appropriate for the particular stain (see list below). Take care when using commercial carpet cleaners, they can change the colour or your carpet, or leave you with a very clean patch that looks strange compared to the rest of your grubby student flooring.

For most staining and soiling on clothes you can rinse thoroughly with water, then use a general stain remover such as Vanish, and place the item straight into a regular wash. There's also a range of Stain Devils that remove specific stains such as grass, so if you do regular sports you could invest in one of them to keep your kit clean.

COMMON STAINS

Red wine: first blot the wine firmly out of the carpet or clothing using kitchen paper and pressing down hard. For carpets sponge the area clean with sparkling water and blot again, then use a carpet cleaner such as Vanish bubbling stain remover and rinse well. For clothes, rinse well in fresh water, then wash as usual.

Vomit: for carpets, first put on rubber gloves then scrape up the lumpy bits with a blunt knife and a dustpan. If you don't have rubber gloves, protect your hands with plastic bags. Blot up the liquid with kitchen paper, then wash the carpet with a mixture of warm water and detergent that has no bleach in it. Blot again. If it's smelly afterwards, sprinkle on a generous amount of Shake'n'Vac or spray on some Febreze. For clothes, rinse thoroughly in cold running water then wash with a biological powder or liquid.

Pasta sauce: for carpets, scrape off the residue gently then rinse with bicarbonate of soda solution, made by mixing 1 teaspoon of powder in 500 ml of water. Remove as much of the stain as you can before using carpet cleaner. For clothes, rinse the stain under the cold tap until it goes pink, rub on a stain remover like Vanish, then wash with biological powder or liquid.

Curry: for carpets, gently scrape up as much food as you can, then use a carpet cleaner. Work from the outside of the stain inwards towards the centre to avoid spreading it. For clothes, sponge with washing-up liquid or other detergent, then rub on a stain remover and wash with biological powder or liquid. Big stains may not come out.

Makeup: for carpets, scrape up any residue or vacuum up powder, then use a carpet stain remover, followed by carpet shampoo. For clothes, try rubbing with washing-up liquid or gentle detergent and rinsing, then rubbing on a stain remover like Vanish before adding to a normal wash.

Blood: for carpets, put on rubber gloves, then blot with kitchen paper before sponging thoroughly with cold water. For clothes and bedding, sponge well with cold water, and if this doesn't remove the stain, soak overnight in a solution of cold water and washing powder. Then machine wash as normal using water that's as hot as the fabric can take.

Ink: for carpets, blot up the ink gently with kitchen paper, then sponge the area with cold water or bicarbonate solution and blot dry. Repeat sponging and blotting process until you've removed as much of the ink as possible, then use carpet cleaner. For clothes, rinse thoroughly under the cold tap, then treat with Vanish stain remover or Stain Devils for ink or ballpoint pen, then wash as normal in hot water.

Candle wax: for carpets, let the wax cool and solidify, then pick off as much as you can. Place a couple of sheets of kitchen paper over the area and place an iron gently over the top. Using a very low heat, melt the wax and let it absorb into the paper. Repeat process with fresh sheets of kitchen paper until all the wax is cleaned up. For clothes, remove the wax in the same way with an iron, then wash in water that's as hot as the fabric allows.

Mud: for carpets, allow to dry then remove with a stiff brush and a vacuum cleaner. For clothes, brush off as much as you can, soak in cold water overnight then machine wash as usual.

Grass stains: for clothes, use a Stain Devil for grass or rub on some Vanish stain remover, then add to your usual wash with some biological liquid or powder.

Coffee/tea: for carpets, blot with kitchen paper then sponge with plenty of cold water. Use a carpet shampoo to get rid of any stubborn marks. For clothes, rinse under the hot tap, then machine wash in water that's as hot as the fabric allows.

GENERAL CLEANING

- **Get a kit together for spills that contains a bowl or bucket, clean cloths, a sponge, some gentle all-purpose cleaning fluid that contains no bleach, rubber gloves and gentle carpet cleaner.**

- **Never mix different cleaning products together because, no matter how harmless they look, many of them combine to produce poisonous gases.**

Dusting:

- **You don't need fancy products to dust. Just use a slightly damp, wrung-out cloth to wipe surfaces such as tables, shelves and windowsills. If the cloth gets dirty, rinse it out and start again.**

Vacuuming:

- **Check that the dust bag or dust collector is empty. If not, replace or empty it.**

- **A quick vacuum involves running the cleaner fairly slowly around all areas of visible carpet.**

- **A thorough vacuum involves moving the furniture to clean under there as well, and using the extra vacuum tool or a damp cloth to get at the dust that collects on the carpet at the edge of the skirting board.**

- **If your vacuum cleaner isn't picking dust up very well, check the bag or dust collector. If that isn't the cause, use the manufacturer's guidelines to check for other blockages in the machine, or contact the landlord.**

Floor cleaning:

- **Laminate floors just need to be swept and wiped down with a damp cloth occasionally.**

- **Floors with vinyl or ceramic tiles need to be swept first, then mopped. Use multi-purpose cleaner or floor cleaner to make up a bucket of hot soapy cleaning solution, then use this to scrub the floor with a clean mop. Use neat cleaner to scrub up small sticky dirty areas. Discard dirty water and rinse mop out thoroughly. Mop again using clean hot water. Squeeze out mop to dry it out and use it to get excess water off the floor. Discard dirty water and rinse out mop again. Leave floor to dry.**

- **Keep floor-cleaning equipment away from other cleaning equipment to prevent the spread of bacteria.**

BATHROOM STUFF

Sinks, baths and showers:

- **Use multi-purpose cleaning fluid to wipe down the inside and outside of sinks, baths, wall tiles and shower trays. Pay extra attention to soap scum and tide marks. Use an old toothbrush to clean around dirty taps. Pull hairs out of plugholes, then rinse everything down thoroughly with clean water.**

- **If your bath is old, or enamel, make sure your cleaning products are gentle and say they're suitable for enamel etc.**

- **If there's mould growing, put on rubber gloves and use a mould and mildew spray to kill it off. Use every now and again to stop mould growing back.**

Toilets:

- **Wipe down the seat, cistern and the outside of the bowl with multi-purpose cleaning fluid.**

- Squirt toilet cleaner into the bowl and up under the rim of the toilet. Leave for a few minutes, then scrub off firmly with a toilet brush. Keep the toilet brush in the bowl and flush the toilet to get rid of cleaning products and to rinse the brush clean.

Limescale:

- Limescale is the chalky whitish stuff that builds up around taps, shower heads, plug holes and toilet bowls.

- The cheapest way to get rid of it is by soaking a cloth in distilled white vinegar and wrapping it around the affected area for a few minutes. Then scrub off with a plastic scourer and rinse with clean water.

- Stubborn deposits can be removed with commercial limescale cleaners such as Limelite. Follow the instructions carefully, wear rubber gloves and avoid getting it on your clothes.

CLEANING TIPS FOR KITCHENS

- Keep your kitchen cleaning equipment separate from other cleaning equipment to prevent the spread of bacteria.

- Wipe down kitchen surfaces, the outside of cookers, fridge doors and the inside of microwaves with a solution of hot water and anti-bacterial cleanser to keep them fresh.

- Stubborn stains on worktops can be removed by dabbing them with weak bleach and leaving it there for a few minutes, then rinsing well with clean water. Wear rubber gloves, don't let it get on your clothes and don't leave it unattended in case flatmates get it all over themselves.

- Keep sink drains free from greasy blockages by using a commercial sink cleaner regularly, or by pouring a solution of soda crystals dissolved in boiling water down the sink once a week. Use rubber gloves and avoid getting any of the solution on your skin as it can burn.

Cooker tops and hobs:

- Take off the removable metal pan holders and any removable control knobs, then scrub down with a plastic scourer and some multi-purpose cleaning solution. Wash pan holders and control knobs in the same solution. Scrape off stubborn food deposits gently with a blunt knife.

- If food is badly burnt-on, use a commercial oven cleaner and handle with extreme caution as it can cause chemical burns to the skin.

Inside ovens:

- Newer ovens are self-cleaning, but the cookers in most student houses are old-fashioned enamelled ones, which do need cleaning occasionally, especially if you want to get your bond back from the landlord at the end of your tenancy.

- Take out metal trays and racks. Scrape food out of the bottom of the oven with a spatula.

- Use a commercial oven cleaner inside the oven, and on metal trays and racks if they're very dirty. Be VERY careful. Wear an old long-sleeved T-shirt, rubber gloves, and an apron if you have one. Get all the windows open for maximum ventilation to get rid of fumes, and follow the instructions on the cleaner packaging exactly. If you get any on your skin, rinse immediately in huge amounts of cold running water for at least five minutes.

- Less-dirty trays and racks can be scrubbed with hot water and washing-up liquid, or soaked in a solution of hot water and half a teacupful of biological washing (laundry) powder.

Pans with burnt-on food:

- Remove from the heat immediately and allow to cool slowly. Adding cold water immediately may damage the pan or make it spit hot food at you.

- Scrape cooled burnt food into the bin, and rinse the pan out with water and washing-up liquid.

- If the food is still burnt-on, leave the pan to soak overnight filled with either distilled white vinegar or hot water mixed with half a teacupful of biological washing powder.

Fridges:

- Take all the food out and switch the fridge off. Wash any stains or sticky deposits with hot water and anti-bacterial cleaning fluid.

- If the fridge is still smelly, mix 2 teaspoons of bicarbonate of soda into 500 ml of hot water, and use to wipe down the inside of the fridge.

Bins:

- Wipe down bin lids regularly with anti-bacterial cleanser.

- If the inside of the bin is gungy and smelly, swill it out with a solution of hot water and washing-up liquid, then wipe down with anti-bacterial cleanser.

FOOD SAFETY

- Check the sell-by and use-by dates when you're buying food. Be especially careful with fish, poultry, meat and dairy products. If in doubt, throw it away.

- Keep your fridge temperature control at 5 degrees or cooler, and don't store raw and cooked food next to each other and uncovered.

- Wash hands with soap before cooking and after handling raw meat, fish or chicken. Wash raw meat, fish or chicken well before preparing it and, preferably, keep an extra chopping board just for these raw foods.

- **Use disposable cloths or kitchen paper to clean up your kitchen, or cloths that are washed regularly and hung up at night to dry completely, rather than old rags that sit around for weeks in pools of water without being washed.**

RECIPES

To get started in the kitchen, you might like to invest in some simple cookbooks to get you started, such as *The Complete Cookery Course* by Delia Smith, BBC Consumer Publishing, £9.99, or *The Essential Student Cookbook* by Cas Clarke, Hodder Headline, £5.99.

QUICK SNACKS FOR ONE

PASTA WITH GARLIC, OLIVE OIL AND CHILLI
Ingredients:
100 g of dried pasta such as fusilli (twists)
1 clove of garlic, peeled, then crushed or finely chopped
1 small crumbled dried chilli, or a pinch of chilli powder
1 tablespoon of olive oil

Method:
Put the pasta on to cook with plenty of boiling water, according to the instructions on the packet.
Make the sauce while the pasta is cooking.
In a frying pan, cook the garlic and olive oil over a very low heat for 4 minutes, then add the chilli. Stir thoroughly for 1 minute longer, then turn off the heat.
Drain the pasta thoroughly and put it back into the pan.
Pour over the oil, garlic and chilli and mix well before serving.

TANGY CHEESE ON TOAST
Ingredients:
100 g of cheddar cheese, grated
2 large slices of bread, toasted
2 teaspoons (10 ml) of mild mustard
Large dash of Worcestershire sauce

Method:
Preheat the grill to a medium heat.
Spread the toast with mild mustard.
Top with grated cheese and a dash of Worcestershire sauce, then grill for a few minutes until the cheese has melted and started to bubble and brown slightly.

HERBY OMELETTE
Ingredients:
2 medium-sized eggs
20 g of butter
2 teaspoons (10 ml) of cold water
Salt and pepper
½ a teaspoon of dried mixed herbs
1 tablespoon of chopped ham (optional)
1 tablespoon of pre-cooked mushrooms (optional)

Method:
Beat the eggs well with salt, pepper, water and mixed herbs.
Stir in ham or mushrooms to the mixture, if using.
Melt the butter in a frying pan over a medium heat and pour in the egg mixture.
Run a plastic or wooden spatula around the edge of the omelette and underneath so that it does not stick to the pan.
Tilt the pan to allow the still-liquid part of the mixture to get underneath the base of the omelette.
Cook until just set, when the top of the omelette is firmer and less shiny.
Fold in half quickly, then slide onto a plate to serve.

FISH FINGER SARNIE
Ingredients:
5 frozen fishfingers
2 thick slices of wholemeal bread
2 heaped teaspoons (15 ml) of mayonnaise or ketchup
2 slices of lettuce, washed, drained and shredded
½ a fresh tomato, washed and sliced

Method:
Preheat the grill, then cook the fishfingers according to the instructions on the packet.
Spread the bread with mayo or ketchup, and arrange the cooked fishfingers on top of the bottom slice.
Top with tomato and lettuce and the remaining slice of bread.

GUACAMOLE

Ingredients:

1 large ripe avocado pear

1 clove of garlic, peeled and crushed, or 2 small spring onions, trimmed and finely chopped

2 teaspoons (10 ml) of lemon or lime juice

1 small tomato, peeled, deseeded and chopped (optional)

Salt

A few drops of Tabasco sauce

1 heaped teaspoon of chopped coriander leaves, or ¼ of a teaspoon of ground coriander

Method:

Cut the avocado in half, discarding the large stone in the middle, then remove the outer peel from the flesh.

Chop and mash with lemon or lime juice, then add all the remaining ingredients and add salt to taste.

Serve with tortilla chips and eat straight away (otherwise the avocado will start going brown).

STUDENT CLASSICS FOR TWO

SPAGHETTI BOLOGNESE

Ingredients:

200 g dried spaghetti

225 g minced beef

2 teaspoons (10 ml) of vegetable oil

1 medium onion, peeled and finely sliced

50 g button mushrooms, wiped clean then sliced

1 small stick of celery, finely chopped (optional)

1/2 a teaspoon of dried mixed herbs

1/4 teaspoon of ground nutmeg (optional)

2 tablespoons (30 ml) of tomato puree

2 tablespoons (30 ml) of red wine (optional)

400 g can of chopped tomatoes

Black pepper to taste

Method:

Fry the onions, celery (if using) and mushrooms in the oil over a medium heat for about 10 minutes until softened.

Add the beef and stir for about 5 minutes until well browned, then mix in the canned tomatoes, tomato puree, wine (if using), herbs and nutmeg (if using).

Bring to the boil, cover and then simmer gently on a medium heat for 15 to 20 minutes.

While the sauce is cooking, cook the spaghetti in plenty of hot water according to the instructions on the packet, then strain and place in a serving bowl.

Top with cooked sauce and ground black pepper.

TUNA PASTA BAKE
Ingredients:
200 g of dried pasta shapes
1 teaspoon of vegetable oil
1 clove of garlic, peeled then crushed or finely chopped
400 g can of chopped tomatoes
200 g can of sweetcorn, drained
200 g of broccoli florets, washed
100 g of canned tuna in brine
1 teaspoon of dried oregano
1 tablespoon of cornflour
100 g of cheddar cheese, grated

Method:
Pre-heat the oven to gas mark 6, 400°F, 200°C.
Boil the broccoli in a little water for 5 minutes, then drain it thoroughly.
Cook the pasta for 1 minute less than the instructions on the packet tell you, then drain.
Grease a large baking dish with vegetable oil, then place the drained pasta, sweetcorn, broccoli and tuna in the dish, mixing them together.
Mix the tomatoes, garlic, oregano, cornflour and cheese together in a separate bowl, and spoon over the pasta mixture.
Cover the dish tightly with foil and bake for 30 minutes, until the cheese has melted and starts to bubble.

VEGETABLE CHILLI
400 g can of kidney beans, drained and rinsed
1 tablespoon of vegetable oil
1 clove of garlic, peeled then crushed or finely chopped
1 small onion, peeled and thickly sliced
1 red pepper, de-seeded and sliced
1 courgette, sliced
400 g can of chopped tomatoes
1/2 a teaspoon of mild chilli powder (or more if you like it hotter)

Method:
In a large pan, fry the onion in the vegetable oil over a medium heat for about 10 minutes, until the onion softens.
Add the garlic and cook for another couple of minutes.
Mix in all the remaining ingredients and cook for 30 minutes, then serve with boiled rice.

CHUNKY LENTIL SOUP

Ingredients:
100 g of split red lentils, washed
2 teaspoons of vegetable oil
1 small onion, peeled then chopped
1 medium carrot, scrubbed then chopped
1 medium potato, peeled and cubed
500 ml of vegetable stock or water
1/2 a teaspoon of dried thyme or oregano, or 1 teaspoon of medium curry powder

Method:
Heat the vegetable oil in a large saucepan and fry onion over a medium heat for about 10 minutes until it softens.
Add the carrot and potato and cook for 5 minutes more, stirring constantly.
Add the lentils and water, plus herbs or curry powder (if using), and bring to the boil.
Simmer for 25 minutes, taste, add salt and pepper if needed, then serve.

SUNDAY LUNCH FOR 6 (ROAST CHICKEN)

This will make enough roast chicken, roast potatoes, stuffing, vegetables and gravy to feed six hungry students. There might be enough for leftovers.

Ingredients:
2.5 kg chicken
1 lemon, scrubbed and cut in half
1 kg of potatoes, washed and peeled, cut in half or quarters
Olive oil
500 g thin green beans, washed
500 g carrots, peeled and sliced
Instant chicken gravy granules
1 packet of stuffing mix

Method:
If you are using a frozen chicken, defrost it thoroughly overnight.
Decide what time you want to eat.
2 hours and 40 minutes before you want to eat, preheat the oven to gas mark 4, 350°F, 180°C. Prepare the chicken by rinsing it thoroughly all over, including inside the cavity. Drain off well then rub the outside with olive oil, sprinkle generously with salt and pepper, and push the two lemon halves into the cavity inside the chicken. Place into a roasting dish and cover with baking foil.
2 hours and 20 minutes before you want to eat, put the chicken into the preheated oven.
1 hour and 5 minutes before you want to eat, put a pan of water on to boil then cook the potatoes for 5 minutes. Drain them thoroughly. While potatoes are boiling, put a 2 mm layer of olive oil into a medium-sized roasting tin and place it into the oven to heat up, then roll the boiled potatoes in the hot oil. Be very careful as the hot oil may spit.
55 minutes before you want to eat, put the prepared potatoes into the oven

to roast. Remove the foil from the chicken and baste it by scooping up its own cooking juices and spooning them over the top of the chicken.

35 minutes before you want to eat, prepare the stuffing mix according to the instructions on the packet, then press into a small ovenproof dish.

30 minutes before you want to eat, turn the roast potatoes over in their oil, and put the stuffing into the oven. Baste the chicken again.

20 minutes before you want to eat, check the chicken. Stick the point of a sharp knife into the chicken at the place where the top of the thigh meets the rest of the body, and look at the juices that run out. If the juices are clear then the chicken is cooked, if they are bloody then cook for 15 more minutes and check again. If the chicken is ready, turn up the heat in the oven to gas mark 6, 400°F, 200°C to crisp up the potatoes. Let the chicken 'rest' on a warm serving plate covered in tinfoil for 20 minutes.

15 minutes before you want to eat, get a pan of water boiling, then 10 minutes before you want to eat, start cooking the beans and carrots.

One minute before you want to eat, make up a pint of gravy by straining the cooking liquid from the vegetables onto the gravy granules. Add extra boiling water if necessary.

Carve the chicken and serve everything together.

APPENDIX 2: CONTACTS

GENERAL
National Union of Students
Nelson Mandela House
461 Holloway Road
London, N7 6LJ
Tel: 020 7272 8900
Fax: 020 7263 5713
Website: www.nusonline.org.uk
email: nusuk@nus.org.uk

Get Connected
Free advice line for the under-25s, covering all subjects, including safety, money, sexuality, housing and much more.
Helpline: 0808 808 4994 (open 1 p.m. to 11 p.m. every day)

Citizens' Advice Bureaux
Your nearest bureau will be listed in your local phone book, or you can look it up online at: www.nacab.org.uk
Advice website: www.adviceguide.org.uk

Student websites
www.virginstudent.com
www.studentUK.com
www.s-k-i-n-t.co.uk
www.uniserveuk.com

HOUSING
Shelter

Shelter, 88 Old Street, London, EC1V 9HU

Shelter Scotland, 4th Floor, Scotiabank House, 6 South Charlotte Street, Edinburgh, EH2 4AW

Shelter Cymru, 25 Walter Road, Swansea, SA1 5NN

Shelterline: 0808 800 4444. Calls are free, and service includes minicom (textphone) and translators.

Main website: www.shelter.org.uk, consumer advice: www.shelternet.co.uk

Housing websites

www.accommodationforstudents.com

www.bunk.com

MONEY

Student Loans Company
100 Bothwell Street
Glasgow, G2 7JD
Tel: 0800 40 50 10
Minicom: 0800 085 3950
Website: www.slc.co.uk

EGAS
501–505 Kingsland Road
London, E8 4AU
Tel: 020 7254 6251, 10 a.m. to 12 noon, and 2 p.m. to 4 p.m., on Monday,
Wednesday and Friday.
Website: www.egas-online.org.uk

National Debtline
Tel: 0808 808 400
Website: www.nationaldebtline.co.uk

The Consumer Credit Counselling Service
Tel: 0800 138 1111
Website: www.cccs.co.uk

The Student Debtline
Tel: 0800 328 1813, open 8 a.m. to 8 p.m., Monday to Friday.

WORK AND CAREERS

Department for Education and Skills
Sanctuary Buildings
Great Smith Street
London, SW1P 3BT
Public Enquiries: 0870 000 2288
Website: www.dfes.gov.uk

UK Socrates–Erasmus Council
Research and Development Building
The University
Canterbury
Kent, CT2 7PD
Tel: 01227 762712
Fax: 01227 762711
Website: www.erasmus.ac.uk

Job websites

www.prospects.ac.uk

www.nases.org.uk

www.doctorjob.com

www.totaljobs.com

www.workthing.com

www.hotrecruit.com

EQUAL OPPORTUNITIES

SKILL, the National Bureau for Students with Disabilities
Chapter House
18–20 Crucifix Lane
London, SE1 3JW
Telephone or minicom: 020 7450 0620
Fax: 020 7450 0650
Information Service, telephone: 0800 328 5050 (freephone) and 020 7657 2337, open Monday to Thursday afternoons.
Website: www.skill.org.uk

London Lesbian and Gay Switchboard
PO Box 7324
London, N1 9QS
Helpline: 020 7837 7324
Admin Line: 020 7837 6768
Fax: 020 7837 7300
Website: www.llgs.org.uk
Email: admin@llgs.org.uk

Commission for Racial Equality
St Dunstan's House
201–211 Borough High Street
London, SE1 1GZ
Tel: 020 7939 0000
Fax: 020 7939 0001
Website: www.cre.gov.uk
email: info@cre.gov.uk

HEALTH

NHS Direct
Speak to a trained nurse for advice and information about anything health-related.
Helpline: 0845 46 47 (open 24 hours daily)
Website: www.nhsdirect.nhs.uk

Brook Advisory Service
Find out about what your contraception options are, and what services are available in your local area.
Tel: 0800 0185 023 (open 9 a.m. to 5 p.m., Monday to Friday)
Website: www.brook.org.uk

Family Planning Association (fpa)
Tel: 0845 310 1334 (England), 028 90 325 488 or 028 71 260 016 (Northern Ireland), 0141 576 5088 (Scotland), open 9 a.m. to 7 p.m., Monday to Friday.
Website: www.fpa.org.uk

CRIME AND SAFETY
Victim Support
Victim Supportline: 0845 30 30 900, open 9 a.m. to 9 p.m., Monday to Friday,
9 a.m. to 7 p.m., weekends and 9 a.m. to 5 p.m. bank holidays.
Minicom: 020 7896 3776
Website: www.victimsupport.com

The Suzy Lamplugh Trust
PO Box 17818
London, SW14 8WW
Tel: 020 8876 0305
Website: www.suzylamplugh.org

THANKS

I would like to thank the following people for reading through the first drafts of this guide, fearlessly risking both their eyesight and their sanity: Lauren Burke, Lara Clifford, Val and Garry Fitzhugh, Frank Huxtable and Dr Alka Mehta. I'm also very grateful to the Suzy Lamplugh Trust and Shelter for their help. Special thanks to Bertrand Man for writing the bike-buying tips at the back of the book, and for making me sit on a sunny beach in Cornwall in between chapters.

INDEX

A

access funds 116
accommodation 1–4
  bathrooms 3, 15–16,
    209–210
  bills 99–101
  buying 107–108
  contracts 96–97
  costs 4
  damp 102
  decoration 15, 98–99
  flatmates 15, 94, 106,
    110
  halls of residence
    91–93
  heating 102
  at home 1
  kitchens 3, 11, 210–211
  noise 98
  renting privately
    93–107
  tenancies 96
  vermin 103
accommodation office
  13–14
acne 167
AIDS 76
alcohol 17, 19, 78–82
  addiction 127
  date rape 178
  poisoning 80, 152
ambulances 152
amphetamines 85
anorexia nervosa 164
anxiety 161–162
application forms, jobs
  142, 148–149
asthma 168
assault 79, 80, 152,
  177–179
assessment 28
assignments 44–46

B

balls 60–61
banks
  accounts 1, 5, 6, 17,
    111–113
  loans 117
bathrooms 3, 15–16,
  209–210
benefits, health 152
bicycles 3, 176, 202–203
bills 6, 99–101, 120–123

books 26, 36–37
  dictionaries 32, 33
breaking up a
  relationship 72
breast screening 153
Bristol Crisis Centre 166
Brook Advisory Service
  74
budgeting 4, 6, 35, 113
  gap years 194
  living expenses
    119–123
  social life 59–60
  travelling 66
bulimia nervosa 164–165
burglary 171–173

C

camping 62–63
cannabis 82, 84–85
carbon monoxide leaks
  104
careers, choosing
  145–150
cars 3, 176, 201–202
cash points 174
cervical smear tests 153
cheating 46
children 135
  childcare 9
Childcare Grant 9
chlamydia 75
cinemas 61
Citizens' Advice Bureaux
  109, 127, 128
cleaning 7, 16, 98, 107,
  207–211
  after parties 65
clothes and toiletries,
  saving on 122–123
clubs and societies
  20–21, 60
cocaine 87
colds 156
competitions 118
compulsive eating 165
computers
  backing up 34–35
  care 201
  centres 27
  email 33–34
  Internet research
    39–40
  skills 6–7

spreadsheets 35
  word processing 34
condoms 70, 73
Consumer Credit
  Counselling Service
  128
contraception 21, 70,
  73–74
contracts
  accommodation 96–97
  work 149–150, 185
cooking 1, 7, 154,
  212–217
  house parties 64
  romantic dinners
    69–70
CORGI gas installation
  104
coughs 156
Council of Mortgage
  Lenders 108
council tax 100
counselling 22, 151, 160
couples 71–72
courses
  assessment 28
  assignments 44–46
  attendance 40–44
  changing 32, 53–54
  coursemates 30–31
  enrolling 16–17
  research 36–40
  structure 27–28
  timetables 25–26
crack 87–88
credit cards 112–113, 126
  fraud 176–177
Cruse helpline 166
Curriculum Vitae 132,
  139–141, 148, 186
cystitis 77

D

dating 67–78
  date rape 177–178
deans 29
debt 111, 124–128
decoration 15
degree grades 28, 53
dentists 151–152
Dependents' Grant 9
deposits 97, 106–107
depression 159–161
Depression Alliance 166

dictionaries 32, 33
diet 153–154
dinner parties 65
directories, web 39–40
disabilities 9, 57
discrimination 57, 106, 135
dissertations 47
doctors 151–152
drinking 17, 19, 22, 51, 68, 78–82
  party drinks 64
Drinkline 82, 127
drugs 19, 22, 51, 82–89
  dependency 88, 127
  drug-assisted rape 81, 178–179
  emergencies 152
  risks 82–83
Drugscope 89
drunkenness 79
dyslexia 33

E
eating disorders 164–164
  helpline 166
ecstasy 82, 86–87
eczema 167
Educational Grants
  Advisory Service 117
electrical know-how 199–201
electricity and gas bills 100
email 33–34
emergency services 152
employment see jobs; work
Endsleigh Insurance 18
Energywatch 100
English, writing 32–33
entertainment
  Freshers' Week 18–19
  social life 59–67
equipment, academic 26
erectile dysfunction 77
essays 44–46
  exams 51–52
eviction, illegal 106
exams 44, 49–53
exercise 22, 50, 155

F
faculty office 16
family 7–8, 14
  accommodation 1
  money from 115–116
festivals 62–63
field trips 43–44
filing 26–27
finance office 17

finances 1, 4–5, 17
  bank accounts 1, 5, 17, 111–113
  credit cards 112–113, 126
  crisis 123–124
  debt 111, 124–128
  expenses 118–124
  incoming money 113–118
  post-graduate funding 192
  savings 113
  stress 111, 128
fire practices 14
fire safety 103–104
first aid 153, 203–204
flat/housemates 94, 106, 110
food
  bills 122
  cooking 1, 7, 212–217
  eating sensibly 153–154
  house parties 64
  preventing stress 22, 50
  recipes 212–217
  romantic dinners 69–70
  safety 211–212
  while drinking 79
food poisoning 158–159
friends 8
  couples 71–72
  coursemates 30–31
  dating 67–78
  girlfriends/boyfriends 7–8, 20
  making 1, 13, 15, 19–20

G
gambling 127
GamCare helpline 127
gap years 193–196
gas and electricity bills 100
gas leaks 104–105
genital herpes 75
genital warts 75
glandular fever 157
gonorrhea 75–76
graduation 183–184
grants and bursaries 116–117
GUM (genito-urinary) clinics 76–77

H
halls of residence 91–93
hangovers 78, 80

harassment 179–180
  by landlords 106
hardship funds 116
hay fever 167–168
health benefits 152
health care 13, 17, 21
  alcohol 79–82
  drugs 82–83
  first aid 153, 203-204
  gap year 195
  helplines 169
  mental health 159–166
  sexually transmitted infections 74–77
  skin problems 166–167
health services 151–152
helplines 21, 71, 74, 77, 82, 89, 100, 109, 127, 155, 166, 169, 179
hepatitis B and C 76
heroin 88
HIV 76
Home Safety Network 109
homesickness 21–22
house buying 107–108
house parties 63–65
house/flatmates 94, 106, 110

I
income tax 134
induction meetings 14
influenza 156–157
Inland Revenue 115
insomnia 154
insurance 1, 4, 17–18, 171
  credit cards 176–177
  gap years 195
international students 8–9
Internet
  banking 112
  connection 101
  research 39–40
interviews, jobs 143–145, 149
inventories 97
IUD/coil 74

J
jobs 116
  abroad 136–137
  application forms 142
  graduate jobs 184–186
  interviews 143–145, 149
  jobhunting 139–145, 146, 186–187
  part-time 131–135
  recruitment fairs 149

summer jobs 4–5,
    135–137
  temping 187–188
  voluntary 61–62, 139,
    186, 194
  work placements
    137–139
Jobseeker's Allowance
  187

K
kitchens 3, 210–211
  equipment 11

L
landlords 97, 101–102,
  105–107
laundry 1, 7, 205–208
law 181
  on drugs 83–84
learning centres 33
lecturers 29–30
lectures 40–42
Lesbian, Gay and
  Bisexual Society 71
libraries 18, 27, 36–37
living expenses 119–123
Local Education
  Authorities 5
loss of libido 77
LSD 86

M
manic depression
  163–164
mature students 9
means-tested grants
  117
meningitis 158
mental health 159–166
MIND 166
mobile phones 121–122,
  173–174
modules 27–28
'morning-after' pill 74,
  152
mortgages 108
motivation 31–32
motorbikes 176
muggings 175
multiple-choice exams 52
mushrooms, magic 86

N
National Debtline 127,
  128
National Federation of
  Enterprise Agencies
  189
national insurance
  134–135

national minimum wage
  135
National Union of
  Students 16, 116
neighbours 105
NetDoctor 169
NHS Direct 169
NHS prescriptions 152
nitrites (poppers) 85
No Panic helpline 166
NSU 76

O
obesity 169
obsessions 162
Officer Training Corps
  118
overdrafts 111–112
overseas study 27, 28,
  192

P
packing 9–12
parking 3, 13
parties 63–66
personal attack alarms
  174
personality, assessment
  145–147
phobias 162
phone harassment 180
pill, contraceptive 73–74
PIN numbers 174
plumbing 105
police 181
  and drugs 84
post-graduate study
  189–193
practicals 43
pregnancy 73
premature ejaculation
  78
presentation of work 34,
  46, 47–49
Prince's Trust 189
private halls of residence
  93
psoriasis 167
pubic lice 76

Q
Quitline 155

R
rag weeks 61
rape 177–179
Rape Crisis 179
recipes 212–217
recruitment fairs 149
registrars 29
Release charity 89

rent 91
renting accommodation
  93–107
renting equipment 101
research 36–40, 45
reviews, writing 46–47
revision 49–50

S
safety 19, 103–104, 134
  at home 171–173
  out at night 174–176
salaries 149
Samaritans 21, 161, 166
sandwich degrees 27
saving 120–123
savings 113
scabies 76
schizophrenia 163–164
science courses 43
search engines 39
security at home 172–173
self-employment
  188–189
self-harm 165
semesters/terms 27
seminars 42–43
septicaemia 158
sex and dating 67–78
  contraception 21, 70,
    73–74
  safe sex 70, 75
sexual assault 152,
  177–179
  helplines 179
sexual harassment 57
sexual problems 77–78
sexuality 71
sexually transmitted
  infections 74–77
Shelterline 109
shopping 67
SKILL 9, 57
skin problems 166–167
sleep 154–155
smoking 155
snoring 154–155
social life 59–67
societies and clubs
  20–21, 60
Socrates-Erasmus
  Scheme 28
solvents 87
spiked drinks 80–81, 152,
  178–179
sponsorship 117
sports 20–21, 61, 155
  injuries 168–169
spreadsheets 35
stalking 180
statistics 35–36, 38

INDEX

stress 21–22, 52, 161–162
  exams 50–51
  money 111, 128
Student Awards Agency
  114
Student Debtline 128
student discounts 59, 61
  travel 66
Student Health Centre
  151–152
student loans 5, 13, 17,
  114–115
Student Loans Company
  114–115, 126
Student Support 5, 114
students' union 60
study areas 26
suicide 161
summer jobs 4–5,
  135–137
Survivors 179
syphilis 76

T
Talk to Frank drugs
  helpline 89, 127
taxis 174–175
teacher training 191
telephone bills 100
tenancies 96
terms/semesters 27
testicular cancer 153
theft 9–10, 17–18, 19,
  92
  burglary 171–173

thrush 77
time management 31,
  55–56
timetables 25–26, 31
  revision 49–50
tranquillisers 88
Transco gas engineers
  105
transport 176
  bicycles 3, 176,
    202–203
  cars 3, 176, 201–202
  costs 4
  parking 3, 13
travelling 66–67, 195
trichomonas 76
tuition fees 118
tutorials 42–43
tutors 29–30, 45

U
unemployment 187
university
  access funds 116
  accommodation office
    13–14, 94
  careers service
    147–148, 186, 190
  faculty office 16
  finance office 17
  health centre 151–152
  learning centres 33
  libraries 18, 27
  staff 29–30, 56
utility bills 100, 120–121

V
valuables 9–10, 17–18,
  62, 173
vermin 103
violence 175–176
  attacks on men 177
  sexual assault 152,
    177–179
viruses 156–159

W
water bills 100
welfare 51
  health care 13, 17, 21
  see also health
word processing 34
work
  abroad 136–137
  application forms 142
  careers, choosing
    145–150
  interviews 143–145
  part-time 131–135
  placements 137–139
  self-employment
    188–189
  summer jobs 135–137
  temping 187–188
  university careers
    service 147–148
  voluntary 61–62, 139
Working Families Tax
  Credit 135
writing skills 32–33,
  45–46